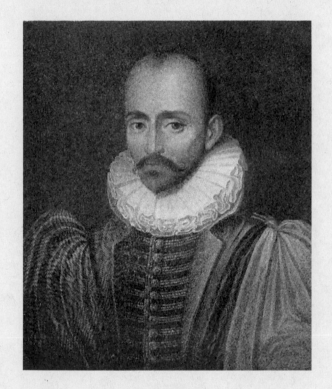

Montaigne

Michel de Montaigne
Selected Essays

Translated by Charles Cotton
Edited by William Carew Hazlitt

DOVER PUBLICATIONS, INC.
Mineola, New York

DOVER THRIFT EDITIONS

GENERAL EDITOR: MARY CAROLYN WALDREP
EDITOR OF THIS VOLUME: JANET BAINE KOPITO

Bibliographical Note

This Dover edition, first published by Dover Publications, Inc., in 2011, is an unabridged republication of the work originally published as *Selected Essays of Michel de Montaigne* by Thomas Y. Crowell & Co., Publishers, New York, in 1903.

International Standard Book Number
ISBN-13: 978-0-486-48603-1
ISBN-10: 0-486-48603-6

Manufactured in the United States by Courier Corporation
48603603
www.doverpublications.com

The Author to the Reader

READER, thou hast here an honest book; it doth at the outset fore-
warn thee that, in contriving the same, I have proposed to myself no
other than a domestic and private end: I have had no cosideration at
all either to thy service or to my glory. My powers are not capable of
any such design. I have dedicated it to the particular commodity of
my kinsfolk and friends, so that, having lost me (which they must do
shortly), they may therein recover some traits of my conditions and
humors, and by that means preserve more whole, and more life-like,
the knowledge they had of me.

Had my intention been to seek the world's favor, I should surely
have adorned myself with borrowed beauties: I desire therein to be
viewed as I appear in mine own genuine, simple, and ordinary manner, without study and artifice: for it is myself I paint. My defects are
therein to be read to the life, and my imperfections and my natural
form, so far as public reverence hath permitted me. If I had lived
among those nations, which (they say) yet dwell under the sweet
liberty of nature's primitive laws, I assure thee I would most willingly
have painted myself quite fully and quite naked. Thus, reader, myself
am the matter of my book: there's no reason thou shouldst employ
thy leisure about so frivolous and vain a subject. Therefore, farewell.

From Montaigne, the 12th June, 1580.

Preface

THE Essays of Montaigne, which are at once the most celebrated and the most permanent of his productions, form a magazine out of which such writers as Bacon and Shakespeare did not disdain to help themselves; and indeed, as Hallam observes, the Frenchman's literary importance largely results from the share which his mind had in influencing other minds, coeval and subsequent. But, at the same time, estimating the value and rank of the essayist, we are not to leave out of the account the drawbacks and the circumstances of the period: the imperfect state of education, the comparative scarcity of books, and the limited opportunities of intellectual intercourse.

Montaigne freely borrowed of others, and he has found men willing to borrow of him as freely. We need not wonder at the reputation which he with seeming facility achieved. He was, without being aware of it, the leader of a new school in letters and morals. His book was different from all others which were at that date in the world. It diverted the ancient currents of thought into new channels. It told its readers with unexampled frankness, what its writer's opinion was about men and things, and threw what must have been a strange kind of new light on many matters but darkly understood. Above all, the Essayist uncased himself, and made his intellectual and physical organism public property. He took the world into his confidence on all subjects. His essays were a sort of literary anatomy, where we get a diagnosis of the writer's mind, made by himself at different levels and under a large variety of operating influences.

The text of these volumes is taken from the first edition of Cotton's version, printed in 3 vols. 8 vo, 1685–6. In the earliest impression the errors of the press are corrected merely as far as page 240 of the first volume, and all the editions follow one another. That of 1685–6 was the only one which the translator lived to see. He died in 1687.

It was considered imperative to correct Cotton's translation by a careful collation with the *variorum* edition of the original, Paris, 1854, with reference also to Florio's earlier undertaking. The besetting sin of both Montaigne's translators seems to have been a propensity for reducing his language and phraseology to the language and phraseology of the age and country to which they belonged, and, moreover, for inserting paragraphs and words, not here and there only, but constantly and habitually, from an evident desire and view to elucidate or strengthen their author's meaning. Nor is redundancy or paraphrase the only form of transgression in Cotton, for there are places in his author which he thought proper to omit, and it is hardly necessary to say that the restoration of all such matter to the text was considered essential to its integrity and completeness.

W. C. H.

Barnes Common, Surrey,
January, 1892.

Contents

The Author to the Reader   v

Preface   vii

Biographical Introduction   xii

That Men by Various Ways arrive
    at the same End   1

Of Sorrow   4

That the Soul discharges her Passions
    upon False Objects, where the
    True are Wanting   7

That the Intention is Judge of
    Our Actions   8

Of Liars   10

Of Quick or Slow Speech   14

Of Constancy   16

Of Fear   18

That Men are not to judge of Our
  Happiness till after Death 20

That it is Folly to measure Truth
  and Error by Our Own Capacity 23

Of Friendship 26

That a Man is soberly to judge
  of the Divine Ordinances 34

Of the Custom of Wearing Clothes 36

That We laugh and cry for the
  Same Thing 39

Of Solitude 41

Of the Inequality Among Us 50

Of Ancient Customs 56

Of the Vanity of Words 59

Of Prayers 62

Of Books 69

Of Cruelty 80

Of the Inconstancy of Our Actions 91

Use makes Perfect 96

Of Glory 105

Of Presumption 115

Of Giving the Lie 140

Of Liberty of Conscience 144

Of Virtue 147

Of Anger 153

Of Profit and Honesty 159

Of Repentance 171

Of the Inconvenience of Greatness 183

Of Managing the Will 187

Biographical Introduction

THE AUTHOR of the Essays was born on the last day of February, 1533, at the château of St. Michel de Montaigne. His father, Pierre Eyquem, écuyer, was successively first jurat of the town of Bordeaux (1530), sub-mayor (1536), jurat for the second time in 1540, procureur in 1546, and at length mayor from 1553 to 1556. He was a man of austere probity, who had "a particular regard for honor and propriety in his person and attire . . . a mighty good faith in his speech, and a conscience and a religious feeling inclining to superstition, rather than to the other extreme." Pierre Eyquem bestowed great care on the education of his children, especially on the practical side of it. To associate closely his son Michel with the people, and attach him to those who stand in need of assistance, he caused him to be held at the font by persons of the meanest position; subsequently he put him out to nurse with a poor villager, and then, at a later period, made him accustom himself to the most common sort of living, taking care, nevertheless, to cultivate his mind, and superintend its development without the exercise of undue rigor or constraint. Michel, who gives us the minutest account of his earliest years, charmingly narrates how they used to awake him by the sound of some agreeable music, and how he learned Latin, without suffering the rod or shedding a tear, before beginning French, thanks to the German teacher whom his father had placed near him, and who never addressed him except in the language of Virgil and Cicero. The study of Greek took precedence.

At six years of age young Montaigne went to the College of Guienne at Bordeaux, where he had as preceptors the most eminent scholars of the sixteenth century, Nicolas Grouchy, Guerente, Muret, and Buchanan. At thirteen he had passed through all the classes, and as he was destined for the law he left school to study that science. The next information that we have is that in 1554 he received the appointment of councillor in the parliament of Bordeaux; in 1559 he was at Bar-le-Duc with the court of Francis II., and in the year following he was present at Rouen to witness the declaration of the majority of Charles IX.

Between 1556 and 1563 commenced his romantic friendship with Etienne de la Boetie, whom he had met, as he tells us, by pure chance at some festive celebration in the town. From their very first interview the two found themselves drawn irresistibly toward one another, and during the six years this alliance was foremost in the heart of Montaigne, as it was afterward in his memory, when death had severed it.

Although in his Essays he blames severely those who, contrary to the advice of Aristotle, marry before five and thirty, Montaigne, in 1566, in his thirty-third year, espoused Françoise de Chassaigne, daughter of a councillor in the Parliament of Bordeaux. The title of Gentleman in Ordinary to the king, which he assumes in a preface, and which Henry III. gives him in a letter; what he says as to the commotions of courts, where he passed a portion of his life; the instructions which he wrote under the dictation of Catherine de Medici for King Charles IX.; and his noble correspondence with Henry IV., leave no doubt as to the part which he played in the transactions of those times; and we find an unanswerable proof of the esteem in which he was held by the most exalted personages in a letter which was addressed to him by Charles at the time he was admitted to the Order of St. Michael, which was, as he informs us himself, the highest honor of the French noblesse.

Several passages in the Essays seem to indicate that Montaigne not only took military service, but that he was actually in numerous campaigns with the Catholic armies; and on his monument he is represented in a coat of mail, with his casque and gauntlets on his right side, and a lion at his feet, alike symbols of a share in military transactions.

But, on his arrival at his thirty-eighth year, he resolved to dedicate to study and contemplation the remaining term of his life; and on his birthday, the last of February, 1571, he caused a Latin inscription to this effect to be placed upon one of the walls of his château.

Montaigne was at this date unknown to the world of letters, except as a translator and an editor. In 1569 he published a translation of the *Natural Theology* of Reymond de Sebonde, which he had undertaken solely to please his father. In 1571 he caused to be printed at Paris certain *opuscula* of Etienne de la Boetie. At the very outset of his retirement from public engagements, Montaigne was exclusively occupied with reading and reflection, and acquired the habit of setting down his thoughts just as they occurred to him. Those thoughts became a book, and the first draft of that book, which was to confer immortality on the writer, appeared at Bordeaux in 1580. Montaigne was then forty-seven; he had suffered for some years past from renal colic and gravel; and it was with the necessity of distraction from his pain, and the hope of deriving relief from the waters, that he undertook at this time his Italian tour of which an itinerary, dictated to his secretary, is extant, and has been separately printed.

Montaigne traveled, just as he wrote, completely at his ease, and without the least constraint, turning, just as he fancied, from the common or ordinary roads taken by tourists. The good inns, the soft beds, the fine views, attracted his notice at every point, and in his observations on men and things he confines himself chiefly to the practical side.

At Rome he at first put up at the Orso, but subsequently hired, at twenty crowns a month, three fine furnished rooms in the house of a Spaniard, who included in these terms the use of the kitchen fire. What most annoyed him in the Eternal City was the number of Frenchmen he met, who all saluted him in his native tongue; but otherwise he was very comfortable, and his stay extended to five months.

Sceptical as Montaigne shows himself in his books, yet during his sojourn at Rome he manifested a great regard for religion. He solicited the honor of being admitted to kiss the feet of the Holy Father, Gregory XIII.; and the pontiff exhorted him always to continue in the devotion which he had hitherto exhibited to the church and the service of the Most Christian King.

"He met at San Sisto a Muscovite ambassador, the second who had come to Rome since the pontificate of Paul III. This minister had despatches from his court for Venice, addressed to the *Grand Governor of the Signory*. The court of Muscovy had at that time such limited relations with the other powers of Europe, and it was so imperfect in its information, that it thought Venice to be a dependency of the Holy See."

Before quitting Rome, Montaigne received his diploma of citizenship, by which he was greatly flattered; and after a visit to Tivoli he set out for Loretto, stopping at Ancona, Fano, and Urbino. He arrived at the beginning of May, 1581, at Bagno della Villa, where he established himself, in order to try the waters.

The greater part of the entries in the Journal, giving the account of these waters, and of the travels, down to Montaigne's arrival at the first French town on his homeward route, are in Italian, because he wished to exercise himself in that language.

The minute and constant watchfulness of Montaigne over his health and over himself might lead one to suspect that excessive fear of death which degenerates into cowardice. But was it not rather the fear of the operation for the stone, at that time really formidable?

He was still at the waters of La Villa, when, on the 7th September, 1581, he learned by letter that he had been elected mayor of Bordeaux on the Ist August preceding. This intelligence made him hasten his departure; and from Lucca he proceeded to Rome. He again made some stay in that city, and he there received the letter of the jurats of Bordeaux, notifying to him officially his election to the mayoralty, and inviting him to return as speedily as possible. He left for France accompanied by young D'Estissac and several other gentlemen, who escorted him a considerable distance; but none went back to France with him, not even his travelling companion. He passed by Padua, Milan, Mont Cenis, and Chambery; thence he went on to Lyons, and lost no time in repairing to his château, after an absence of seventeen months and eight days.

"The gentlemen of Bordeaux," says he, "elected me mayor of their town while I was at a distance from France, and far from the thought of such a thing. I excused myself; but they gave me to understand that I was wrong in so doing, it being also command of the king that I should stand." This is the letter which Henry III. wrote to him on the occasion:

"MONSIEUR DE MONTAIGNE:- Inasmuch as I hold in great esteem your fidelity and zealous devotion to my service, it has been a pleasure to me to learn that you have been chosen mayor of my town of Bordeaux. I have had the agreeable duty of confirming the selection, and I did so the more willingly, seeing that it was made during your distant absence; wherefore it is my desire, and I require and command you expressly, that you proceed without delay to enter on the duties to which you have received so legitimate a call. And so you will act in a manner very agreeable to me, while the contrary will displease me greatly. Praying God, M. de Montaigne, to have you in his holy keeping.

"Written at Paris, the 25th day of November,1581.

"HENRI.

"To Monsieur de MONTAIGNE,

"Knight of my Order, Gentleman in Ordinary of
"my Chamber, being at present in Rome."

Montaigne in his new employment, the most important in the province, obeyed the axiom that a man may not refuse a duty, though it absorb his time and attention and even involve the sacrifice of his blood. Placed between two extreme parties ever on the point of getting to blows, he showed himself in practice what he is in his book, the friend of a middle and temperate policy.

He applied himself in an especial manner to the maintenance of peace between the two religious factions which at that time divided the town of Bordeaux; and at the end of his two first years of office his grateful fellow-citizens conferred on him (in 1583) the mayoralty for two years more, a distinction which had been enjoyed, as he tells us, only twice before. On the expiration of his official career, after four years' duration, he could say fairly enough of himself, that he left behind him neither hatred nor cause of offence.

In the midst of the cares of government, Montaigne found leisure to revise and enlarge his Essays, which since their appearance in 1580, had been continually receiving augmentations in the form of additional chapters or papers. Two more editions were printed in 1582 and 1587; and during this time the author, while making alterations in the original text, composed part of the third book. He went to Paris to make arrangements for the publication of his enlarged labors, and a fourth impression in 1588 was the result. He remained in the capital some time on this occasion, and it was now that he met for the first time Mademoiselle de Gournay. Gifted with an active and inquiring spirit, and, above all, possessing a sound and healthy tone of mind, Mademoiselle de Gournay had been carried from her childhood with that tide which set in with the sixteenth century toward controversy, learning, and knowledge. She learned Latin without a master; and when, at the age of eighteen, she accidentally became possessor of a copy of the Essays, she was transported with delight and admiration.

She quitted the château of Gournay, to come to see him. We cannot do better, in connection with this journey of sympathy, than to repeat the words of Pasquier: "That young lady, allied to several great and noble families of Paris, proposed to herself no other marriage than with her honor, enriched with the knowledge gained from good books, and, beyond all others from the Essays of M. de Montaigne, who making in the year 1588, a lengthened stay in the town of Paris, she went there for the purpose of forming his personal acquaintance; and her mother, Madame de Gournay, and herself took him back with them to their château, where, at two or three different times, he spent three months altogether, most welcome of visitors." It was from this moment that Mademoiselle de Gournay dated her adoption as Montaigne's daughter, a circumstance which has tended to confer immortality upon her in a far greater measure than her own literary productions.

Montaigne, on leaving Paris, stayed a short time at Blois, to attend the meeting of the States-General; and it is known that he was commissioned, about this period, to negotiate between Henry of Navarre (afterward Henry IV.) and the duke of Guise. De Thou assures us that Montaigne enjoyed the confidence of the principal persons of this time. The president, who calls him a frank man without constraint, tells us that, walking with him and Pasquier in the court at the castle of Blois, he heard him pronounce some very remarkable opinions on contemporary events, and he adds that Montaigne had foreseen that the troubles in France could not end without witnessing the death of either the king of Navarre or of the duke of Guise. He had made himself so completely master of the views of these two princes, that he told De Thou that the king of Navarre would have been prepared to embrace Catholicism, if he had not been afraid of being abandoned by his party, and that the duke of Guise, on his part, had no particular repugnance to the confession of Augsburg, for which the cardinal of Lorraine, his uncle, had inspired him with a liking, if it had not been for the peril involved in quitting the Romish communion. It would have been easy for Montaigne to play, as we call it, a great part in politics, and create for himself a lofty position; but his motto was, *Otio et libertati*; and he returned quietly home to compose a chapter for his next edition on "The Inconveniences of Greatness."

The author of the Essays was now fifty-five. The malady which tormented him grew only worse and worse with years; and yet he occupied himself continually with reading, meditating, and composition. He employed the years 1589, 1590, and 1591, in making fresh additions to his book; and even in the approaches of old age he might fairly anticipate many happy hours, when he was attacked by quinsy, depriving him of the power of utterance. Pasquier, who has left us some details of his last hours, narrates that he remained three days in full possession of his faculties, but unable to speak, so that, in order to make known his desires he was obliged to resort to writing; and as he felt his end drawing near, he begged his wife to summon certain of the gentlemen who resided in the neighborhood to bid them a last farewell. When they had arrived, he caused mass to be celebrated in his apartment; and just as the priest was elevating the host, Montaigne fell forward, with his arms extended in front of him, on the bed, and so expired. He was in his sixtieth year. It was the 13th of September, 1592.

Montaigne was buried near his own house; but a few months after his decease, his remains were removed to the church of a Commandery of St. Antoine at Bordeaux.[1] His monument was restored in 1803 by

[1] The Paris correspondent of the *Daily News*, under date of the 13th March, 1886, writes: "The remains of Montaigne were on Thursday morning removed to the vault of the new University buildings at Bordeaux. Several speeches were made, and M. de Brons, a descendant of Montaigne, thanked the Municipal Council who defrayed the cost of the monument. That illustrious Bordelais, who much more than Descartes may be regarded as the father of French philosophy, had a direct action on the mind of Shakespeare. Victor Hugo claimed for Montaigne the honor of having led the greatest English poet from the *concetti* of the Italian school to the graver form of thought of which 'Hamlet' is an example. Shakespeare having possessed a copy of Montaigne's Essays, Victor Hugo concluded that he marked, learned, and inwardly digested them—a good modern book being a rarity in those days."

a descendant. It was seen about 1858 by an English traveler (Mr. St. John), and was then in good preservation.

In 1595 Mademoiselle de Gournay published a new edition of Montaigne's Essays, and the first with the latest emendations of the author, from a copy presented to her by his widow, and which has not been recovered, although it is known to have been in existence some years after the date of the impression made on its authority.

Coldly as Montaigne's literary productions appear to have been received by the generation immediately succeeding his own age, his genius grew into just appreciation in the seventeenth century, when such great spirits arose as La Bruyère, Molière, La Fontaine, and Madame de Sévigné. "Oh," exclaimed the Chatelaine des Rochers, "what capital company he is, the dear man! He is my old friend; and just for the reason that he is so, he always seems new. Mon Dieu! how full is that book of sense!" Balzac said that he had carried human reason as far and as high as it could go, both in politics and in morals. On the other hand, Malebranche and the writers of Port Royal were against him; some reprehended the licentiousness of his writings; others their impiety, materialism, and Epicureanism. Even Pascal, who had carefully read the Essays, and gained no small profit by them, did not spare his reproaches. But Montaigne has outlived detraction. As time has gone on, his admirers and borrowers have increased in number, and his Jansenism, which recommended him to the eighteenth century, may not be his least recommendation in the nineteenth. Here we have certainly, on the whole, a first-class man, and one proof of his masterly genius seems to be, that his merits and his beauties are sufficient to induce us to leave out of consideration blemishes and faults which would have been fatal to an inferior writer.

ESSAYS OF MONTAIGNE

THAT MEN BY VARIOUS WAYS ARRIVE
AT THE SAME END.

THE MOST usual way of appeasing the indignation of such as we have any way offended, when we see them in possession of the power of revenge, and find that we absolutely lie at their mercy, is by submission, to move them to commiseration and pity; and yet bravery, constancy, and resolution, however quite contrary means, have sometimes served to produce the same effect.

Edward, Prince of Wales (the same who so long governed our Guienne, a personage whose condition and fortune have in them a great deal of the most notable and most considerable parts of grandeur), having been highly incensed by the Limousins, and taking their city by assault, was not, either by the cries of the people, or the prayers and tears of the women and children abandoned to slaughter and prostrate at his feet for mercy, to be stayed from prosecuting his revenge; till, penetrating further into the town, he at last took notice of three French gentlemen, who with incredible bravery alone sustained the whole power of his victorious army. Then it was that consideration and respect unto so remarkable a valor first stopped the torrent of his fury, and that his clemency, beginning with these three cavaliers, was afterward extended to all the remaining inhabitants of the city.

Scanderbeg, Prince of Epirus, pursuing one of his soldiers with the purpose to kill him, the soldier, having in vain tried by all the ways of humility and supplication to appease him, resolved, as his last refuge, to face about and await him sword in hand; which behavior of his gave a sudden stop to his captain's fury, who, for seeing him assume so notable a resolution, received him into grace; an example, however, that might suffer another interpretation with such as have not read of the prodigious force and valor of that prince.

The Emperor Conrad III. having besieged Guelph, Duke of Bavaria [1140], would not be prevailed upon, what mean and unmanly satisfactions soever were tendered to him, to condescend to milder conditions than that the ladies and gentlewomen only who were in the town with the duke might go out without violation of their honor, on foot, and with so much only as they could carry about them. Whereupon they, out of magnanimity of heart, presently contrived to carry out, upon their shoulders, their husbands and children, and the duke himself; a sight at which the emperor was so pleased, that, ravished with the generosity of the action, he wept for joy, and immediately extinguishing in his heart the mortal and capital hatred he had conceived against this duke, he from that time forward treated him and his with all humanity.

The one and the other of these two ways would with great facility work upon my nature; for I have a marvellous propensity to mercy and mildness, and to such a degree that I fancy of the two I should sooner surrender my anger to compassion than to esteem. And yet pity is reputed a vice among the Stoics, who will that we succor the afflicted, but not that we should be so affected with their sufferings as to suffer with them. I conceived these examples not ill suited to the question in hand, and the rather because therein we observe these great souls assaulted and tried by these two several ways, to resist the one without relenting, and to be shaken and subjected by the other. It may be true that to suffer a man's heart to be totally subdued by compassion may be imputed facility, effeminacy, and over-tenderness; whence it comes to pass that the weaker natures, as of women, children, and the common sort of people, are the most subject to it; but after having resisted and disdained the power of groans and tears, to yield to the sole reverence of the sacred image of Valor, this can be no other than the effect of a strong and inflexible soul enamored of and honoring masculine and obstinate courage.

Nevertheless, astonishment and admiration may, in less generous minds, beget a like effect: witness the people of Thebes, who, having put two of their generals upon trial for their lives for having continued in arms beyond the precise term of their commission, very hardly pardoned Pelopidas, who, bowing under the weight of so dangerous an accusation, made no manner of defence for himself, nor produced other arguments than prayers and supplications; whereas, on the contrary, Epaminondas, falling to recount magniloquently the exploits he had performed in their service, and, after a haughty and arrogant manner reproaching them with ingratitude and injustice, they had not the heart to proceed any further in his trial, but broke up the court and departed, the whole assembly highly commending the high courage of this personage.

Dionysius the elder, after having, by a tedious siege and through exceeding great difficulties, taken the city of Reggio, and in it the governor Phyton, a very gallant man, who had made so obstinate a defence, was resolved to make him a tragical example of his revenge: in order whereunto he first told him, "That he had the day before caused his son and all his kindred to be drowned." To which Phyton returned no other answer but this: "That they were then by one day happier than he." After which, causing him to be stripped, and delivering him into the hands of the tormentors, he was by them not only dragged through the streets of the town, and most ignominiously and cruelly whipped, but moreover villified with most bitter and contumelious language; yet still he maintained his courage entire all the way, with a strong voice and undaunted countenance proclaiming the honorable and glorious cause of his death; namely, for that he would not deliver up his country into the hands of a tyrant; at the same time denouncing against him a speedy chastisement from the offended gods. At which Dionysius, reading in his soldiers' looks, that instead of being incensed at the haughty language of this conquered enemy, to the contempt of their captain and his triumph, they were not only struck with admiration of so rare a virtue, but moreover inclined to mutiny, and were even ready to rescue the prisoner out of the hangman's hands, he caused the torturing to cease, and afterward privately caused him to be thrown into the sea.

Man (in good earnest) is a marvellous vain, fickle, and unstable subject, and on whom it is very hard to form any certain and uniform judgment. For Pompey could pardon the whole city of the Mamertines, though furiously incensed against it, upon the single account of the virtue and magnanimity of one citizen, Zeno, who took the fault of the public wholly upon himself; neither entreated other favor, but alone to undergo the punishment for all: and yet Sylla's host having in the city of Perugia manifested the same virtue, obtained nothing by it, either for himself or his fellow-citizens.

And, directly contrary to my first examples, the bravest of all men, and who was reputed so gracious to all those he overcame, Alexander, having, after many great difficulties, forced the city of Gaza, and, entering, found Betis, who commanded there, and of whose valor in the time of this siege he had most marvellous manifest proof, alone forsaken by all his soldiers, his armor hacked and hewed to pieces, covered all over with blood and wounds, and yet still fighting in the crowd of a number of Macedonians, who were laying on him on all sides, he said to him, nettled at so dear-bought a victory (for, in addition to the other damage, he had two wounds newly received in his own person), "Thou shalt not die, Betis, as thou dost intend; be sure thou shalt suffer all the torments that can be inflicted on a captive." To which menace the other returning no other answer, but only a fierce and disdainful look: "What," says Alexander, observing his haughty and obstinate silence, "is he too stiff to bend a knee? Is he too proud to utter one suppliant word? Truly, I will conquer this silence; and if I cannot force a word from his mouth, I will at least extract a groan from his heart." And thereupon converting his anger into fury, presently commanded his heels to be bored through, causing him, alive, to be dragged, mangled, and dismembered at a cart's tail.

Was it that the height of courage was so natural and familiar to this conqueror, that because he could not admire, he respected it the less? Or was it that he conceived valor to be a virtue so peculiar to himself, that his pride could not, without envy, endure it in another? Or was it that the natural impetuosity of his fury was incapable of opposition? Certainly, had it been capable of moderation, it is to be believed that in the sack and desolation of Thebes, to see so many valiant men, lost and totally destitute of any further defence, cruelly massacred before his eyes, would have appeased it: where there were above six thousand put to the sword, of whom not one was seen to fly, or heard to cry out for quarter; but, on the contrary, every one running here and there to seek out and to provoke the victorious enemy to help them to an honorable end. Not one was seen who, however weakened with wounds, did not in his last gasp yet endeavor to revenge himself, and with all the arms of a brave despair, to sweeten his own death in the death of an enemy. Yet did their valor create no pity, and the length of one day was not enough to satiate the thirst of the conqueror's revenge, but the slaughter continued to the last drop of blood that was capable of being shed, and stopped not till it met with none but unarmed persons, old men, women, and children, of them to carry away to the number of thirty thousand slaves.

OF SORROW.

No man living is more free from this passion than I, who yet neither like it in myself nor admire it in others, and yet generally the world, as a settled thing, is pleased to grace it with a particular esteem, clothing therewith wisdom, virtue, and conscience. Foolish and sordid guise! The Italians have more fitly baptized by this name malignity; for 'tis a quality always hurtful, always idle and vain; and as being cowardly, mean, and base, it is by the Stoics expressly and particularly forbidden to their sages.

But the story says that Psammenitus, king of Egypt, being defeated and taken prisoner by Cambyses, king of Persia, seeing his own daughter pass by him as prisoner, and in a wretched habit, with a bucket to draw water, though his friends about him were so concerned as to break out into tears and lamentations, yet he himself remained unmoved, without uttering a word, his eyes fixed upon the ground; and seeing, moreover, his son immediately after led to execution, still maintained the same countenance; till spying at last one of his domestic and familiar friends dragged away among the captives, he fell to tearing his hair and beating his breast, with all the other extravagances of extreme sorrow.

A story that may very fitly be coupled with another of the same kind, of recent date, of a prince of our own nation, who being at Trent, and having news there brought him of the death of his elder brother, a brother on whom depended the whole support and honor of his house, and soon after of that of a younger brother, the second hope of his family, and having withstood these two assaults with an exemplary resolution; one of his servants happening a few days after to die, he suffered his constancy to be overcome by this last accident; and, parting with his courage, so abandoned himself to sorrow and mourning, that some from thence were forward to conclude that he was only touched to the quick by this last stroke of fortune; but, in truth, it was, that being before brimful of grief, the least addition overflowed the bounds of all patience. Which, I think, might also be said of the former example, did not the story proceed to tell us that Cambyses asking Psammenitus, "Why, not being moved at the calamity of his son and daughter, he should with so great impatience bear the misfortune of his friend?" "It is," answered he, "because only this last affliction was to be manifested by tears, the two first far exceeding all manner of expression."

And, peradventure, something like this might be working in the fancy of the ancient painter, who having, in the sacrifice of Iphigenia, to represent the sorrow of the assistants proportionably to the several degrees of interest every one had in the death of this fair innocent virgin, and having, in the other figures, lain out to the utmost power of his art, when he came to that of her father, he drew him with a veil over his face, meaning thereby that no kind of countenance was capable of expressing such a degree of sorrow. Which is also the reason why the poets feign the miserable mother, Niobe having first lost seven sons, and then afterwards as many daughters (overwhelmed with her losses), to be at last transformed into a rock, thereby to express that melancholic, dumb and deaf stupefaction, which benumbs all our faculties, when oppressed with accidents greater than we are able to bear. And, indeed, the violence and impression of an excessive grief must of necessity astonish the soul, and wholly deprive her of her ordinary functions: as it happens to every one of us, who, upon any sudden alarm of very ill news, find ourselves surprised, stupefied, and in a manner deprived of all power of motion, so that the soul, beginning to vent itself in tears and lamentations, seems to free and disengage itself from the sudden oppression, and to have obtained some room to work itself out at greater liberty. Says the *Æneid*: "And at length and with difficulty is a passage opened by grief for words."

In the war that Ferdinand made upon the widow of King John of Hungary, about Buda, a man-at-arms was particularly taken notice of by every one for his singular gallant behavior in a certain encounter; and, unknown, highly commended, and lamented, being left dead upon the place: but by none so much as by Raisciac, a German lord, who was infinitely enamored of so rare a valor. The body being brought off, and the count, with the common curiosity coming to view it, the armor was no sooner taken off but he immediately knew him to be his own son, a thing that added a second blow to the compassion of all the beholders; only he, without uttering a word, or turning away his eyes from the woful object, stood fixedly contemplating the body of his son, till the vehemency of sorrow having overcome his vital spirits made him sink down stone-dead to the ground. "He who can express in words the ardor of his love, has but little love to express" say the Innamoratos when they would represent an insupportable passion.

Says Seneca: "Light griefs can speak; deep sorrows are dumb."

A surprise of unexpected joy does likewise often produce the same effect: "When she beheld me advancing, and saw, with stupefaction, the Trojan arms around me, terrified with so great a prodigy, she fainted away at the very sight: vital warmth forsook her limbs: she sinks down, and, after a long interval, with difficulty speaks" [*Æneid*].

Besides the examples of the Roman lady, who died for joy to see her son safe returned from the defeat of Cannæ; and of Sophocles and of Dionysius the Tyrant, who died of joy; and of Thalna, who died in Corsica, reading news of the honors the Roman senate had decreed in his favor, we have, moreover, one in our time, of Pope Leo X., who, upon news of the taking of Milan, a thing he had so ardently desired, was rapt with so sudden an excess of joy that he immediately fell into a fever and died. And for a more notable testimony of the imbecility of human nature it is recorded by the ancients that Diodorus the dialectician died upon the spot, out of an extreme passion of shame, for not having been able in his own school, and in the presence of a great auditory, to disengage himself from a nice argument that was propounded to him. I, for my part, am very little subject to these violent passions; I am naturally of a stubborn apprehension, which also, by reasoning, I every day harden and fortify.

THAT THE SOUL DISCHARGES HER PASSIONS UPON FALSE OBJECTS, WHERE THE TRUE ARE WANTING.

A gentleman of my country, marvellously tormented with the gout, being importuned by his physicians totally to abstain from all manner of salt meats, was wont pleasantly to reply, that in the extremity of his fits he must needs have something to quarrel with, and that railing at and cursing, one while the Bologna sausages, and another the dried tongues and the hams, was some mitigation to his pain. But, in good earnest, as the arm when it is advanced to strike, if it miss the blow, and goes by the wind, it pains us; and as also that, to make a pleasant prospect, the sight should not be lost and dilated in vague air, but have some bound and object to limit and circumscribe it at a reasonable distance.

"As winds lose their force, and are dispersed in empty space, when not confined by dense woods" [Lucan].

So it seems that the soul, being transported and discomposed, turns its violence upon itself, if not supplied with something to oppose it, and therefore always requires an object at which to aim and whereon to act. Plutarch says of those who are delighted with little dogs and monkeys, that the amorous part that is in us, for want of a legitimate object, rather than lie idle, does after that manner forge and create one false and frivolous. And we see that the soul, in its passions, inclines rather to deceive itself, by creating a false and fantastical subject, even contrary to its own belief, than not to have something to work upon. After this manner brute beasts direct their fury to fall upon the stone or weapon that has hurt them, and with their teeth even execute revenge upon themselves for the injury they have received from another.

"As the bear, made fiercer by the wound from the Lybian's thong-hurled dart, turns round upon the wound, and attacking the received spear, contorts it, as she flies" [Lucan].

What causes of the misadventures that befall us do we not invent? what is it that we do not lay the fault to, right or wrong, that we may have something to quarrel with? It is not those beautiful tresses you tear, nor is it the white bosom that in your anger you so unmercifully beat, that with an unlucky bullet have slain your beloved brother; quarrel with something else. Livy, speaking of the Roman army in Spain, says that for the loss of the two brothers [Publius and Cneius Scipio], their great captains "all at once wept and tore their hair." 'Tis

a common practice. And the philosopher Bion said, pleasantly, of the
king, who by handfuls pulled his hair off his head for sorrow, "Does
this man think that baldness is a remedy for grief?" Who has not seen
peevish gamesters chew and swallow the cards and swallow the dice in
revenge for the loss of their money? Xerxes whipped the sea, and wrote
a challenge to Mount Athos; Cyrus employed a whole army, several
days at work, to revenge himself of the river Gyndas, for the fright it
had put him into in passing over it; and Caligula demolished a very
beautiful palace for the pleasure his mother had once enjoyed there.

I remember there was a story current, when I was a boy, that one
of our neighboring kings having received a blow from the hand of
God, swore he would be revenged, and, in order to do it, made proc-
lamation that for ten years to come no one should pray to Him, or so
much as mention Him throughout his dominions, or, so far as his
authority went, believe in Him; by which they meant to paint not so
much the folly as the vainglory of the nation of which this tale was
told. They are vices that always go together, but in truth such actions
as these have in them still more of presumption than want of wit.

Augustus Cæsar, having been tossed with a tempest at sea, fell to
defying Neptune, and, in the pomp of the Circensian games, to be
revenged, deposed his statue from the place it had among the other
deities. Wherein he was still less excusable than the former, and less
than he was afterward when, having lost a battle under Quintilius
Varus in Germany, in rage and despair he went running his head
against the wall, crying out, "O Varus! give me back my legions!" for
these exceed all folly, forasmuch as impiety is joined therewith, in-
vading God himself, or at least Fortune, as if she had ears that were
subject to our batteries; like the Thracians, who when it thunders or
lightens, fall to shooting against heaven with Titanian vengeance, as
if by flights of arrows they intended to bring God to reason. Though
the ancient poet in Plutarch tells us: "We must not trouble the gods
with our affairs; they take no heed of our angers and disputes."

But we can never enough decry the disorderly sallies of our
minds.

THAT THE INTENTION IS JUDGE OF OUR ACTIONS.

'Tis a saying, "that death discharges us of all our obligations." I know
some who have taken it in another sense. Henry VII., king of
England, articled with Don Philip, son to Maximilian the emperor,
or (to place him more honorably) father to the Emperor Charles V.,
that the said Philip should deliver up the duke of Suffolk of the White
Rose, his enemy, who was fled into the low countries, into his hands;

which Philip accordingly did, but upon condition, nevertheless, that Henry should attempt nothing against the life of the said duke; but coming to die, the king in his last will commanded his son to put him to death immediately after his decease. And, lately, in the tragedy that the duke of Alva presented to us in the persons of the Counts Horn and Egmont at Brussels, there were very remarkable passages, and one among the rest, that Count Egmont (upon the security of whose word and faith Count Horn had come and surrendered himself to the duke of Alva) earnestly entreated that he might first mount the scaffold, to the end that death might disengage him from the obligation he had passed to the other. In which case, methinks, death did not acquit the former of his promise, and that the second was discharged from it without dying.

We cannot be bound beyond what we are able to perform, by reason that effect and performance are not at all in our power, and that, indeed, we are masters of nothing but the will, in which, by necessity, all the rules and whole duty of mankind are founded and established: therefore Count Egmont, conceiving his soul and will indebted to his promise, although he had not the power to make it good, had doubtless been absolved of his duty, even though he had outlived the other; but the king of England wilfully and premeditately breaking his faith, was no more to be excused for deferring the execution of his infidelity till after his death than Herodotus' mason, who having inviolably, during the time of his life, kept the secret of the treasure of the king of Egypt, his master, at his death discovered it to his children.

I have taken notice of several in my time, who, convicted by their consciences of unjustly detaining the goods of another, have endeavored to make amends by their will, and after their decease; but they had as good do nothing, as either in taking so much time in so pressing an affair, or in going about to remedy a wrong with so little dissatisfaction or injury to themselves. They owe, over and above, something of their own; and by how much their payment is more strict and incommodious to themselves, by so much is their restitution more just and meritorious.

Penitency requires penalty; but they yet do worse than these, who reserve the declaration of a mortal animosity against their neighbor to the last gasp, having concealed it during their life, wherein they manifest little regard of their own honor, irritating the party offended in their memory; and less to their conscience, not having the power, even out of respect to death itself, to make their malice die with them, but extending the life of their hatred even beyond their own. Unjust judges, who defer judgment to a time wherein they can have no knowledge of the cause! For my part, I shall take care, if I can, that my death discover nothing that my life has not first and openly declared.

OF LIARS.

There is not a man living whom it would so little become to speak from memory as myself, for I have scarcely any at all, and do not think that the world has another so marvellously treacherous as mine. My other faculties are all sufficiently ordinary and mean; but in this I think myself very rare and singular and deserving to be thought famous. Besides the natural inconvenience I suffer by it (for, certes, the necessary use of memory considered, Plato had reason when he called it a great and powerful goddess), in my country, when they would say a man has no sense, they say, such a one has no memory; and when I complain of the defect of mine, they do not believe me, and reprove me, as though I accused myself for a fool: not discerning the difference between memory and understanding, which is to make matters still worse for me.

But they do me wrong; for experience, rather, daily shows us on the contrary, that a strong memory is commonly coupled with infirm judgment. They do me, moreover (who am so perfect in nothing as in friendship), a great wrong in this, that they make the same words which accuse my infirmity, represent me for an ungrateful person: they bring my affections into question upon the account of my memory, and from a natural imperfection, make out a defect of conscience. "He has forgot," says one, "this request or that promise; he no more remembers his friends; he has forgot to say or do, or conceal such and such a thing, for my sake." And, truly, I am apt enough to forget many things, but to neglect anything my friend has given me in charge, I never do it. And it should be enough, methinks, that I feel the misery and inconvenience of it, without branding me with malice, a vice so contrary to my humor.

However, I derive these comforts from my infirmity: first, that it is an evil from which principally I have found reason to correct a worse, that would easily enough have grown upon me, namely, ambition; the defect being intolerable in those who take upon them public affairs. That, as several like examples in the progress of nature demonstrate to us, she has fortified me in my other faculties proportionably as she has left me unfurnished in this; I should otherwise have been apt implicitly to have reposed my mind and judgment upon the bare report of other men, without ever setting them to work upon their own force, had the inventions and opinions of others been ever present with me by the benefit of memory. That by this means I am not so talkative, for the magazine of the memory is ever better furnished with matter than that of the invention. Had mine been faithful to me, I had ere this deafened all my friends with my babble, the subjects themselves arousing and stirring up the little faculty I have of handling and employing them, heating and extending my discourse, which were a pity: as I have observed in several of my intimate friends, who, as their memories supply them with an entire and full view of things, begin their narrative so far back, and crowd it with so many impertinent circumstances, that though the story be good in itself, they make a shift to spoil it; and if otherwise, you are either to curse the strength of their memory or the weakness of their judgment: and it is a hard thing to close up a discourse, and to cut it short, when you have once started; there is nothing wherein the force of a horse is so much seen as in a round and sudden stop.

I see even those who are pertinent enough, who would, but cannot stop short in their career; for while they are seeking out a handsome period to conclude with, they go on at random, straggling about upon impertinent trivialities, as men staggering upon weak legs. But, above all, old men who retain the memory of things past, and forget how often they have told them, are dangerous company; and I have known stories from the mouth of a man of very great quality, otherwise very pleasant in themselves, become very wearisome by being repeated a hundred times over and over again to the same people.

Secondly, that, by this means, I the less remember the injuries I have received; insomuch that, as the ancient said, I should have a register of injuries, or a prompter, as Darius, who, that he might not forget the offence he had received from those of Athens, so oft as he sat down to dinner, ordered one of his pages three times to repeat in his ear, "Sir, remember the Athenians;" and then, again, the places which I revisit, and the books I read over again, still smile upon me with a fresh novelty.

It is not without good reason said "that he who has not a good memory should never take upon him the trade of lying." I know very well that the grammarians distinguish between an *untruth* and a *lie*, and say that to tell an *untruth* is to tell a thing that is false, but that we ourselves believe to be true; and that the definition of the word *to lie* in Latin, from which our French is taken, is to tell a thing which we know in our conscience to be untrue; and it is of this last sort of liars only that I now speak. Now, these do either wholly contrive and invent the untruths they utter, or so alter and disguise a true story that it ends in a lie. When they disguise and often alter the same story according to their own fancy, 'tis very hard for them, at one time or another, to escape being trapped, by reason that the real truth of the thing, having first taken possession of the memory, and being there lodged and impressed by the medium of knowledge and science, it will be difficult that it should not represent itself to the imagination, and shoulder out false-hood, which cannot there have so sure and settled footing as the other; and the circumstances of the first true knowledge evermore running in their minds, will be apt to make them forget those that are illegitimate, and only forged by their own fancy. In what they wholly invent, for-asmuch as there is no contrary impression to jostle their invention, there seems to be less danger of tripping; and yet even this also, by reason it is a vain body, and without any hold, is very apt to escape the memory, if it be not well assured. Of which I have had very pleasant experience, at the expense of such as profess only to form and accom-modate their speech to the affair they have in hand, or to the humor of the great folks to whom they are speaking; for the circumstances to which these men stick not to enslave their faith and conscience being subject to several changes, their language must vary accordingly: whence it happens that of the same thing they tell one man that it is this, and another that it is that, giving it several colors; which men, if they once come to confer notes, and find out the cheat, what becomes of this fine art? To which may be added, that they must of necessity very often ridiculously trap themselves; for what memory can be suf-ficient to retain so many different shapes as they have forged upon one and the same subject? I have known many in my time very ambitious of the repute of this fine wit; but they do not see that if they have the reputation of it, the effect can no longer be.

In plain truth, lying is an accursed vice. We are not men, nor have other tie upon one another, but by our word. If we did but discover the horror and gravity of it, we should pursue it with fire and sword, and more justly than other crimes. I see that parents commonly, and with indiscretion enough, correct their children for little innocent faults, and torment them for wanton tricks, that have neither impres-sion nor consequence; whereas, in my opinion, lying only, and which is of something a lower form, obstinacy, are the faults which are to be severely whipped out of them, both in their infancy and in their progress, otherwise they grow up and increase with them; and after a tongue has once got the knack of lying, 'tis not to be imagined how impossible it is to reclaim it: whence it comes to pass that we see some, who are otherwise very honest men, so subject and enslaved to this vice. I have an honest lad to my tailor, whom I never knew guilty of one truth, no, not when it had been to his advantage.

If *falsehood* had, like *truth*, but one face only, we should be upon better terms; for we should then take for certain the contrary to what the liar says: but the reverse of *truth* has a hundred thousand forms, and a field indefinite, without bound or limit. The Pythagoreans make *good* to be certain and finite, and *evil*, infinite and uncertain. There are a thousand ways to miss the white, there is only one to hit it. For my own part, I have this vice in so great horror, that I am not sure I could prevail with my conscience to secure myself from the most manifest and extreme danger by an impudent and solemn lie. An ancient father says "that a dog we know is better company than a man whose language we do not understand." "As a foreigner cannot be said to supply to us the place of a man" [Pliny]. And how much less sociable is false speaking than silence?

King Francis I. bragged that he had, by this means, nonplussed Francisco Taverna, ambassador of Francisco Sforza, duke of Milan, a man very famous for his science in talking in those days. This gentleman had been sent to excuse his master to his majesty about a thing of very great consequence, which was this: the king, still to maintain some intelligence with Italy, out of which he had lately been driven, and particularly with the duchy of Milan, had thought it convenient to have a gentleman on his behalf to be with that duke: an ambassador in effect, but in outward appearance a private person who pretended to reside there upon his own particular affairs; for the duke, much more depending upon the emperor, especially at a time when he was in a treaty of a marriage with his niece, daughter to the king of Denmark, and now dowager of Lorraine, could not manifest any practice and conference with us, but very much to his own prejudice.

For this commission one Merveille, a Milanese gentleman, and an equerry to the king, being thought very fit, was accordingly despatched thither with private credentials, and instructions as ambassador, and with other letters of recommendation to the duke about his own private concerns, the better to mask and color the business; and was so long in that court, that the emperor at last had some inkling of his real employment there; which was the occasion of what followed after, as we suppose; which was, that under pretence of some murder, his trial was in two days despatched, and his head in the night struck off in prison.

Messire Francisco being come, and prepared with a long counterfeit history of the affair (for the king had applied himself to all the princes of Christendom, as well as to the duke himself, to demand satisfaction), had his audience at the morning council; where, after he had for the support of his cause laid open several plausible justifications of the fact, that his master never looked upon this Merveille for other than a private gentleman, and his own subject, who was there only in order to his own business, neither had he ever lived after any other aspect; absolutely disowning that he had ever heard he was one of the king's household, or that his majesty so much as knew him, so far was he from taking him for an ambassador: the king, in his turn, pressing him with several objections and demands, and sifting him on all hands, gravelled him at last by asking, why, then, the execution was performed by night, and as it were by stealth? At which the poor confounded ambassador, the more handsomely to disengage himself, made answer, that the duke would have been very loath, out of respect to his majesty, that such an execution should have been performed by day. Any one may guess if he was not well rated when he came home, for having so grossly tripped in the presence of a prince of so delicate a nostril as King Francis.

Pope Julius II. having sent an ambassador to the king of England to animate him against King Francis, the ambassador having had his audience, and the king, before he would give an answer, insisting upon the difficulties he should find in setting on foot so great a preparation as would be necessary to attack so potent a king, and urging some reasons to that effect, the ambassador, very unseasonably, replied that he had also himself considered the same difficulties, and had represented them to the pope. From which saying of his, so directly opposite to the thing propounded, and the business he came about, which was immediately to incite him to war, the king first derived argument (which also he afterward found to be true), that this ambassador, in his own mind, was on the side of the French; of which having advertised the pope, his estate at his return home was confiscated, and he himself very narrowly escaped the losing of his head.

OF QUICK OR SLOW SPEECH.

"All graces were never yet given to any one man," so we see in the gift of eloquence, wherein some have such a facility and promptness, and that which we call a *present* wit so easy, that they are ever ready upon all occasions, and never to be surprised; and others more heavy and slow, never venture to utter anything but what they have long premeditated, and taken great care and pains to fit and prepare.

Now, as we teach young ladies those sports and exercises which are most proper to set out the grace and beauty of those parts wherein their chiefest ornament and perfection lie, so it should be in these two advantages of eloquence, to which the lawyers and preachers of our age seem principally to pretend. If I were worthy to advise, the slow speaker, methinks, should be more proper for the pulpit, and the other for the bar: and that because the employment of the first does naturally allow him all the leisure he can desire to prepare himself, and besides, his career is performed in an even and unintermitted line, without stop or interruption; whereas the pleader's business and interest compels him to enter the lists upon all occasions, and the unexpected objections and replies of his adverse party jostle him out of his course, and put him, upon the instant, to pump for new and extempore answers and defences.

Yet, at the interview between Pope Clement and King Francis at Marseilles, it happened, quite contrary, that Monsieur Poyet, a man bred up all his life at the bar, and in the highest repute for eloquence, having the charge of making the harangue to the pope committed to him, and having so long meditated on it beforehand, as, so they said, to have brought it ready made along with him from Paris; the very day it was to have been pronounced, the pope, fearing something might be said that might give offence to the other prince's ambassadors who were there attending on him, sent to acquaint the king with the argument which he conceived most suiting to the time and place, but, by chance, quite another thing to that Monsieur de Poyet had taken so much pains about: so that the fine speech he had prepared was of no use, and he was upon the instant to contrive another; which finding himself unable to do, Cardinal du Bellay was constrained to perform that office.

The pleader's part is, doubtless, much harder than that of the preacher, and, yet, in my opinion, we see more passable lawyers than preachers, at all events in France. It should seem that the nature of wit is to have its operation prompt and sudden, and that of judgment, to have it more deliberate and more slow. But he who remains totally silent, for want of leisure to prepare himself to speak well, and he also whom leisure does noways benefit to better speaking, are equally unhappy.

'Tis said of Severus Cassius that he spoke best extempore; that he stood more obliged to fortune than to his own diligence; that it was an advantage to him to be interrupted in speaking, and that his adversaries were afraid to nettle him, lest his anger should redouble his eloquence. I know experimentally, the disposition of nature so impatient of a tedious and elaborate premeditation, that if it do not go frankly and gayly to work, it can perform nothing to purpose. We say of some compositions that they stink of oil and of the lamp, by reason of a certain rough harshness that laborious handling imprints upon those where it has been employed.

But besides this, the solicitude of doing well, and a certain striving and contending of a mind too far strained and overbent upon its undertaking, breaks and hinders itself like water, that by force of its own pressing violence and abundance, cannot find a ready issue through the neck of a bottle or a narrow sluice. In this condition of nature, of which I am now speaking, there is this also, that it would not be disordered and stimulated with such passions as the fury of Cassius (for such a motion would be too violent and rude); it would not be jostled but solicited; it would be roused and heated by unexpected, sudden, and accidental occasions. If it be left to itself, it flags and languishes; agitation, only, gives it grace and vigor.

I am always worst in my own possession: and when wholly at my own disposition: accident has more title to anything that comes from me than I; occasion, company, and even the very rising and falling of my own voice, extract more from my fancy than I can find when I sound and employ it by myself. By which means, the things I say are better than those I write, if either were to be preferred, where neither is worth anything. This, also, befalls me, that I do not find myself where I seek myself, and I light upon things more by chance than by any inquisition of my own judgment. I perhaps sometimes hit upon something when I write, that seems quaint and sprightly to me, though it will appear dull and heavy to another.

But let us leave these fine compliments; every one talks thus of himself according to his talent. But when I come to speak, I am already so lost that I know not what I was about to say, and in such cases a stranger often finds it out before me. If I should make erasures so often as this inconvenience befalls me, I should make clean work; occasion will, at some other time, lay it as visible to me as the light, and make me wonder what I should stick at.

OF CONSTANCY.

The law of resolution and constancy does not imply that we ought not, as much as in us lies, to decline and secure ourselves from the mischiefs and inconveniences that threaten us; nor, consequently, that we shall not fear lest they should surprise us: on the contrary, all decent and honest ways and means of securing ourselves from harms, are not only permitted, but, moreover, commendable, and the business of constancy chiefly is, bravely to stand to, and stoutly to suffer those inconveniences which are not possibly to be avoided. So that there is no supple motion of body, nor any movement in the handling of arms, how irregular or ungraceful soever, that we need condemn, if they serve to protect us from the blow that is made against us.

Several very warlike nations have made use of a retreating and flying way of fight as a thing of singular advantage, and, by so doing, have made their backs more dangerous to their enemies than their faces. Of which kind of fighting the Turks still retain something in their practice of arms; and Socrates, in Plato, laughs at Laches, who had defined fortitude to be a standing firm in the ranks against the enemy. "What!" says he, "would it, then, be a reputed cowardice to overcome them by giving ground?" urging, at the same time, the authority of Homer, who commends in Æneas the science of flight. And whereas Laches, considering better o' it, admits the practice as to the Scythians, and, in general, all cavalry whatever, he again attacks him with the example of the Lacedæmonian foot — a nation of all other the most obstinate in maintaining their ground — who, in the battle of Platæa, not being able to break into the Persian phalanx, bethought themselves to disperse and retire, that by the enemy supposing they fled, they might break and disunite that vast body of men in the pursuit, and by that stratagem obtained the victory.

As for the Scythians, 'tis said of them, that when Darius went his expedition to subdue them, he sent, by a herald, highly to reproach their king, that he always retired before him, and declined a battle; to which Idanthyrses, for that was his name, returned answer, that it was not for fear of him, or of any man living, that he did so, but that it was the way of marching in practice with his nation, who had neither tilled fields, cities, nor houses to defend, or to fear the enemy should make any advantage of; but that if he had such a stomach to fight, let him but come to view their ancient places of sepulture, and there he should have his fill.

Nevertheless, as to cannon-shot, when a body of men are drawn up in the face of a train of artillery, as the occasion of war often requires, it is unhandsome to quit their post to avoid the danger, forasmuch as by reason of its violence and swiftness we account it inevitable; and many a one, by ducking, stepping aside, and such other motions of fear, has been, at all events, sufficiently laughed at by his companions. And yet, in the expedition that the Emperor Charles V. made against us into Provence, the Marquis de Guast going to reconnoitre the city of Arles, and advancing out of the cover of a windmill, under favor of which he had made his approach, was perceived by the Seigneurs de Bonneval and the seneschal of Agenois, who were walking upon the *théâtre aux arènes*; who having shown him to the Sieur de Villiers, commissary of the artillery, he pointed a culverin so admirably well, and levelled it so exactly right against him, that had not the marquis, seeing fire given to it, slipped aside, it was certainly concluded the shot had taken him full in the body. And, in like manner, some years before, Lorenzo de Medici, duke of Urbino [Florence] and father to the queen-mother [Catherine de Medici, mother of Henry III.], laying siege to Mondolpho, a place in the territories of the vicariat in Italy, seeing the cannoneer give fire to a

piece that pointed directly against him, it was well for him that he
ducked, for otherwise the shot, that only razed the top of his head,
had doubtless hit him full in the breast. To say truth, I do not think
that these evasions are performed upon the account of judgment; for
how can any man living judge of high or low aim on so sudden an
occasion? And it is much more easy to believe that Fortune favored
their apprehension, and that it might be as well at another time to
make them face the danger, as to seek to avoid it. For my own part,
I confess I cannot forbear starting when the rattle of a arquebus thunders in my ears on a sudden, and in a place where I am not to expect
it, which I have also observed in others, braver fellows than I.

Neither do the Stoics pretend that the soul of their philosopher
need be proof against the first visions and fantasies that surprise him;
but, as to a natural subjection, consent that he should tremble at the
terrible noise of thunder, or the sudden clatter of some falling ruin,
and be affrighted even to paleness and convulsion; and so in other
passions, provided his judgment remain sound and entire, and that the
seat of his reason suffer no concussion nor alteration, and that he yield
no consent to his fright and discomposure. To him who is not a philosopher a fright is the same thing in the first part of it, but quite
another thing in the second; for the impression of passions does not
remain superficially in him, but penetrates farther, even to the very
seat of reason, infecting and corrupting it, so that he judges according
to his fear, and conforms his behavior to it. In this verse you may see
the true state of the wise Stoic learnedly and plainly expressed,
"Though tears flow, the mind remains unmoved" [Virgil].

The peripatetic sage does not exempt himself totally from pertur-
bations of mind, but he moderates them.

OF FEAR.

"I was amazed, my hair stood on end, and my voice stuck in my
throat" [Virgil].

I am not so good a naturalist (as they call it) as to discern by what
secret springs fear has its motion in us; but, be this as it may, 'tis a
strange passion, and such a one that the physicians say there is no
other whatever that sooner dethrones our judgment from its proper
seat; which is so true, that I myself have seen very many become
frantic through fear; and, even in those of the best settled temper, it
is most certain that it begets a terrible astonishment and confusion
during the fit. I omit the vulgar sort, to whom it one while represents
their great-grandsires risen out of their graves in their shrouds, another while hobgoblins, spectres, and chimeras; but even among

soldiers, a sort of men over whom, of all others, it ought to have the least power, how often has it converted flocks of sheep into armed squadrons, reeds and bulrushes into pikes and lances, friends into enemies, and the French white cross into the red cross of Spain!

When Monsieur de Bourbon took Rome [1527], an ensign who was upon guard at Borgo San Pietro was seized with such a fright upon the first alarm, that he threw himself out at a breach with his colors upon his shoulder, and ran directly upon the enemy, thinking he had retreated toward the inward defences of the city, and with much ado, seeing Monsieur de Bourbon's people, who thought it had been a sally upon them, draw up to receive him, at last came to himself, and saw his error; and then facing about, he retreated full speed through the same breach by which he had gone out, but not till he had first blindly advanced above three hundred paces into the open field.

It did not, however, fall out so well with Captain Julio's ensign, at the time when St. Paul was taken from us by the Count de Bures and Monsieur de Reu, for he, being so astonished with fear as to throw himself, colors and all, out at a porthole, was immediately cut to pieces by the enemy; and in the same siege, it was a very memorable fear that so seized, contracted, and froze up the heart of a gentleman, that he sank down, stone-dead, in the breach, without any manner of wound or hurt at all.

The like madness does sometimes push on a whole multitude; for in one of the encounters that Germanicus had with the Germans, two great parties were so amazed with fear that they ran two opposite ways, the one to the same place from which the other had fled. Sometimes it adds wings to the heels, as in the two first: sometimes it nails them to the ground, and fetters them from moving; as we read of the Emperor Theophilus, who, in a battle he lost against the Agarenes, was so astonished and stupefied that he had no power to fly; till such time as Manuel, one of the principal commanders of his army, having jogged and shaked him so as to rouse him out of his trance, said to him, "Sir, if you will not follow me, I will kill you; for it is better you should lose your life than, by being taken, lose your empire."

But fear does then manifest its utmost power when it throws us upon a valiant despair, having before deprived us of all sense both of duty and honor. In the first pitched battle the Romans lost against Hannibal, under the consul Sempronius, a body of ten thousand foot, that had taken fright, seeing no other escape for their cowardice, went and threw themselves headlong upon the great battalion of the enemies, which with marvellous force and fury they charged through and through, and routed with a very great slaughter of the Carthaginians, thus purchasing an ignominious flight at the same price they might have gained a glorious victory.

The thing in the world I am most afraid of is fear, that passion alone, in the trouble of it, exceeding all other accidents. What affliction could be greater or more just than that of Pompey's friends, who, in his ship, were spectators of that horrible murder? Yet so it was, that the fear of the Egyptian vessels they saw coming to board them, possessed them with so great alarm that it is observed they thought of nothing but calling upon the mariners to make haste, and by force of oars to escape away, till being arrived at Tyre, and delivered from fear, they had leisure to turn their thoughts to the loss of their captain, and to give vent to those tears and lamentations that the other more potent passion had till then suspended.

Such as have been well banged in some skirmish, may yet, all wounded and bloody as they are, be brought on again the next day to charge; but such as have once conceived a good sound fear of the enemy, will never be made so much as to look him in the face. Such as are in immediate fear of losing their estates, of banishment, or of slavery, live in perpetual anguish, and lose all appetite and repose; whereas such as are actually poor, slaves, or exiles, ofttimes live as merrily as other folk. And the many people who, impatient of the perpetual alarms of fear, have hanged or drowned themselves, or dashed themselves to pieces, give us sufficiently to understand that fear is more importunate and insupportable than death itself.

The Greeks acknowledge another kind of fear, differing from any we have spoken of yet, that surprises us without any visible cause, by an impulse from heaven, so that whole nations and whole armies have been struck with it. Such a one was that which brought so wonderful a desolation upon Carthage, where nothing was to be heard but affrighted voices and outcries; where the inhabitants were seen to sally out of their houses as to an alarm, and there to charge, wound, and kill one another, as if they had been enemies come to surprise their city. All things were in disorder and fury till, with prayers and sacrifices, they had appeased their gods; and this is that they call a panic terror.

THAT MEN ARE NOT TO JUDGE OF OUR HAPPINESS TILL AFTER DEATH.

"We should all look forward to our last day; no one can be called happy till he is dead and buried" [Ovid].

The very children know the story of King Crœsus to this purpose, who being taken prisoner by Cyrus, and by him condemned to die, as he was going to execution cried out, "O Solon, Solon!" which being presently reported to Cyrus, and he sending to inquire of him what it meant, Crœsus gave him to understand that he now found the teaching Solon had formerly given him true to his cost, which was, "That men, however fortune may smile upon them, could never be said to be happy till they had been seen to pass over the last day of their lives," by reason of the uncertainty and mutability of human things, which, upon very light and trivial occasions, are subject to be totally changed into a quite contrary condition.

And so it was that Agesilaus made answer to one who was saying what a happy young man the king of Persia was, to come so young to so mighty a kingdom; "'Tis true," said he, "but neither was Priam unhappy at his years." In a short time, kings of Macedon, successors to that mighty Alexander, became joiners and scriveners at Rome; a tyrant of Sicily, a pedant at Corinth; a conqueror of one-half of the world and general of so many armies, a miserable suppliant to the rascally officers of a king of Egypt: so much did the prolongation of five or six months of life cost the great Pompey; and, in our fathers' days, Ludovico Sforza, the tenth duke of Milan, whom all Italy had so long truckled under, was seen to die a wretched prisoner at Loches, but not till he had lived ten years in captivity, which was the worst part of his fortune. The fairest of all queens,[1] widow to the greatest king in Europe, did she not come to die by the hand of an executioner? Unworthy and barbarous cruelty! And a thousand more examples there are of the same kind; for, it seems, that as storms and tempests have a malice against the proud and overtowering heights of our lofty buildings, there are also spirits above that are envious of the grandeurs here below.

And it should seem, also, that Fortune sometimes lies in wait to surprise the last hour of our lives, to show the power she has, in a moment, to overthrow what she was so many years in building, making us cry out with Laberius, "I have lived longer by this one day than I should have done."

And, in this sense, this good advice of Solon may reasonably be taken; but he, being a philosopher (with which sort of men the favors and disgraces of Fortune stand for nothing, either to the making a man happy or unhappy, and with whom grandeurs and powers are accidents of a quality almost indifferent) I am apt to think that

---

[1] Mary, Queen of Scots.

he had some further aim, and that his meaning was, that the very felicity of life itself, which depends upon the tranquillity and contentment of a well-descended spirit, and the resolution and assurance of a well-ordered soul, ought never to be attributed to any man till he has first been seen to play the last and doubtless the hardest act of his part. There may be disguise and dissimulation in all the rest: where these fine philosophical discourses are only put on, and where accident, not touching us to the quick, gives us leisure to maintain the same gravity of aspect; but, in this last scene of death, there is no more counterfeiting: we must speak out plain, and discover what there is of pure and clean in the bottom of the pot. Lucretius says, "Then at last truth issues from the heart; the visor's gone, the man remains."

Wherefore, at this last, all the other actions of our life ought to be tried and sifted; 'tis the master-day, 'tis the day that is judge of all the rest, "'tis the day," says one of the ancients [Seneca], "that must be judge of all my foregoing years." To death do I refer the assay of the fruit of all my studies: we shall then see whether my discourses came only from my mouth or from my heart. I have seen many by their death give a good or an ill repute to their whole life. Scipio, the father-in-law of Pompey, in dying, well wiped away the ill opinion that till then every one had conceived of him. Epaminondas being asked which of the three he had in greatest esteem, Chabrias, Iphicrates, or himself, "You must first see us die," said he, "before that question can be resolved." And, in truth, he would infinitely wrong that man who would weigh him without the honor and grandeur of his end.

God has ordered all things as it has best pleased Him; but I have, in my time, seen three of the most execrable persons that ever I knew in all manner of abominable living, and the most infamous to boot, who all died a very regular death, and in all circumstances composed, even to perfection. There are brave and fortunate deaths: I have seen death cut the thread of the progress of a prodigious advancement, and in the height and flower of its increase, of a certain person, with so glorious an end that, in my opinion, his ambitious and generous designs had nothing in them so high and great as their interruption. He arrived, without completing his course, at the place to which his ambition aimed, with greater glory than he could either have hoped or desired, anticipating by his fall the name and power to which he aspired in perfecting his career. In the judgment I make of another man's life, I always observe how he carried himself at his death; and the principal concern I have for my own is that I may die well — that is, patiently and tranquilly.

THAT IT IS FOLLY TO MEASURE TRUTH AND ERROR BY OUR OWN CAPACITY.

'Tis not, perhaps, without reason, that we attribute facility of belief and easiness of persuasion, to simplicity and ignorance; for I fancy I have heard belief compared to the impression of a seal upon the soul, which by how much softer and of less resistance it is, is the more easy to be impressed upon. Says Cicero: "As the scale of the balance must give way to the weight that presses it down, so the mind must of necessity yield to demonstration." By how much the soul is more empty and without counterpoise, with so much greater facility it yields under the weight of the first persuasion. And this is the reason that children, the common people, women, and sick folks, are most apt to be led by the ears.

But then, on the other hand, 'tis a foolish presumption to slight and condemn all things for false that do not appear to us probable; which is the ordinary vice of such as fancy themselves wiser than their neighbors. I was myself once one of those; and if I heard talk of dead folks walking, of prophecies, enchantments, witchcrafts, or any other story I had no mind to believe: "Dreams, magic terrors, marvels, sorceries, hobgoblins, and Thessalian prodigies," I presently pitied the poor people that were abused by these follies. Whereas I now find, that I myself was to be pitied as much, at least, as they; not that experience has taught me anything to alter my former opinions, though my curiosity has endeavored that way; but reason has instructed me, that thus resolutely to condemn anything for false and impossible, is arrogantly and impiously to circumscribe and limit the will of God, and the power of our mother nature, within the bounds of my own capacity, than which no folly can be greater. If we give the names of monster and miracle to everything our reason cannot comprehend, how many are continually presented before our eyes? Let us but consider through what clouds, and as it were groping in the dark, our teachers lead us to the knowledge of most of the things about us; assuredly we shall find that it is rather custom than knowledge that takes away their strangeness, and that if those things were now newly presented to us, we should think them as incredible, if not more, than any others.

He that had never seen a river, imagined the first he met with to be the sea; and the greatest things that have fallen within our knowledge, we conclude the extremes that nature makes of the kind.

"Things grow familiar to men's minds by being often seen; so that they neither admire, nor are inquisitive about, things they daily see" [Cicero]. The novelty, rather than the greatness of things, tempts us to inquire into their causes. We are to judge with more reverence,

and with greater acknowledgment of our own ignorance and infirmity, of the infinite power of nature. How many unlikely things are
there testified by people worthy of faith, which, if we cannot persuade ourselves absolutely to believe, we ought at least to leave them
in suspense; for, to condemn them as impossible, is by a temerarious
presumption to pretend to know the utmost bounds of possibility.
Did we rightly understand the difference between the impossible and
the unusual, and between that which is contrary to the order and
course of nature, and contrary to the common opinion of men, in not
believing rashly, and on the other hand, in not being too incredulous,
we should observe the rule of *Ne quid nimis*, enjoined by Chilo.

When we find in Froissart, that the Count de Foix knew in Bearn
the defeat of John, king of Castile, at Juberoth the next day after it
happened, and the means by which he tells us he came to do so, we
may be allowed to be a little merry at it, as also at what our annals
report, that Pope Honorius, the same day that King Philip Augustus
died at Mantes, performed his public obsequies at Rome, and commanded the like throughout Italy, the testimony of these authors not
being, perhaps, of authority enough to restrain us. But what if
Plutarch, besides several examples that he produces out of antiquity,
tells us, he knows of certain knowledge, that in the time of Domitian,
the news of the battle lost by Anthony in Germany, was published at
Rome, many days' journey from thence, and dispersed throughout
the whole world, the same day it was fought; and if Cæsar was of
opinion, that it has often happened, that the report has preceded the
incident, shall we not say, that these simple people have suffered
themselves to be deceived with the vulgar, for not having been so
clear-sighted as we? Is there anything more delicate, more clear, more
sprightly, than Pliny's judgment, when he is pleased to set it to work?
Anything more remote from vanity? Setting aside his learning, of
which I make less account, in which of these excellences do any of
us excel him? And yet there is scarce a young schoolboy that does not
convict him of untruth, and that pretends not to instruct him in the
progress of the works of nature.

When we read in Bouchet the miracles of St. Hilary's relics, away
with them: his authority is not sufficient to deprive us of the liberty of
contradicting him; but generally and offhand to condemn all such like
stories seems to me a singular impudence. That great St. Augustin
testifies to have seen a blind child recover sight upon the relics of
St. Gervaise and St. Protasius at Milan; a woman at Carthage cured of
a cancer, by the sign of the cross made upon her by a woman newly
baptized; Hesperius, a familiar friend of his, to have driven away the
spirits that haunted his house, with a little earth of the sepulchre of our

Lord; which earth, being also transported thence into the church, a paralytic to have there been suddenly cured by it; a woman in a procession, having touched St. Stephen's shrine with a nosegay, and rubbing her eyes with it, to have recovered her sight, lost many years before; with several other miracles of which he professes himself to have been an eyewitness; of what shall we accuse him and the two holy bishops, Aurelius and Maximinus, both of whom he attests to the truth of these things? Shall it be of ignorance, simplicity, and facility; or of malice and imposture? Is any man now living so impudent as to think himself comparable to them in virtue, piety, learning, judgment, or any kind of perfection? "Who, though they should give me no reason for what they affirm, convince me with their sole authority" [Cicero].

'Tis a presumption of great danger and consequence, besides the absurd temerity it draws after it, to contemn what we do not comprehend. For after, according to your fine understanding, you have established the limits of truth and error, and that, afterward, there appears a necessity upon you of believing stranger things than those you have contradicted, you are already obliged to quit your limits. Now, that which seems to me so much to disorder our consciences in the commotions we are now in concerning religion, is the Catholics dispensing so much with their belief. They fancy they appear moderate, and wise, when they grant to their opponents some of the articles in question; but, besides that they do not discern what advantage it is to those with whom we contend, to begin to give ground and to retire, and how much this animates our enemy to follow his blow; these articles which they select as things indifferent are sometimes of very great importance.

We are either wholly and absolutely to submit ourselves to the authority of our ecclesiastical polity, or totally throw off all obedience to it: 'tis not for us to determine what and how much obedience we owe to it. And this I can say, as having myself made trial of it, that having formerly taken the liberty of my own swing and fancy, and omitted or neglected certain rules of the discipline of our church, which seemed to me vain and strange: coming afterward to discourse of it with learned men, I have found those same things to be built upon very good and solid ground and strong foundation; and that nothing but stupidity and ignorance makes us receive them with less reverence than the rest.

Why do we not consider what contradictions we find in our own judgments; how many things were yesterday articles of our faith, that to-day appear no other than fables? Glory and curiosity are the scourges of the soul; the last prompts us to thrust our noses into everything, the other forbids us to leave anything doubtful and undecided.

OF FRIENDSHIP.

Having considered the proceedings of a painter that serves me, I had a mind to imitate his way. He chooses the fairest place and middle of any wall, or panel, wherein to draw a picture, which he finishes with his utmost care and art, and the vacuity about it he fills with grotesques, which are odd fantastic figures without any grace but what they derive from their variety, and the extravagance of their shapes. And in truth, what are these things I scribble, other than grotesques and monstrous bodies, made of various parts, without any certain figure, or any other than accidental order, coherence, or proportion?

In this second part I go hand in hand with my painter; but fall very short of him in the first and the better, my power of handling not being such, that I dare to offer at a rich piece, finely polished, and set off according to art. I have therefore thought fit to borrow one of Estienne de la Boetie, and such a one as shall honor and adorn all the rest of my work—namely, a discourse that he called Voluntary Servitude; but, since, those who did not know him have properly enough called it "Le contre Un." He wrote in his youth by way of essay, in honor of liberty against tyrants; and it has since run through the hands of men of great learning and judgment, not without singular and merited commendation; for it is finely written, and as full as anything can possibly be.

And yet one may confidently say it is far short of what he was able to do; and if in that more mature age, wherein I had the happiness to know him, he had taken a design like this of mine, to commit his thoughts to writing, we should have seen a great many rare things, and such as would have gone very near to have rivalled the best writings of antiquity: for in natural parts especially, I know no man comparable to him. But he has left nothing behind him, save this treatise only (and that, too, by chance, for I believe he never saw it after it first went out of his hands), and some observations upon that edict of January,[1] made famous by our civil wars, which also shall elsewhere, peradventure, find a place. These were all I could recover of his remains, I to whom, with so affectionate a remembrance, upon his deathbed, he by his last will bequeathed his library and papers, the little book of his works only excepted, which I committed to the press. And this particular obligation I have to this treatise of his, that it was the occasion of my first coming acquainted with him; for it was showed to me long before I had the good fortune to know him; and gave me the first knowledge of his name, proving the first cause and foundation of a friendship

---

[1] 1562, which granted to the Huguenots the public exercise of their religion.

which we afterward improved and maintained, so long as God was pleased to continue us together, so perfect, inviolate, and entire, that certainly the like is hardly to be found in story, and among the men of this age there is no sign nor trace of any such thing in use; so much concurrence is required to the building of such a one, that 'tis much, if fortune bring it but once to pass in three ages.

There is nothing to which nature seems so much to have inclined us as to society; and Aristotle says, that the good legislators had more respect to friendship than to justice. Now the most supreme point of its perfection is this: for, generally, all those that pleasure, profit, public or private interest create and nourish, are so much the less beautiful and generous, and so much the less friendships, by how much they mix another cause, and design, and fruit in friendship, than itself. Neither do the four ancient kinds, natural, social, hospitable, venerian, either separately or jointly, make up a true and perfect friendship.

That of children to parents is rather respect: friendship is nourished by communication, which cannot, by reason of the great disparity, be betwixt these, but would rather perhaps offend the duties of nature; for neither are all the secret thoughts of fathers fit to be communicated to children, lest it beget an indecent familiarity between them; nor can the advices and reproofs, which is one of the principal offices of friendship, be properly performed by the son to the father. There are some countries where 'twas the custom for children to kill their fathers; and others, where the fathers killed their children, to avoid their being an impediment one to another in life; and naturally the expectations of the one depend upon the ruin of the other.

This name of brother does indeed carry with it a fine and delectable sound, and for that reason, he and I called one another brothers, but the complication of interests, the division of estates, and that the wealth of the one should be the poverty of the other, strangely relax and weaken the fraternal tie: brothers pursuing their fortune and advancement by the same path, 'tis hardly possible but they must of necessity often jostle and hinder one another. Besides, why is it necessary that the correspondence of manners, parts, and inclinations, which begets the true and perfect friendships, should always meet in these relations? The father and the son may be of quite contrary humors, and so of brothers: he is my son, he is my brother; but he is passionate, ill-natured, or a fool. And moreover, by how much these are friendships that the law and natural obligation impose upon us, so much less is there of our own choice and voluntary freedom; whereas that voluntary liberty of ours has no production more promptly and properly its own than affection and friendship. Not that I have not in my own person experimented all that can possibly be expected of that kind, having had the best and most indulgent father, even to his extreme old age, that ever was, and who was himself descended from a family for many generations famous and exemplary for brotherly concord.

We are not here to bring the love we bear to women, though it be an act of our own choice, into comparison; nor rank it with the others. "Nor is the goddess unknown to me, who mixes a pleasing sorrow with my love's flame" [Catullus]. The fire of this, I confess, is more active, more eager, and more sharp; but withal, 'tis more precipitant, fickle, moving, and inconstant; a fever subject to intermissions and paroxysms, that has seized but on one part of us. Whereas in friendship, 'tis a general and universal fire, but temperate and equal, a constant established heat, all gentle and smooth, without poignancy or roughness. Moreover, in love, 'tis no other than frantic desire for that which flies from us: "As the hunter pursues the hare, through cold and heat, over hill and dale, but, so soon as it is taken, no longer cares for it, and only delights in chasing that which flees from him" [Ariosto], so soon as it enters into the terms of friendship, that is to say, into a concurrence of desires, it vanishes and is gone, fruition destroys it, as having only a fleshly end, and such a one as is subject to satiety. Friendship, on the contrary, is enjoyed proportionably as it is desired; and only grows up, is nourished and improves by enjoyment, as being of itself spiritual, and the soul growing still more refined by practice. Under this perfect friendship, the other fleeting affections have in my younger years found some place in me, to say nothing of him, who himself so confesses but too much in his verses; so that I had both these passions, but always so, that I could myself well enough distinguish them, and never in any degree of comparison with one another; the first maintaining its flight in so lofty and so brave a place, as with disdain to look down, and see the other flying at a far humbler pitch below.

As concerning marriage, besides that it is a covenant, the entrance into which only is free, but the continuance in it forced and compulsory, having another dependence than that of our own freewill, and a bargain commonly contracted to other ends, there almost always happens a thousand intricacies in it to unravel, enough to break the thread and to divert the current of a lively affection: whereas friendship has no manner of business or traffic with aught but itself. Moreover, to say truth, the ordinary talent of women is not such as is sufficient to maintain the conference and communication required to the support of this sacred tie; nor do they appear to be endued with constancy of mind, to sustain the pinch of so hard and durable a knot. And doubtless, if without this, there could be such a free and voluntary familiarity contracted where not only the souls might have this entire fruition, but the bodies also might share in the alliance, and a man be engaged throughout, the friendship would certainly be more full and perfect; but it is without example that this sex has ever yet arrived at such perfection; and by the common consent of the ancient schools, it is wholly rejected from it.

I return to my own more just and true description. "Those are only to be reputed friendships, that are fortified and confirmed by judgment and length of time" [Cicero]. For the rest, what we commonly call friends and friendships, are nothing but acquaintance and familiarities, either occasionally contracted or upon some design, by means of which there happens some little intercourse between our souls. But in the friendship I speak of, they mix and work themselves into one piece, with so universal a mixture, that there is no more sign of the seam by which they were first conjoined. If a man should importune me to give a reason why I loved him, I find it could no otherwise be expressed, than by making answer: because it was he, because it was I. There is, beyond all that I am able to say, I know not what inexplicable and fated power that brought on this union. We sought one another long before we met, and by the characters we heard of one another, which wrought upon our affections more than, in reason, mere reports should do; I think 'twas by some secret appointment of heaven. We embraced in our names; and at our first meeting, which was accidentally at a great city entertainment, we found ourselves so mutually taken with one another, so acquainted, and so endeared between ourselves, that from thenceforward nothing was so near to us as one another. He wrote an excellent Latin satire, since printed, wherein he excuses the precipitation of our intelligence, so suddenly come to perfection, saying, that destined to have so short a continuance, as begun so late (for we were both full-grown men, and he some years the older), there was no time to lose, nor were we tied to conform to the example of those slow and regular friendships that require so many precautions of long preliminary conversation. This has no other idea than that of itself, and can only refer to itself: this is no one special consideration, nor two, nor three, nor four, nor a thousand; 'tis I know not what quintessence of all this mixture, which, seizing my whole will, carried it to plunge and lose itself in his, and that having seized his whole will, brought it back with equal concurrence and appetite to plunge and lose itself in mine. I may truly say lose, reserving nothing to ourselves, that was either his or mine.[1]

---

[1] All this relates to Estienne de la Boetie.

When Lælius, in the presence of the Roman consuls, who after they had sentenced Tiberius Gracchus, prosecuted all those who had had any familiarity with him also, came to ask Caius Blosius, who was his chiefest friend how much he would have done for him, and that he made answer: "All things." "How! All things!" said Lælius. "And what if he had commanded you to fire our temples?" "He would never have commanded me that," replied Blosius. "But what if he had?" said Lælius. "I would have obeyed him," said the other. If he was so perfect a friend to Gracchus, as the histories report him to have been, there was yet no necessity of offending the consuls by such a bold confession, though he might still have retained the assurance he had of Gracchus' disposition. However, those who accuse this answer as seditious, do not well understand the mystery; nor presuppose, as it was true, that he had Gracchus' will in his sleeve, both by the power of a friend, and the perfect knowledge he had of the man: they were more friends than citizens, more friends to one another than either friends or enemies to their country, or than friends to ambition and innovation; having absolutely given up themselves to one another, either held absolutely the reins of the other's inclination; and suppose all this guided by virtue, and all this by the conduct of reason, which also without these it had not been possible to do, Blosius' answer was such as it ought to be. If any of their actions flew out of the handle, they were neither (according to my measure of friendship) friends to one another, nor to themselves.

As to the rest, this answer carries no worse sound, than mine would do to one that should ask me: "If your will should command you to kill your daughter, would you do it?" and that I should make answer, that I would; for this expresses no consent to such an act, forasmuch as I do not in the least suspect my own will, and as little that of such a friend. 'Tis not in the power of all the eloquence in the world to dispossess me of the certainty I have of the intentions and resolutions of my friend: nay, no one action of his, what face soever it might bear, could be presented to me, of which I could not presently, and at first sight, find out the moving cause. Our souls had drawn so unanimously together, they had considered each other with so ardent an affection, and with the like affection laid open the very bottom of our hearts to one another's view, that I not only knew his as well as my own; but should certainly in any concern of mine have trusted my interest much more willingly with him than with myself.

Let no one, therefore, rank other common friendships with such a one as this. I have had as much experience of these as another, and of the most perfect of their kind; but I do not advise that any should confound the rules of the one and the other, for they would find themselves much deceived. In those other ordinary friendships, you are to walk with bridle in your hand, with prudence and circumspection, for in them the knot is not so sure, that a man may not half suspect it will slip. "Love him," said Chilo, "so, as if you were one day to hate him; and hate him so, as you were one day to love him." This precept, though abominable in the sovereign and perfect friendship I speak of, is nevertheless very sound, as to the practice of the ordinary and customary ones, and to which the saying that Aristotle had so frequent in his mouth, "Oh, my friends, there is no friend;" may very fitly be applied.

In this noble commerce, good offices, presents, and benefits, by which other friendships are supported and maintained, do not deserve so much as to be mentioned; and the reason is the concurrence of our wills; for as the kindness I have for myself receives no increase, for anything I relieve myself withal in time of need (whatever the Stoics say), and as I do not find myself obliged to myself for any service I do myself: so the union of such friends, being truly perfect, deprives them of all idea of such duties, and makes them loathe and banish from their conversation these words of division and distinction, benefit, obligation, acknowledgment, entreaty, thanks, and the like. All things, wills, thoughts, opinions, goods, wives, children, honors, and lives, being in effect common between them, and that absolute concurrence of affections being no other than one soul in two bodies (according to that very proper definition of Aristotle), they can neither lend nor give anything to one another. This is the reason why the lawgivers, to honor marriage with some resemblance of this divine alliance, interdict all gifts between man and wife; inferring by that, that all should belong to each of them, and that they have nothing to divide or to give to each other.

If, in the friendship of which I speak, one could give to the other, the receiver of the benefit would be the man that obliged his friend; for each of them contending and above all things studying how to be useful to the other, he that administers the occasion is the liberal man, in giving his friend the satisfaction of doing that toward him, which above all things he most desires. When the philosopher Diogenes wanted money, he used to say that he redemanded it of his friends, not that he demanded it. And to let you see the practical working of this, I will here produce an ancient and singular example: Eudamidas a Corinthian had two friends, Charixenus a Sycionian, and Areteus a Corinthian; this man coming to die, being poor, and his two friends rich, he made his will after this manner. "I bequeath to Areteus the maintenance of my mother, to support and provide for her in her old age; and to Charixenus I bequeath the care of marrying my daughter, and to give her as good a portion as he is able; and in case one of these chance to die, I hereby substitute the survivor in his place." They who first saw this will, made themselves very merry at the contents: but the legatees being made acquainted with it, accepted it with very great content; and one of them, Charixenus, dying within five days after, and Areteus, by that means, having the charge of both duties devolved solely to him, he nourished the old woman with very great care and tenderness, and of five talents he had in estate, he gave two and a half in marriage with an only daughter he had of his own, and two and a half in marriage with the daughter of Eudamidas, and in one and the same day solemnized both their nuptials.

This example is very full, if one thing were not to be objected, namely, the multitude of friends: for the perfect friendship I speak of is indivisible; each one gives himself so entirely to his friend, that he has nothing left to distribute to others: on the contrary, is sorry that he is not double, treble, or quadruple, and that he has not many souls, and many wills, to confer them all upon this one object. Common friendships will admit of division; one may love the beauty of this person, the good-humor of that, the liberality of a third, the paternal affection of a fourth, the fraternal love of a fifth, and so of the rest: but this friendship that possesses the whole soul, and there rules and sways with an absolute sovereignty, cannot possibly admit of a rival. If two at the same time should call to you for succor, to which of them would you run? Should they require of you contrary offices, how could you serve them both? Should one commit a thing to your silence, that it were of importance to the other to know, how would you disengage yourself?

A unique and particular friendship dissolves all other obligations whatsoever: the secret I have sworn not to reveal to any other, I may without perjury communicate to him who is not another, but myself. 'Tis miracle enough certainly, for a man to double himself, and those that talk of tripling, talk they know not of what. Nothing is extreme, that has its like; and he who shall suppose, that of two, I love one as much as the other, that they mutually love one another too, and love me as much as I love them, multiplies into a confraternity the most single of units, and whereof, moreover, one alone is the hardest thing in the world to find. The rest of this story suits very well with what I was saying; for Eudamidas, as a bounty and favor, bequeaths to his friends a legacy of employing themselves in his necessity; he leaves them heirs to this liberality of his, which consists in giving them the opportunity of conferring a benefit upon him; and doubtless, the force of friendship is more eminently apparent in this act of his, than in that of Areteus.

In short, these are effects not to be imagined nor comprehended by such as have not experience of them, and which make me infinitely honor and admire the answer of that young soldier to Cyrus, by whom being asked how much he would take for a horse with which he had won the prize of a race, and whether he would exchange him for a kingdom? "No, truly, sir," said he, "but I would give him with all my heart, to get thereby a true friend, could I find out any man worthy of that alliance." He did not say ill in saying, "could I find"; for though one may almost everywhere meet with men sufficiently qualified for a superficial acquaintance, yet in this, where a man is to deal from the very bottom of his heart, without any manner of reservation, it will be requisite that all the wards and springs be truly wrought, and perfectly sure.

In confederations that hold but by one end, we are only to provide against the imperfections that particularly concern that end. It can be of no importance to me of what religion my physician or my lawyer is; this consideration has nothing in common with the offices of friendship which they owe me; and I am of the same indifference in the domestic acquaintance my servants must necessarily contract with me. I never inquire, when I am to take a footman, if he be chaste, but if he be diligent; and am not solicitous if my muleteer be given to gaming, as if he be strong and able; or if my cook be a swearer, if he be a good cook. I do not take upon me to direct what other men should do in the government of their families (there are plenty that meddle enough with that), but only give an account of my method in my own. Terence says, "This has been my way; as for you, do as you think fit."

For table-talk, I prefer the pleasant and witty before the learned and the grave; in bed, beauty before goodness; in common discourse, the ablest speaker, whether or no there be sincerity in the case. And, as he that was found astride upon a hobby-horse, playing with his children, entreated the person who had surprised him in that posture to say nothing of it till himself came to be a father,[1] supposing that the fondness that would then possess his own soul, would render him a fairer judge of such an action; so I, also, could wish to speak to such as have had experience of what I say: though, knowing how remote a thing such a friendship is from the common practice, and how rarely it is to be found, I despair of meeting with any such judge. For even these discourses left us by antiquity upon this subject, seem to me flat and poor in comparison of the sense I have of it, and in this particular, the effects surpass even the precepts of philosophy. "While I have

---

[1] Plutarch, *Life of Agesilaus*, c. 9.

sense left to me, there will never be anything more acceptable to me than an agreeable friend" [Horace].

The ancient Menander declared him to be happy that had had the good fortune to meet with but the shadow of a friend: and doubtless he had good reason to say so, especially if he spoke by experience; for in good earnest, if I compare all the rest of my life, though, thanks be to God, I have passed my time pleasantly enough, and at my ease, and the loss of such a friend excepted, free from any grievous affliction, and in great tranquillity of mind, having been contented with my natural and original commodities, without being solicitous after others; if I should compare it all, I say, with the four years I had the happiness to enjoy the sweet society of this excellent man, 'tis nothing but smoke, an obscure and tedious night. From the day that I lost him, "A day to me forever sad, forever sacred, so have you willed, ye gods" [Æneid], I have only led a languishing life; and the very pleasures that present themselves to me, instead of administering anything of consolation, double my affliction for his loss. We were halves throughout, and to that degree, that methinks, by outliving him, I defraud him of his part. "I have determined that it will never be right for me to enjoy any pleasure, so long as he, with whom I shared in all pleasures, is away" [Terence].

I was so grown and accustomed to be always his double in all places and in all things, that methinks I am no more than half of myself. As Horace says: "If that half of my soul were snatched away from me by an untimely stroke, why should the other stay? That which remains will not be equally dear, will not be a whole: the same day will involve the destruction of both." There is no action or imagination of mine wherein I do not miss him; as I know that he would have missed me: for as he surpassed me by infinite degrees in virtue and all other accomplishments, so he also did in the duties of friendship. "What shame can there be, or measure, in lamenting so dear a friend?"

THAT A MAN IS SOBERLY TO JUDGE OF
THE DIVINE ORDINANCES.

The true field and subject of imposture are things unknown, forasmuch as, in the first place, their very strangeness lends them credit, and moreover, by not being subjected to our ordinary reasons, they deprive us of the means to question and dispute them. For which reason, says Plato, it is much more easy to satisfy the hearers, when speaking of the nature of the gods than of the nature of men, because the ignorance of the auditory affords a fair and large career and all manner of liberty in the handling of abstruse things. Thence it comes to pass, that nothing is so firmly believed, as what we least know; nor any people so confident, as those who entertain us with fables, such as your alchemists, judicial astrologers, fortunetellers, and physicians, *id genus omne*; to which I would willingly, if I durst, join a pack of people that take upon them to interpret and control the designs of God himself, pretending to find out the cause of every accident, and to pry into the secrets of the divine will, there to discover the incomprehensible motives of His works; and although the variety, and the continual discordance of events, throw them from corner to corner, and toss them from east to west, yet do they still persist in their vain inquisition, and with the same pencil to paint black and white.

In a nation of the Indies, there is this commendable custom, that when anything befalls them amiss in any encounter or battle, they publicly ask pardon of the sun, who is their god, as having committed an unjust action, always imputing their good or evil fortune to the divine justice, and to that submitting their own judgment and reason. 'Tis enough for a Christian to believe that all things come from God, to receive them with acknowledgment of His divine and inscrutable wisdom, and also thankfully to accept and receive them, with what face soever they may present themselves. But I do not approve of what I see in use, that is, to seek to affirm and support our religion by the prosperity of our enterprises.

Our belief has other foundation enough, without going about to authorize it by events: for the people being accustomed to such plausible arguments as these and so proper to their taste, it is to be feared, lest when they fail of success they should also stagger in their faith; as in the war wherein we are now engaged upon the account of religion, those who had the better in the business of Rochelabeille; making great brags of that success, as an infallible approbation of their cause, when they came afterward to excuse their misfortunes of Moncontour and Jarnac, by saying they were fatherly scourges and corrections that they had not a people wholly at their mercy, they make it manifestly enough appear, what it is to take two sorts of grist out of the same sack, and with the same mouth to blow hot and cold. It were better to possess the vulgar with the solid and real foundations of truth. 'Twas a fine naval battle that was gained under the command of Don John of Austria a few months since[1] against the Turks; but it has also pleased God at other times to let us see as great victories at our own expense.

In fine, 'tis a hard matter to reduce divine things to our balance, without waste and losing a great deal of the weight. And who would

---

[1] That of Lepanto, October 7, 1571.

take upon him to give a reason, that Arius, and his Pope Leo, the principal heads of the Arian heresy, should die, at several times, of so like and strange deaths, and would aggravate this divine vengeance by the circumstances of the place, might as well add the similar death of Heliogabalus. And, indeed, Irenæus was involved in the same fortune. God, being pleased to show us, that the good have something else to hope for and the wicked something else to fear, than the fortunes or misfortunes of this world, manages and applies these according to His own occult will and pleasure, and deprives us of the means foolishly to make thereof our own profit. And those people abuse themselves who will pretend to dive into these mysteries by the strength of human reason. They never give one hit that they do not receive two for it; of which St. Augustine makes out a great proof upon his adversaries.

'Tis a conflict, that is more decided by strength of memory than by the force of reason. We are to content ourselves with the light it pleases the sun to communicate to us, by virtue of his rays; and who will lift up his eyes to take in a greater, let him not think it strange, if for the reward of his presumption, he there lose his sight. "Who among men can know the counsel of God? or who can think what the will of the Lord is?"

OF THE CUSTOM OF WEARING CLOTHES.

Whatever I shall say upon this subject, I am of necessity to invade some of the bounds of custom, so careful has she been to shut up all the avenues. I was disputing with myself in this shivering season, whether the fashion of going naked in those nations lately discovered is imposed upon them by the hot temperature of the air, as we say of the Indians and Moors, or whether it be the original fashion of mankind. Men of understanding, forasmuch as all things under the sun, as the holy writ declares, are subject to the same laws, were wont in such considerations as these, where we are to distinguish the natural laws from those that have been imposed by man's invention, to have recourse to the general polity of the world, where there can be nothing counterfeit. Now all other creatures being sufficiently furnished with all things necessary for the support of their being, it is not to be imagined that we only should be brought into the world in a defective and indigent condition, and in such a state as cannot subsist without external aid.

Therefore it is that I believe, that as plants, trees, and animals, and all things that have life, are seen to be by nature sufficiently clothed and covered to defend them from the injuries of weather, so were we;

but as those who by artificial light put out that of the day, so we by borrowed forms and fashions have destroyed our own. And 'tis plain enough to be seen that 'tis custom only which renders that impossible that otherwise is nothing so; for of those nations who have no manner of knowledge of clothing, some are situated under the same temperature that we are, and some in much colder climates. And besides, our most tender parts are always exposed to the air, as the eyes, mouth, nose, and ears; and our country laborers, like our ancestors in former times, go with their breasts and bellies open. Had we been born with a necessity upon us of wearing petticoats and breeches there is no doubt but nature would have fortified those parts she intended should be exposed to the fury of the seasons with a thicker skin, as she has done the finger-ends, and the soles of the feet.

And why should this seem hard to believe? I observe much greater distance between my habit and that of one of our country boors, than between his and that of a man who has no other covering but his skin. How many men, especially in Turkey, go naked upon the account of devotion? Some one asked a beggar, whom he saw in his shirt in the depth of winter as brisk and frolic as he who goes muffled up to the ears in furs, how he was able to endure to go so. "Why, sir," he answered, "you go with your face bare: I am all face." The Italians have a story of the duke of Florence's fool, whom his master asking, how, being so thinly clad, he was able to support the cold, when he himself, warmly wrapped up as he was, was hardly able to do it. "Why," replied the fool, "use my receipt to put on all your clothes you have at once, and you'll feel no more cold than I."

King Massinissa, to an extreme old age, could never be prevailed upon to go with his head covered, how cold, stormy, or rainy soever the weather might be; which also is reported of the Emperor Severus. Herodotus tells us, that in the battles fought between the Egyptians and the Persians, it was observed both by himself and by others, that of those who were left dead upon the field, the heads of the Egyptians were without comparison harder than those of the Persians, by reason that the last had gone with their heads always covered from their infancy, first with biggins, and then with turbans, and the others always shaved and bare. King Agesilaus continued to a decrepit age, to wear always the same clothes in winter that he did in summer. Cæsar, says Suetonius, marched always at the head of his army, for the most part on foot, with his head bare, whether it was rain or sunshine, and as much is said of Hannibal.

A Venetian who had long lived in Pegu, and has lately returned thence, writes that the men and women of that kingdom, though they cover all their other parts, go always barefoot and ride so, too;

and Plato very earnestly advises for the health of the whole body, to give the head and the feet no other clothing than what nature has bestowed. He whom the Poles have elected for their king,[1]—since ours came thence,—who is, indeed, one of the greatest princes of this age, never wears any gloves, and in winter or whatever weather can come, never wears other cap abroad than that he wears at home. Whereas I cannot endure to go unbuttoned or untied; my neighboring laborers would think themselves in chains, if they were so braced.

Varo is of opinion, that when it was ordained we should be bare in the presence of the gods and before the magistrate, it was so ordered rather upon the score of health, and to inure us to the injuries of the weather, than upon the account of reverence; and since we are now talking of cold, and Frenchmen use to wear variety of colors (not I myself, for I seldom wear other than black or white in imitation of my father), let us add another story out of Captain Martin du Bellay, who affirms that in the march to Luxembourg he saw so great frost, that the munition wine was cut with hatchets and wedges, and delivered out to the soldiers by weight and that they carried it away in baskets; and Ovid says, "The wine when out of the cask, retains the form of the cask; and is given out not in cups, but in bits."

At the mouth of Lake Mæotis, the frosts are so very sharp, that in the very same place where Mithridates' lieutenant had fought the enemy dry-foot and given them a notable defeat, the summer following he obtained over them a naval victory. The Romans fought at a very great disadvantage, in the engagement they had with the Carthaginians near Placentia, by reason that they went to the charge with their blood fixed and their limbs numbed with cold; whereas Hannibal had caused great fires to be dispersed quite through his camp to warm his soldiers, and oil to be distributed among them, to the end that anointing themselves, they might render their nerves more supple and active, and fortify the pores against the violence of the air and freezing wind, which raged in that season.

The retreat the Greeks made from Babylon into their own country is famous for the difficulties and calamities they had to overcome; of which this was one, that being encountered in the mountains of Armenia with a horrible storm of snow, they lost all knowledge of the country and of the ways, and being driven up, were a day and a night without eating or drinking; most of their cattle died, many of themselves starved to death, several struck blind with the driving hail and the glittering of the snow, many of them maimed in their fingers and

---

[1] Stephen Bathory.

toes, and many stiff and motionless with the extremity of the cold, who had yet their understanding entire.

Alexander saw a nation, where they bury their fruit-trees in winter, to protect them from being destroyed by the frost, and we also may see the same.

But, so far as clothes go, the king of Mexico changed four times a day his apparel, and never put it on again, employing that he left off in his continual liberalities and rewards; and neither pot, dish, nor other utensil of his kitchen or table was ever served twice.

THAT WE LAUGH AND CRY FOR THE SAME THING.

When we read in history, that Antigonus was very much displeased with his son for presenting him the head of King Pyrrhus his enemy, but newly slain fighting against him, and that seeing it, he wept: and that René, Duke of Lorraine, also lamented the death of Charles, Duke of Burgundy, whom he had himself defeated, and appeared in mourning at his funeral: and that in the battle of d'Auray (which Count Montfort obtained over Charles de Blois, his competitor for the duchy of Brittany), the conqueror meeting the dead body of his enemy, was very much afflicted at his death, we must not presently cry out, "And thus it happens that the mind of each veils its passion under a different appearance, sad beneath a smiling visage, gay beneath a sombre air" [Petrarch].

When Pompey's head was presented to Cæsar, the histories tell us that he turned away his face, as from a sad and unpleasing object. There had been so long an intelligence and society between them in the management of the public affairs, so great a community of fortunes, so many mutual offices, and so near an alliance, that this countenance of his ought not to suffer under any misinterpretation; or to be suspected for either false or counterfeit, as this other seems to believe, "And now he thought it safe to play the kind father-in-law, he shed forced tears, and from a joyful breast sent forth sighs and groans" [Lucan]; for though it be true that the greatest part of our actions are no other than visor and disguise, and that it may sometimes be true that "The heir's tears behind the mask are smiles," yet, in judging of these accidents, we are to consider how much our souls are oftentimes agitated with divers passions.

And as they say that in our bodies there is a congregation of divers humors, of which that is the sovereign which, according to the complexion we are of, is commonly most predominant in us: so, though the soul have in it divers motions to give it agitation, yet must there of necessity be one to overrule all the rest, though not with so necessary and absolute a dominion but that through the flexibility and inconstancy of the soul, those of less authority may upon occasion reassume their place and make a little sally in turn. Thence it is, that we see not only children, who innocently obey and follow nature, often laugh and cry at the same thing, but not one of us can boast, what journey soever he may have in hand that he has the most set his heart upon, but when he comes to part with his family and friends, he will find something that troubles him within; and though he refrain his tears yet he puts his foot in the stirrup with a sad and cloudy countenance.

Neither is it strange to lament a person dead, whom a man would by no means should be alive. When I rattle my man, I do it with all the mettle I have, and load him with no feigned, but downright real curses; but the heat being over, if he should stand in need of me, I should be very ready to do him good: for I instantly turn the leaf. When I call him calf and coxcomb, I do not pretend to entail those titles upon him forever; neither do I think I give myself the lie in calling him an honest fellow presently after. No one quality engrosses us purely and universally. Were it not the sign of a fool to talk to one's self, there would hardly be a day or hour wherein I might not be heard to grumble and mutter to myself and against myself, "Confound the fool!" and yet I do not think that to be my definition. Who for seeing me one while cold and presently very fond toward my wife, believes the one or the other to be counterfeited, is an ass.

Nero, taking leave of his mother whom he was sending to be drowned, was nevertheless sensible of some emotion at this farewell, and was struck with horror and pity. 'Tis said that the light of the sun is not one continuous thing, but that he darts new rays so thick one upon another that we cannot perceive the intermission. Says Lucretius, "Exhaustless source of liquid light, the ethereal sun, inundates the heavens with splendor, ever renewing itself, still replacing its rays with new rays." Just so the soul variously and imperceptibly darts out her passions.

Artabanus coming by surprise once upon his nephew Xerxes, chid him for the sudden alteration of his countenance. He was considering the immeasurable greatness of his forces passing over the Hellespont for the Grecian expedition: he was first seized with a palpitation of joy, to see so many millions of men under his command, and this appeared in the gayety of his looks: but his thoughts at the same instant suggesting to him that of so many lives, within a century at most, there would not be one left, he presently knit his brows and grew sad, even to tears.

We have resolutely pursued the revenge of an injury received, and been sensible of a singular contentment for the victory; but we shall weep notwithstanding. 'Tis not for the victory, though, that we shall weep: there is nothing altered in that: but the soul looks upon things with another eye and represents them to itself with another kind of face; for everything has many faces and several aspects.

Relations, old acquaintance, and friendships possess our imaginations and make them tender for the time, according to their condition; but the turn is so quick, that 'tis gone in a moment. "Nothing therefore so prompt as the soul when it propounds anything to be done and begins to do it. It is more active than anything which we see in nature" [Lucretius], and therefore, if we would make one continued thing of all this succession of passions, we deceive ourselves. When Timoleon laments the murder he had committed upon so mature and generous deliberation, he does not lament the liberty restored to his country, he does not lament the tyrant, but he laments his brother; one part of his duty is performed; let us give him leave to perform the other.

OF SOLITUDE.

Let us pretermit that long comparison between the active and the solitary life; and as for the fine saying with which ambition and avarice palliate their vices, that we are not born for ourselves but for the public, let us boldly appeal to those who are in public affairs; let them lay their hands upon their hearts, and then say whether, on the contrary, they do not rather aspire to titles and offices and that tumult of the world to make their private advantage at the public expense. The corrupt ways by which in this our time they arrive at the height to which their ambitions aspire, manifestly enough declare that their ends cannot be very good. Let us tell ambition that it is she herself who gives us a taste of solitude; for what does she so much avoid as society? What does she so much seek as elbow-room? A man may do well or ill everywhere: but if what Bias says be true, that the greatest part is the worse part, or what the Preacher says: there is not one good of a thousand, the contagion is very dangerous in the crowd. Says Juvenal, "Good men are scarce: we could hardly reckon up as many as there are gates to Thebes, or mouths to the Nile." A man must either imitate the vicious or hate them: both are dangerous things, either to resemble them because they are many or to hate many because they are unresembling to ourselves.

Merchants who go to sea are in the right, when they are cautious that those who embark with them in the same bottom be neither dissolute blasphemers nor vicious other ways, looking upon such society as unfortunate. And therefore it was that Bias pleasantly said to some, who being with him in a dangerous storm implored the assistance of the gods: "Peace, speak softly," said he, "that they may not know you are here in my company." And of more pressing example, Albuquerque, viceroy in the Indies for Emmanuel, king of Portugal, in an extreme peril of shipwreck took a young boy upon his shoulders, for this only end that, in the society of their common danger, his innocence might serve to protect him, and to recommend him to the divine favor, that they might get safe to shore. 'Tis not that a wise man may not live everywhere content, and be alone in the very crowd of a palace: but if it be left to his own choice, the schoolman will tell you that he should fly the very sight of the crowd: he will endure it, if need be; but if it be referred to him, he will choose to be alone. He cannot think himself sufficiently rid of vice, if he must yet contend with it in other men. Charondas punished those as evil men who were convicted of keeping ill company. There is nothing so unsociable and sociable as man, the one by his vice, the other by his nature. And Antisthenes, in my opinion, did not give him a satisfactory answer, who reproached him with frequenting ill company, by saying that the physicians lived well enough among the sick: for if they contribute to the health of the sick, no doubt but by the contagion, continual sight of, and familiarity with diseases, they must of necessity impair their own.

Now the end, I take it, is all one, to live at more leisure and at one's ease: but men do not not always take the right way. They often think they have totally taken leave of all business, when they have only exchanged one employment for another: there is little less trouble in governing a private family than a whole kingdom. Whenever the mind is perplexed it is in an entire disorder, and domestic employments are not less troublesome for being less important. Moreover, for having shaken off the court and the exchange, we have not taken leave of the principal vexations of life. "Reason and prudence, not a place with a commanding view of the great ocean, banish care" [Horace]. Ambition, avarice, irresolution, fear, and inordinate desires do not leave us because we forsake our native country: they often follow us even to cloisters and philosophical schools; nor deserts, nor caves, hair-shirts, nor fasts, can disengage us from them.

One telling Socrates that such a one was nothing improved by his travels: "I very well believe it," said he, "for he took himself along with him." Says Horace: "Why do we seek climates warmed by another sun? Who is the man that by fleeing from his country, can also flee from himself?" If a man do not first discharge both himself and his mind of the burden with which he finds himself oppressed, motion will but make it press the harder and sit the heavier, as the lading of a ship is of less encumbrance when fast and bestowed in a settled posture. You do a sick man more harm than good in removing him from place to place; you fix and establish the disease by motion, as stakes sink deeper and more firmly into the earth by being moved up and down in the place where they are designed to stand. Therefore, it is not enough to get remote from the public; 'tis not enough to shift the soil only; a man must flee from the popular conditions that have taken possession of his soul, he must sequester and come again to himself. "You say, perhaps, you have broken your chain: the dog who after long efforts has broken his chain, still in his flight drags a heavy portion of it after him" [Persius].

We still carry our fetters along with us. 'Tis not an absolute liberty; we yet cast back a look upon what we have left behind us; the fancy is still full of it. "But unless the mind is purified, what internal combats and dangers must we incur in spite of all our efforts! How many bitter anxieties, how many terrors, follow upon unregulated passion! What destruction befalls us from pride, lust, petulant anger! What evils arise from luxury and sloth!" [Lucretius]. Our disease lies in the mind, which cannot escape from itself; and therefore is to be called home and confined within itself: that is the true solitude, and that may be enjoyed even in populous cities and the courts of kings, though more commodiously apart.

Now, since we will attempt to live alone, and to waive all manner of conversation among men, let us so order it that our content may depend wholly upon ourselves; let us dissolve all obligations that ally us to others; let us obtain this from ourselves, that we may live alone in good earnest, and live at our ease too.

Stilpo having escaped from the fire that consumed the city where he lived, and wherein he had lost his wife, children, goods, and all that ever he was master of, Demetrius Poliorcetes seeing him, in so great a ruin of his country, appear with a serene and undisturbed countenance, asked him if he had received no loss? To which he made answer, no; and that, thanks be to God, nothing was lost of his. This also was the meaning of the philosopher Antisthenes, when he pleasantly said, that "men should furnish themselves with such things as would float, and might with the owner escape the storm;" and certainly a wise man never loses anything if he have himself. When the city of Nola was ruined by the barbarians, Paulinus, who was bishop of that place, having there lost all he had, and himself a prisoner, prayed after this manner: "O Lord, defend me from being sensible of this loss; for Thou knowest they have yet touched nothing of that which is mine." The riches that made him rich, and the goods

that made him good, were still kept entire. This it is to make choice
of treasures that can secure themselves from plunder and violence,
and to hide them in such a place into which no one can enter, and
that is not to be betrayed by any but ourselves. Wives, children, and
goods must be had, and especially health, by him that can get it; but
we are not so to set our hearts upon them that our happiness must
have its dependence upon them; we must reserve a backshop, wholly
our own and entirely free, wherein to settle our true liberty, our
principal solitude and retreat. And in this we must for the most part
entertain ourselves with ourselves, and so privately that no exotic
knowledge or communication be admitted there; there to laugh and
to talk, as if without wife, children, goods, train, or attendance, to the
end, that when it shall so fall out that we must lose any or all of these,
it may be no new thing to be without them. We have a mind pliable
in itself, that will be company; that has herewithal to attack and to
defend, to receive and to give: let us not then fear in this solitude to
languish under an uncomfortable vacuity. "In solitude, be company
for thyself" [Tibullus].

Virtue is satisfied with herself, without discipline, without words,
without effects. In our ordinary actions there is not one of a thousand
that concerns ourselves. He that thou seest scrambling up the ruins of
that wall, furious and transported, against whom so many harquebus-
shots are levelled; and that other all over scars, pale, and fainting with
hunger, and yet resolved rather to die than to open the gates to him;
dost thou think that these men are there upon their own account?
No; peradventure in the behalf of one whom they never saw and who
never concerns himself for their pains and danger, but lies wallowing
the while in sloth and pleasure; this other slavering, blear-eyed, slov-
enly fellow, that thou seest come out of his study after midnight, dost
thou think he has been tumbling over books, to learn how to become
a better man, wiser, and more content? No such matter; he will there
end his days, but he will teach posterity the measure of Plautus' verses
and the true orthography of a Latin word. Who is it that does not
voluntarily exchange his health, his repose, and his very life for reputation and glory, the most useless, frivolous, and false coin that passes
current among us. Our own death does not sufficiently terrify and
trouble us; let us, moreover, charge ourselves with those of our wives,
children, and family: our own affairs do not afford us anxiety enough;
let us undertake those of our neighbors and friends, still more to break
our brains and torment us. "Ah, can any man discover or devise anything dearer than he is to himself?" [Terence].

Solitude seems to me to wear the best favor, in such as have already
employed their most active and flourishing age in the world's service;

after the example of Thales. We have lived enough for others, let us at least live out the small remnant of life for ourselves; let us now call in our thoughts and intentions to ourselves, and to our own ease and repose. 'Tis no light thing to make a sure retreat; it will be enough for us to do without mixing other enterprises. Since God gives us leisure to order our removal, let us make ready, truss our baggage, take leave betimes of the company, and disentangle ourselves from those violent importunities that engage us elsewhere and separate us from ourselves.

We must break the knot of our obligations, how strong soever, and hereafter love this or that, but espouse nothing but ourselves: that is to say, let the remainder be our own, but not so joined and so close as not to be forced away without flaying us or tearing out part of our whole. The greatest thing in the world is for a man to know that he is his own. 'Tis time to wean ourselves from society, when we can no longer add anything to it; he who is not in a condition to lend must forbid himself to borrow. Our forces begin to fail us: let us call them in and concentrate them in and for ourselves. He that can cast off within himself and resolve the offices of friendship and company, let him do it. In this decay of nature which renders him useless, burden-some, and importunate to others, let him take care not to be useless, burdensome, and importunate to himself. Let him soothe and caress himself, and above all things be sure to govern himself with reverence to his reason and conscience to that degree as to be ashamed to make a false step in their presence. "For 'tis rarely seen that men have re-spect and reverence enough for themselves" [Quintilian]. Socrates says that boys are to cause themselves to be instructed, men to exer-cise themselves in well-doing, and old men to retire from all civil and military employments, living at their own discretion, without the obligation to any office.

There are some complexions more proper for these precepts of retirement than others. Such as are of a soft and dull apprehension, and of a tender will and affection not readily to be subdued or em-ployed, whereof I am one, both by natural condition and by reflec-tion, will sooner incline to this advice, than active and busy souls, which embrace all, engage in all, are hot upon everything, which offer, present, and give themselves up to every occasion. We are to use these accidental and extraneous commodities, so far as they are pleasant to us, but by no means to lay our principal foundation there; 'tis no true one: neither nature nor reason allows it so to be. Why therefore should we, contrary to their laws, enslave our own content-ment to the power of another? To anticipate also the accidents of fortune, to deprive ourselves of the conveniences we have in our own power, as several have done upon the account of devotion, and some philosophers by reasoning; to be one's own servant, to lie hard, to put out our own eyes, to throw our wealth into the river, to seek out grief; these, by the misery of this life, aiming at bliss in another; those, by laying themselves low to avoid the danger of falling: all such are acts of an excessive virtue. The stoutest and most resolute natures render even their hiding away glorious and exemplary: "When I run short, I laud a humble and safe condition, content with little: when things turn round, then I change my note, and say that none are wise or know how to live, but those who have plenty of money to lay out in shining villas" [Horace].

A great deal less would serve my turn well enough. 'Tis enough for me, under fortune's favor, to prepare myself for her disgrace, and, being at my ease, to represent to myself, as far as my imagination can stretch, the ill to come; as we do at jousts and tiltings, where we counterfeit war in the greatest calm of peace. I do not think Arcesilaus the philosopher the less temperate and virtuous, for knowing that he made use of gold and silver vessels, when the condition of his fortune allowed him so to do; I have indeed a better opinion of him, than if he had denied himself what he used with liberality and moderation. I see the utmost limits of natural necessity: and considering a poor man begging at my door, ofttimes more jocund and more healthy than I myself am, I put myself into his place, and attempt to dress my mind after his mode; and running, in like manner, over other examples, though I fancy death, poverty, contempt, and sickness treading on my heels, I easily resolve not to be affrighted, forasmuch as a less than I takes them with so much patience; and am not willing to believe that a less understanding can do more than a greater, or that the effects of precept cannot arrive to as great a height as those of custom. And knowing of how uncertain duration these accidental conveniences are, I never forget, in the height of all my enjoyments, to make it my chiefest prayer to Almighty God, that he will please to render me content with myself and the condition wherein I am. I see young men very gay and frolic, who nevertheless keep a mass of pills in their trunk at home, to take when they've got a cold, which they fear so much the less, because they think they have remedy at hand. Every one should do in like manner, and, moreover, if they find themselves subject to some more violent disease, should furnish themselves with such medicines as may numb and stupefy the part.

The employment a man should choose for such a life, ought neither to be a laborious nor an unpleasing one; otherwise 'tis to no purpose at all to be retired. And this depends upon every one's liking and humor. Mine has no manner of complacency for husbandry, and such as love it ought to apply themselves to it with moderation. Husbandry is otherwise a very servile employment, as Sallust calls it; though some parts of it are more excusable than the rest, as the care of gardens, which Xenophon attributes to Cyrus; and a mean may be found out between the sordid and low application, so full of perpetual solicitude, which is seen in men who make it their entire business and study, and the stupid and extreme negligence, letting all things go at random, which we see in others. But let us hear what advice the younger Pliny gives his friend Caninius Rufus upon the subject of solitude: "I advise thee, in the full and plentiful retirement wherein thou art, to leave to thy hinds the care of thy husbandry, and to addict thyself to the study of letters, to extract from thence something that may be entirely and absolutely thine own." By which he means reputation; like Cicero, who says, that he would employ his solitude and retirement from public affairs, to acquire by his writings an immortal life.

"Is all thy learning nothing, unless another knows that thou knowest?" asks Persius. It appears to be reason, when a man talks of retiring from the world, that he should look quite out of himself. These do it but by halves: they design well enough for themselves when they shall be no more in it; but still they pretend to extract the fruits of that design from the world, when absent from it, by a ridiculous contradiction.

The imagination of those who seek solitude upon the account of devotion, filling their hopes and courage with certainty of divine promises in the other life, is much more rationally founded. They propose to themselves God, an infinite object in goodness and power; the soul has there wherewithal, at full liberty, to satiate her desires: afflictions and sufferings turn to their advantage, being undergone for the acquisition of eternal health and joy; death is to be wished and longed for, where it is the passage to so perfect a condition; the asperity of the rules they impose upon themselves is immediately softened by custom, and all their carnal appetites baffled and subdued, by refusing to humor and feed them, these being only supported by use and exercise. This sole end therefore of another happy and immortal life is that which really merits that we should abandon the pleasures and conveniences of this; and he who can really and constantly inflame his soul with the ardor of this vivid faith and hope, erects for himself in solitude a more voluptuous and delicious life than any other sort of living whatever.

Neither the end then nor the means of this advice pleases me, for we often fall out of the frying-pan into the fire. This book employment is as painful as any other, and as great an enemy to health, which ought to be the first thing considered; neither ought a man to be al-lured with the pleasure of it, which is the same that destroys the frugal, the avaricious, the voluptuous, and the ambitious man. The sages give us caution enough to beware the treachery of our desires, and to distinguish true and entire pleasures from such as are mixed and complicated with greater pain. For the most of our pleasures, say they, wheedle and caress only to strangle us, like those thieves the Egyptians called Philistæ; if the headache should come before drunk-enness, we should have a care of drinking too much: but pleasure, to deceive us, marches before and conceals her train. Books are pleasant, but if, by being over-studious, we impair our health and spoil our good-humor, the best pieces we have, let us give it over; I, for my part, am one of those who think that no fruit derived from them can recompense so great a loss. As men, who have long felt themselves weakened by indisposition, give themselves up at last to the mercy of medicine and submit to certain rules of living, which they are for the future never to transgress; so he who retires, weary of, and disgusted with, the common way of living, ought to model this new one he enters into by the rules of reason, and to institute and establish it by premeditation and reflection. He ought to have taken leave of all sorts of labor, what advantage soever it may promise, and generally to have shaken off all those passions which disturb the tranquillity of body and soul, and then choose the way that best suits with his own humor.

In husbandry, study, hunting, and all other exercises, men are to proceed to the utmost limits of pleasure, but must take heed of engag-ing further, where trouble begins to mix with it. We are to reserve so much employment only as is necessary to keep us in breath and de-fend us from the inconveniences that the other extreme of a dull and stupid laziness brings along with it. There are sterile knotty sciences, chiefly hammered out for the crowd; let such be left to them who are engaged in the world's service. I for my part care for no other books, but either such as are pleasant and easy, to amuse me, or those that comfort and instruct me how to regulate my life and death, "Silently meditating in the healthy groves, what best becomes a wise and hon-est man" [Horace].

Wiser men, having great force and vigor of soul, may propose to themselves a rest wholly spiritual: but for me, who have a very ordi-nary soul, it is very necessary to support myself with bodily conve-niences; and age having of late deprived me of those pleasures that were more acceptable to me, I instruct and whet my appetite to those that remain, but more suitable to this other season. We ought to hold with all our force, both of hands and teeth, the use of the pleasures of life that our years, one after another, snatch away from us. "Let us pluck life's sweets, 'tis for them we live: by and by we shall be ashes, a ghost, a mere subject of talk" [Persius]. Now, as to the end that Pliny and Cicero propose to us, of glory; 'tis infinitely wide of my account. Ambition is of all others the most contrary humor to solitude; glory and repose are things that cannot possibly inhabit in one and the same place. For so much as I understand, these have only their arms and legs disengaged from the crowd; their soul and intention remain engaged behind more than ever: they have only retired to take a better leap, and by a stronger motion to give a brisker charge into the crowd. Will you see how they shoot short?

Let us put into the counterpoise the advice of two philosophers,[1] of two very different sects, writing, the one to Idomeneus, the other to Lucilius, their friends, to retire into solitude from worldly honors and affairs. "You have," say they, "hitherto lived swimming and floating; come now, and die in the harbor; you have given the first part of your life to the light, give what remains to the shade. It is impossible to give over business, if you do not also quit the fruit; therefore disengage yourselves from all concern of name and glory; 'tis to be feared the lustre of your former actions will give you but too much light, and follow you into your most private retreat. Quit with other pleasures that which proceeds from the approbation of another man: and as to your knowledge and parts, never concern yourselves; they will not lose their effect if yourselves be the better for them. Remember him, who being asked why he took so much pains in an art that could come to the knowledge of but few persons? 'A few are enough for me,' replied he; 'I have enough with one, I have enough with never an one.' He said true; you and a companion are theatre enough to one another, or you to yourself. Let the people be to you one, and be you one to the whole people. 'Tis an unworthy ambition to think to derive glory from a man's sloth and privacy: you are to do like the beasts of chase, who efface the track at the entrance into their den. You are no more to concern yourself how the world talks of you, but how you are to talk to yourself. Retire yourself into yourself, but first prepare yourself there to receive yourself: it were a folly to trust yourself in your own hands, if you cannot govern yourself.

"A man may miscarry alone as well as in company. Till you have rendered yourself one before whom you dare not trip, and till you have a bashfulness and respect for yourself, 'Let just and honest things be ever present to the mind' [Cicero]. Present continually to your imagination Cato, Phocion, and Aristides, in whose presence the fools themselves will hide their faults, and make them controllers of

[1] Epicurus and Seneca.

all your intentions; should these deviate from virtue, your respect to those will set you right; they will keep you in the way to be contented with yourself; to borrow nothing of any other but yourself; to stay and fix your soul in certain and limited thoughts, wherein she may please herself, and having understood the true and real goods, which men the more enjoy the more they understand, to rest satisfied, without desire of prolongation of life or name."

This is the precept of the true and natural philosophy, not of a boasting and prating philosophy, such as that of the two former.[1]

OF THE INEQUALITY AMONG US.

Plutarch says that he does not find so great a difference between beast and beast as he does between man and man; which he says in reference to the internal qualities and perfections of the soul. And, in truth I find so vast a distance between Epaminondas, according to my judgment of him, and some that I know, who are yet men of good sense, that I could willingly enhance upon Plutarch, and say that there is more difference between such and such a man than there is between such a man and such a beast. Terence exclaims, "Ah! how much may one man surpass another!" and that there are as many and innumerable degrees of minds as there are cubits between this and heaven. But as touching the estimate of men, 'tis strange that, ourselves excepted, no other creature is esteemed beyond its proper qualities; we commend a horse for his strength and sureness of foot, and not for his rich caparison; a greyhound for his speed of heels, not for his fine collar; a hawk for her wing, not for her jesses and bells. Why, in like manner, do we not value a man for what is properly his own? He has a great train, a beautiful palace, so much credit, so many thousand pounds a year: all these are about him, but not in him.

You will not buy a pig in a poke: if you cheapen a horse, you will see him stripped of his housing-cloths, you will see him naked and open to your eye; or if he be clothed, as they anciently were wont to present them to princes to sell, 'tis only on the less important parts, that you may not so much consider the beauty of his color or the breadth of his crupper, as principally to examine his legs, eyes, and feet, which are the members of greatest use: why, in giving your estimate of a man, do you prize him wrapped and muffled up in clothes? He then discovers nothing to you but such parts as are not in the least his own, and conceals those by which alone one may rightly judge of his value. 'Tis the price of the blade that you inquire into,

---

[1] Pliny the younger and Cicero.

not of the scabbard: you would not peradventure bid a farthing for him, if you saw him stripped. You are to judge him by himself, and not by what he wears; and, as one of the ancients very pleasantly said: "Do you know why you repute him tall? You reckon withal the height of his pattens." The pedestal is no part of the statue. Measure him without his stilts; let him lay aside his revenues and his titles, let him present himself in his shirt. Then examine if his body be sound and sprightly, active and disposed to perform its functions. What soul has he?

Is she beautiful, capable, and happily provided of all her faculties? Is she rich of what is her own or of what she has borrowed? Has Fortune no hand in the affair? Can she, without winking, stand the lightning of swords? is she indifferent whether her life expire by the mouth or through the throat? Is she settled, even, and content? This is what is to be examined, and by that you are to judge of the vast differences between man and man. Is he "the wise man, who has command over himself: whom neither poverty, nor death, nor chains affright; who has the strength and courage to restrain his appetites and to contemn honors; who has his all within himself; a mind well turned and even balanced, like a smooth and perfect ball, which nothing external can stop in its course; whom fortune assails in vain?" [Horace]. Such a man is five hundred cubits above kingdoms and duchies; he is an absolute monarch in and to himself. "The wise man is the master of his own fortune" [Plautus]. What remains for him to covet or desire? "Do we not see that man's nature asks no more than that, free from bodily pain, he may exercise his mind agreeably, exempt from fear and anxiety?" [Lucretius].

Compare with such a one the common rabble of mankind, stupid and mean-spirited, servile, instable, and continually floating with the tempest of various passions, that tosses and tumbles them to and fro, and all depending upon others, and you will find a greater distance than between heaven and earth; and yet the blindness of common usage is such that we make little or no account of it; whereas, if we consider a peasant and a king, a nobleman and a vassal, a magistrate and a private man, a rich man and a poor, there appears a vast disparity, though they differ no more, as a man may say, than in their breeches.

In Thrace the king was distinguished from his people after a very pleasant and especial manner; he had a religion by himself, a god all his own, and which his subjects were not to presume to adore, which was Mercury, while, on the other hand, he disdained to have anything to do with theirs, Mars, Bacchus, and Diana. And yet they are no other than pictures that make no essential dissimilitude; for as you see actors in a play representing the person of a duke or an emperor upon

the stage, and immediately after return to their true and original condition of valets and porters, so the emperor, whose pomp and lustre so
dazzle you in public,—do but peep behind the curtain, and you will
see nothing more than an ordinary man, and peradventure more contemptible than the meanest of his subjects. "True happiness lies within,
the other is but a counterfeit felicity," says Seneca. Cowardice, irresolution, ambition, spite, and envy agitate him as much as another. Care
and fear attack him even in the centre of his battalions. "The fears and
pursuing cares of men fear not the clash of arms nor points of darts,
and mingle boldly with great kings and potentates, and respect not
their purple and glittering gold" [Lucretius].

Do fevers, gout, and apoplexies spare him any more than one of
us? When old age hangs heavy upon his shoulders, can the yeomen
of his guard ease him of the burden? When he is astounded with the
apprehension of death, can the gentlemen of his bedchamber comfort
and assure him? When jealousy or any other caprice swings in his
brain, can our compliments and ceremonies restore him to his good-
humor? The canopy embroidered with pearl and gold he lies under
has no virtue against a violent fit of the colic. "Fevers quit a man no
sooner because he is stretched on a couch of rich tapestry than if he
be in a coarse blanket" [Lucretius].

The flatterers of Alexander the Great possessed him that he was the
son of Jupiter; but being one day wounded, and observing the blood
stream from his wound: "What say you now, my masters," said he, "is
not this blood of a crimson color and purely human? This is not of the
complexion of that which Homer makes to issue from the wounded
gods." He is but a man at best, and if he be deformed or ill qualified
from his birth, the empire of the universe cannot set him to rights.
What of all that, if he be a fool? Even pleasure and good fortune are
not relished without vigor and understanding. "Things are, as are the
souls of their possessors; good, if well used; ill, if abused" [Terence].

Whatever the benefits of fortune are, they yet require a palate fit
to relish them. Horace says: "'Tis not lands, or heaps of gold and
silver, that can banish fevers from the body of the sick owner, or cares
from his mind. The possessor must be sound and healthy, if he would
have the true realization of his wealth. To him who is covetous, or
timorous, his house and land are as a picture to a blind man, or a
fomentation to a gouty man."

He is a sot, his taste is palled and flat; he no more enjoys what he
has than one that has a cold relishes the flavor of canary, or than a
horse is sensible of his rich caparison. Plato is in the right when he
tells us that health, beauty, vigor, and riches, and all the other things
called goods, are equally evil to the unjust as good to the just, and the

evil on the contrary the same. And therefore where the body and the mind are in disorder, to what use serve these external conveniences; considering that the least prick with a pin, or the least passion of the soul, is sufficient to deprive one of the pleasure of being sole monarch of the world. At the first twitch of the gout it signifies much to be called Sir and Your Majesty. Does he not forget his palaces and grandeurs? If he be angry, can his being a prince keep him from looking red and looking pale, and grinding his teeth like a madman? Now, if he be a man of parts and of right nature, royalty adds very little to his happiness. Horace says: "If your stomach is sound, your lungs and feet in good order, you need no regal riches to make you happy." He discerns 'tis nothing but counterfeit and gullery. Nay, perhaps he would be of King Seleucus' opinion, that he who knew the weight of a sceptre would not stoop to pick it up, if he saw it lying before him, so great and painful are the duties incumbent upon a good king.

Assuredly it can be no easy task to rule others, when we find it so hard a matter to govern ourselves; and as to dominion, that seems so charming, the frailty of human judgment and the difficulty of choice in things that are new and doubtful considered, I am very much of opinion that it is far more easy and pleasant to follow than to lead; and that it is a great settlement and satisfaction of mind to have only one path to walk in, and to have none to answer for but a man's self; "'Tis much better calmly to obey than wish to rule" [Lucretius]. To which we may add that saying of Cyrus, that no man was fit to rule but he who in his own worth was of greater value than those he was to govern.

Can we think that the singing boys of the choir take any great delight in music? the satiety rather renders it troublesome and tedious to them. Feasts, balls, masquerades, and tiltings delight such as but rarely see, and desire to see them; but having been frequently at such entertainments, the relish of them grows flat and insipid. He who will not give himself leisure to be thirsty can never find the true pleasure of drinking. Farces and tumbling tricks are pleasant to the spectators, but a wearisome toil to those by whom they are performed. And that this is so, we see that princes divert themselves sometimes in disguising their quality, awhile to depose themselves, and to stoop to the poor and ordinary way of living of the meanest of their people. "The rich and great are often pleased with variety; and a plain supper in a poor cottage, where there are neither tapestry nor beds of purple, has made their anxious brow smooth" [Horace].

Nothing is so distasteful and clogging as abundance. What appetite would not be baffled to see three hundred women at its mercy, as the grand signor has in his seraglio? And, of his ancestors, what fruition or taste of sport did he reserve to himself, who never went hawking without seven thousand falconers? And besides all this, I fancy that this lustre of grandeur brings with it no little disturbance and uneasiness upon the enjoyment of the most tempting pleasures; the great are too conspicuous and lie too open to every one's view. Neither do I know to what end a man should more require of them to conceal their errors, since what is only reputed indiscretion in us, the people in them brand with the names of tyranny and contempt of the laws, and, besides their proclivity to vice, are apt to hold that it is a heightening of pleasure to them, to insult over and to trample upon public observances. Plato, indeed, in his *Gorgias*, defines a tyrant to be one who in a city has license to do whatever his own will leads him to do; and by reason of this impunity, the display and publication of their vices do ofttimes more mischief than the vice itself. Every one fears to be pried into and overlooked; but princes are so, even to their very gestures, looks, and thoughts, the people conceiving they have right and title to be judges of them: besides that the blemishes of the great naturally appear greater by reason of the eminence and lustre of the place where they are seated, and that a mole or a wart appears greater in them than a wide gash in others. And this is the reason why the poets feign the amours of Jupiter to be performed in the disguises of so many borrowed shapes, and that among the many amorous practices they lay to his charge, there is only one, as I remember, where he appears in his own majesty and grandeur.

But let us return to Hiero, who complains of the inconveniences he found in his royalty, in that he could not look abroad and travel the world at liberty, being as it were a prisoner in the bounds and limits of his own dominion, and that in all his actions he was evermore surrounded with an importunate crowd. And in truth, to see our kings sit all alone at table, environed with so many people prating about them, and so many strangers staring upon them, as they always are, I have often been moved rather to pity than to envy their condition. King Alfonso was wont to say, that in this, asses were in a better condition than kings, their masters permitting them to feed at their own ease and pleasure, a favor that kings cannot obtain of their servants. And it has never come into my fancy that it could be of any great benefit to the life of a man of sense to have twenty people prating about him when he is at stool; or that the services of a man of ten thousand livres a year, or that has taken Casale or defended Siena, should be either more commodious or more acceptable to him, than those of a good groom of the chamber who understands his place.

The advantages of sovereignty are in a manner but imaginary: every degree of fortune has in it some image of principality. Cæsar calls all the lords of France, having free franchise within their own demesnes, roitelets or petty kings; and in truth, the name of sire excepted, they go pretty far toward kingship; for do but look into the provinces remote from court, as Brittany, for example, take notice of the train, the vassals, the officers, the employment, service, ceremony, and state of a lord who lives retired from court in his own house, among his own tenants and servants; and observe withal, the flight of his imagination, there is nothing more royal; he hears talk of his master once a year, as of a king of Persia, without taking any further recognition of him, than by some remote kindred his secretary keeps in some musty record. And, to speak the truth, our laws are easy enough, so easy that a gentleman of France scarce feels the weight of sovereignty pinch his shoulders above twice in his life. Real and effectual subjection only concerns such among us as voluntarily thrust their necks under the yoke, and who design to get wealth and honors by such services: for a man that loves his own fireside, and can govern his house without falling by the ears with his neighbors or engaging in suits of law, is as free as a duke of Venice. "Servitude enchains few, but many enchain themselves to servitude" [Seneca].

But that which Hiero is most concerned at is, that he finds himself stripped of all friendship, deprived of all mutual society, wherein the true and most perfect fruition of human life consists. For what testimony of affection and good will can I extract from him that owes me, whether he will or no, all that he is able to do? Can I form any assurance of his real respect to me, from his humble way of speaking and submissive behavior, when these are ceremonies it is not in his choice to deny? The honor we receive from those that fear us, is not honor; those respects are paid to royalty and not to me. Do I not see that the wicked and the good king, he that is hated and he that is beloved, have the one as much reverence paid him as the other? My predecessor was, and my successor shall be, served with the same ceremony and state. If my subjects do me no harm, 'tis no evidence of any good affection; why should I look upon it as such, seeing it is not in their power to do it if they would? No one follows me or obeys my commands, upon the account of any friendship between him and me; there can be no contracting of friendship, where there is so little relation and correspondence: my own height has put me out of the familiarity of and intelligence with men: there is too great disparity and disproportion between us. They follow me either upon the account of decency or custom; or rather my fortune, than me, to increase their own. All they say to me, or do for me, is but outward paint, appearance, their liberty being on all parts restrained by the great power and authority I have over them. I see nothing about me but what is dissembled and disguised.

The Emperor Julian being one day applauded by his courtiers for
his exact justice: "I should be proud of these praises," said he, "did
they come from persons that durst condemn or disapprove the contrary, in case I should do it." All the real advantages of princes are
common to them with men of meaner condition ('tis for the gods to
mount winged horses and feed upon ambrosia): they have no other
sleep, nor other appetite than we; the steel they arm themselves
withal, is of no better temper than that we also use; their crowns
neither defend them from the rain nor the sun.

Diocletian, who wore a crown so fortunate and revered, resigned
it to retire to the felicity of a private life; and some time after, the
necessity of public affairs requiring that he should reassume his charge,
he made answer to those who came to court him to it: "You would
not offer," said he, "to persuade me to this had you seen the fine
order of the trees I have planted in my orchard, and the fair melons I
have sown in my garden."

In Anacharsis' opinion, the happiest state of government would be
where, all other things being equal, precedency should be measured
out by the virtues, and repulses by the vices of men.

When King Pyrrhus prepared for his expedition into Italy, his wise
counsellor Cyneas, to make him sensible of the vanity of his ambition:
"Well, sir," said he, "to what end do you make all this mighty preparation?" "To make myself master of Italy," replied the king. "And
what after that is done?" said Cyneas. "I will pass over into Gaul and
Spain," said the other. "And what then?" "I will then go to subdue
Africa; and lastly, when I have brought the whole world to my subjection, I will sit down and rest content at my own ease." "For God's
sake, sir," replied Cyneas, "tell me what hinders that you may not, if
you please, be now in the condition you speak of? Why do you not
now at this instant settle yourself in the state you seem to aim at, and
spare all the labor and hazard you interpose?"

Lucretius would reply, "Truly because one does not know what is
the proper limit of acquisition, and how far real pleasure extends."

I will conclude with an old versicle, that I think very apt to the
purpose. "Every man frames his own fortune" [Cornelius Nepos].

OF ANCIENT CUSTOMS.

I should willingly pardon our people for admitting no other pattern
or rule of perfection than their own peculiar manners and customs;
for 'tis a common vice, not of the vulgar only, but almost of all men,
to walk in the beaten road their ancestors have trod before them. I
am content, when they see Fabricius or Lælius, that they look upon

their countenance and behavior as barbarous, seeing they are neither clothed nor fashioned according to our mode. But I find fault with their singular indiscretion in suffering themselves to be so blinded and imposed upon by the authority of the present usage, as every month to alter their opinion, if custom so required, and that they should so vary their judgment in their own particular concern.

When they wore the busk of their doublets up as high as their breasts, they stiffly maintained that it was in its proper place; some years after, it was slipped down between their thighs, and then they could laugh at the former fashion as uneasy and intolerable. The fashion now in use makes them absolutely condemn the other two with so great resolution and so universal consent, that a man would think there was a certain kind of madness crept in among them, that infatuates their understandings to this strange degree. Now, seeing that our change of fashions is so prompt and sudden, that the inventions of all the tailors in the world cannot furnish out new whim-whams enow to feed our vanity withal, there will often be a necessity that the despised forms must again come in vogue, and these immediately after fall into the same contempt; and that the same judgment must, in the space of fifteen or twenty years, take up half-a-dozen not only divers but contrary opinions, with an incredible lightness and inconstancy; there is not any of us so discreet, who suffers not himself to be gulled with this contradiction, and both in external and internal sight to be insensibly blinded.

I will here muster up some old customs that I have in memory, some of them the same with ours, the others different, to the end, that bearing in mind this continual variation of human things, we may have our judgment more clearly and firmly settled.

The thing in use among us of fighting with rapier and cloak, was in practice among the Romans also: "They wrapped their cloaks upon the left arm, and drew their swords," says Cæsar; and he observes a vicious custom of our nation, that continues yet among us, which is to stop passengers we meet upon the road, to compel them to give an account who they are, and to take it for an affront and just cause of quarrel if they refuse to do it.

At the baths, which the ancients made use of every day before they went to dinner, and as frequently as we wash our hands, they at first only bathed their arms and legs; but afterward, and by a custom that has continued for many ages in most nations of the world, they bathed stark naked in mixed and perfumed water, looking upon it as a great simplicity to bathe in mere water. The most delicate and affected perfumed themselves all over three or four times a day. They often caused their hair to be pinched off, as the women of France have some time since taken up a custom to do their foreheads, though they had ointments proper for that purpose.

They delighted to lie soft, and alleged it as a great testimony of hardiness, to lie upon a mattress. They ate lying upon beds, much after the manner of the Turks in this age. And 'tis said of the younger Cato, that after the battle of Pharsalia, being entered into a melancholy disposition at the ill posture of the public affairs, he took his repasts always sitting, assuming a strict and austere course of life. It was also their custom to kiss the hands of great persons; the more to honor and caress them. And meeting with friends, they always kissed in salutation, as do the Venetians.

In petitioning or saluting any great man, they used to lay their hands upon his knees. Pasicles, the philosopher, brother of Crates, instead of laying his hand upon his knee laid it upon the private parts, and being roughly repulsed by him to whom he made that indecent compliment: "What," said he, "is not that part your own as well as the other?" They used to eat fruit, as we do, after dinner.

They had collation between meals, and had, in summer, cellars of snow to cool their wine; and some there were who made use of snow in winter, not thinking their wine cool enough, even at that cold season of the year. The men of quality had their cupbearers and carvers, and their buffoons to make them sport. They had their meat served up in winter upon chafing dishes, which were set upon the table; and had portable kitchens (of which I myself have seen some) wherein all their service was carried about with them.

In summer, they had a contrivance to bring fresh and clear rills through their lower rooms, wherein were great store of living fish which the guests took out with their own hands to be dressed every man according to his own liking. Fish have ever had this preëminence, and keep it still, that the grandees, as to them, all pretend to be cooks; and indeed the taste is more delicate than that of flesh, at least to my fancy. But in all sorts of magnificence, debauchery, and voluptuous inventions of effeminacy and expense, we do, in truth, all we can to parallel them, for our wills are as corrupt as theirs: but we want ability to equal them; our force is no more able to reach them in their vicious, than in their virtuous qualities, for both the one and the other proceeded from a vigor of soul which was without comparison greater in them than in us. And souls, by how much the weaker they are, by so much have they less power to do either very well or very ill.

The highest place of honor among them was the middle. The name going before, or following after, either in writing or speaking, had no signification of grandeur, as is evident by their writings; they will as soon say Oppius and Cæsar, as Cæsar and Oppius; and me and thee, as thee and me. This is the reason that made me formerly take notice in the life of Flaminius, in our French Plutarch,[1] of one passage, where it seems as if the author, speaking of the jealousy of honor between the Ætolians and Romans, about the winning of a battle they had with their joined forces obtained, made it of some importance, that in the Greek songs they had put the Ætolians before the Romans: if there be no amphibology in the words of the French translation.

The ancient Gauls, says Sidonius Apollinaris, wore their hair long before, and the hinder part of the head shaved, a fashion that begins to revive in this vicious and effeminate age.

The Romans used to pay the watermen their fare at their first stepping into the boat, which we never do till after landing. The women used to lie on the side of the bed next the wall: and for that reason they called Cæsar, "*spondum regis Nicomedis.*" They took breath in their drinking, and watered their wine. And the roguish looks and gestures of our lackeys were also in use among them. The Argian and Roman ladies mourned in white, as ours did formerly and should do still, were I to govern in this point. But there are whole books on this subject.

OF THE VANITY OF WORDS.

A rhetorician of times past said, that to make little things appear great was his profession. This was a shoe-maker, who can make a great shoe for a little foot. They would in Sparta have sent such a fellow to be whipped for making profession of a tricky and deceitful art; and I fancy that Archidamus, who was king of that country, was a little surprised at the answer of Thucydides, when inquiring of him, which was the better wrestler, Pericles or he, he replied, that it was hard to affirm; for when I have thrown him, said he, he always persuades the spectators that he had no fall and carries away the prize. The women who paint, pounce, and plaster up their ruins, filling up their wrinkles and deformities, are less to blame, because it is no great matter whether we see them in their natural complexions; whereas these make it their business to deceive not our sight only but our judgments, and to adulterate and corrupt the very essence of things.

The republics that have maintained themselves in a regular and well-modelled government, such as those of Lacedæmon and Crete, had orators in no very great esteem. Aristo wisely defined rhetoric to be "a science to persuade the people;" Socrates and Plato "an art to

---

[1] Amyot.

flatter and deceive." And those who deny it in the general description, verify it throughout in their precepts. The Mohammedans will not suffer their children to be instructed in it, as being useless, and the Athenians, perceiving of how pernicious consequence the practice of it was, it being in their city of universal esteem, ordered the principal part, which is to move the affections, with their exordiums and perorations, to be taken away. 'Tis an engine invented to manage and govern a disorderly and tumultuous rabble, and that never is made use of, but, like physic to the sick, in a discomposed state.

In those where the vulgar or the ignorant, or both together, have been all-powerful and able to give the law, as in those of Athens, Rhodes, and Rome, and where the public affairs have been in a continual tempest of commotion, to such places have the orators always repaired. And in truth, we shall find few persons in those republics who have pushed their fortunes to any great degree of eminence without the assistance of eloquence. Pompey, Cæsar, Crassus, Lucullus, Lentulus, Metellus, thence took their chiefest spring, to mount to that degree of authority at which they at last arrived, making it of greater use to them than arms, contrary to the opinion of better times; for, L. Volumnius speaking publicly in favor of the election of Q. Fabius and Pub. Decius, to the consular dignity: "These are men," said he, "born for war and great in execution; in the combat of the tongue altogether wanting; spirits truly consular. The subtle, eloquent, and learned are only good for the city, to make praetors of, to administer justice."

Eloquence most flourished at Rome when the public affairs were in the worst condition and most disquieted with intestine commotions; as a free and untilled soil bears the worst weeds. By which it should seem that a monarchical government has less need of it than any other: for the stupidity and facility natural to the common people, and that render them subject to be turned and twined and led by the ears by this charming harmony of words, without weighing or considering the truth and reality of things by the force of reason: this facility, I say, is not easily found in a single person, and it is also more easy by good education and advice to secure him from the impression of this poison. There was never any famous orator known to come out of Persia or Macedon.

I have entered into this discourse upon the occasion of an Italian I lately received into my service, and who was clerk of the kitchen to the late Cardinal Caraffa till his death. I put this fellow upon an account of his office; when he fell to discourse of this palate-science, with such a settled countenance and magisterial gravity, as if he had been handling some profound point of divinity. He made a learned distinction of the several sorts of appetites; of that a man has before he begins to eat, and of those after the second and third service; the means simply to satisfy the first, and then to raise and actuate the other two; the ordering of the sauces, first in general, and then proceeded to the qualities of the ingredients and their effects; the differences of salads according to their seasons, those which ought to be served up hot, and which cold; the manner of their garnishment and decoration to render them acceptable to the eye.

After which he entered upon the order of the whole service, full of weighty and important considerations. And all this set out with lofty and magnificent words, the very same we make use of when we discourse of the government of an empire. Which learned lecture of my man brought this of Terence into my memory: "This is too salt, that's burned, that's not washed enough, that's well; remember to do so another time. Thus do I ever advise them to have things done properly, according to my capacity; and lastly, Demea, I command my cooks to look into every dish as if it were a mirror, and tell them what they should do." And yet even the Greeks themselves very much admired and highly applauded the order and disposition that Paulus Æmilius observed in the feast he gave them at his return from Macedon. But I do not here speak of effects, I speak of words only.

I do not know whether it may have the same operation upon other men that it has upon me, but when I hear our architects thunder out their bombast words of pilasters, architraves, and cornices, of the Corinthian and Doric orders, and such like jargon, my imagination is presently possessed with the palace of Apollidon; when, after all, I find them but the paltry pieces of my own kitchen door.

To hear men talk of metonymies, metaphors, and allegories, and other grammar words, would not one think they signified some rare and exotic form of speaking? And yet they are phrases that are no better than the chatter of my chambermaid.

And this other is a gullery of the same stamp, to call the officers of our kingdom by the lofty titles of the Romans, though they have no similitude of function, and still less of authority and power. And this also, which I doubt will one day turn to the reproach of this age of ours, unworthily and indifferently to confer upon any we think fit the most glorious surnames with which antiquity honored but one or two persons in several ages. Plato carried away the surname of Divine, by so universal a consent that never any one repined at it, or attempted to take it from him; and yet the Italians, who pretend, and with good reason, to more sprightly wits and sounder sense than the other nations of their time, have lately bestowed the same title upon Aretin, in whose writings, save tumid phrases set out with smart periods,

ingenious indeed but far-fetched and fantastic, and the eloquence, be
it what it may, I see nothing in him above the ordinary writers of his
time, so far is he from approaching the ancient divinity. And we make
nothing of giving the surname of great to princes who have nothing
more than ordinary in them.

OF PRAYERS.

I propose formless and undetermined fancies, like those who publish doubtful questions, to be after disputed upon in the schools, not
to establish truth but to seek it; and I submit them to the judgments
of those whose office it is to regulate, not my writings and actions
only, but moreover my very thoughts. Let what I here set down meet
with correction or applause, it shall be of equal welcome and utility
to me, myself beforehand condemning as absurd and impious, if anything shall be found, through ignorance or inadvertency, couched in
this rhapsody, contrary to the holy resolutions and prescriptions of the
Catholic Apostolic and Roman Church, into which I was born and
in which I will die. And yet, always submitting to the authority of
their censure, which has an absolute power over me, I thus rashly
venture at everything, as in treating upon this present subject.

I know not if or no I am wrong; but since, by a particular favor of
the divine bounty, a certain form of prayer has been prescribed and
dictated to us, word by word, from the mouth of God Himself, I have
ever been of opinion that we ought to have it in more frequent use
than we yet have; and if I were worthy to advise, at the sitting down
to and rising from our tables, at our rising from and going to bed, and
in every particular action wherein prayer is used, I would that
Christians always make use of the Lord's Prayer, if not alone, yet at
least always. The Church may lengthen and diversify prayers, according to the necessity of our instruction, for I know very well that it is
always the same in substance and the same thing: but yet such a
privilege ought to be given to that prayer, that the people should have
it continually in their mouths; for it is most certain that all necessary
petitions are comprehended in it, and that it is infinitely proper for all
occasions. 'Tis the only prayer I use in all places and conditions, and
which I still repeat instead of changing; whence it also happens that I
have no other so entirely by heart as that.

It just now came into my mind, whence it is we should derive that
error of having recourse to God in all our designs and enterprises, to
call Him to our assistance in all sorts of affairs, and in all places where
our weakness stands in need of support, without considering whether
the occasion be just or otherwise; and to invoke His name and power,

in what state soever we are, or action we are engaged in, however vicious. He is, indeed, our sole and unique protector, and can do all things for us: but though He is pleased to honor us with his sweet paternal alliance, He is, notwithstanding, as just as He is good and mighty; and more often exercises His justice than His power, and favors us according to that, and not according to our petitions.

Plato, in his Laws, makes three sorts of belief injurious to the gods; "that there are none; that they concern not themselves about our affairs; that they never refuse anything to our vows, offerings, and sacrifices." The first of these errors (according to his opinion), never continued rooted in any man from his infancy to his old age; the other two, he confesses, men might be obstinate in.

God's justice and His power are inseparable; 'tis in vain we invoke His power in an unjust cause. We are to have our souls pure and clean, at that moment at least wherein we pray to Him, and purified from all vicious passions; otherwise we ourselves present Him the rods wherewith to chastise us; instead of repairing anything we have done amiss, we double the wickedness and the offence when we offer to Him, to whom we are to sue for pardon, an affection full of irreverence and hatred. Which makes me not very apt to applaud those whom I observe to be so frequent on their knees, if the actions nearest to the prayer do not give me some evidence of amendment and reformation. And the practice of a man who mixes devotion with an execrable life seems in some sort more to be condemned than that of a man conformable to his own propension, and dissolute throughout; and for that reason it is that our Church denies admittance to and communion with men obstinate and incorrigible in any notorious wickedness. We pray only by custom and for fashion's sake; or, rather, we read or pronounce our prayers aloud, which is no better than an hypocritical show of devotion; and I am scandalized to see a man cross himself thrice at the Benedicite, and as often at Grace (and the more, because it is a sign I have in great veneration and continual use, even when I yawn), and to dedicate all the other hours of the day to acts of malice, avarice, and injustice. One hour to God, the rest to the devil, as if by composition and compensation. 'Tis a wonder to see actions so various in themselves succeed one another with such an uniformity of method as not to interfere nor suffer any alteration, even upon the very confines and passes from the one to the other. What a prodigious conscience must that be that can be at quiet within itself while it harbors under the same roof, with so agreeing and so calm a society, both the crime and the judge?

A man whose whole meditation is continually working upon nothing but impurity which he knows to be so odious to Almighty God, what can he say when he comes to speak to Him? He draws back, but immediately falls into a relapse. If the object of divine justice and the presence of his Maker did, as he pretends, strike and chastise his soul, how short soever the repentance might be, the very fear of offending the infinite Majesty would so often present itself to his imagination that he would soon see himself master of those vices that are most natural and vehement in him. But what shall we say of those who settle their whole course of life upon the profit and emolument of sins, which they know to be mortal? How many trades and vocations have we admitted and countenanced among us, whose very essence is vicious? And he that confessing himself to me, voluntarily told me that he had all his lifetime professed and practised a religion, in his opinion damnable and contrary to that he had in his heart, only to preserve his credit and the honor of his employments, how could his courage suffer so infamous a confession? What can men say to the divine justice upon this subject? Their repentance consisting in a visible and manifest reparation, they lose the color of alleging it both to God and man. Are they so impudent as to sue for remission without satisfaction and without penitence? I look upon these as in the same condition with the first: but the obstinacy is not there so easy to be overcome. This contrariety and volubility of opinion so sudden, so violent, that they feign, are a kind of miracle to me: they present us with the state of an indigestible agony of mind.

It seemed to me a fantastic imagination in those who, these late years past, were wont to reproach every man they knew to be of any extraordinary parts, and made profession of the Catholic religion, that it was but outwardly; maintaining, moreover, to do him honor forsooth, that whatever he might pretend to the contrary he could not but in his heart be of their reformed opinion. An untoward disease, that a man should be so riveted to his own belief as to fancy that others cannot believe otherwise than as he does; and yet worse, that they should entertain so vicious an opinion of such great parts as to think any man so qualified, should prefer any present advantage of fortune to the promises of eternal life and the menaces of eternal damnation. They may believe me: could anything have tempted my youth, the ambition of the danger and difficulties in the late commotions had not been the least motives.

It is not without very good reason, in my opinion, that the Church interdicts the promiscuous, indiscreet, and irreverent use of the holy and divine Psalms, with which the Holy Ghost inspired King David. We ought not to mix God in our actions, but with the highest reverence and caution; that poesy is too holy to be put to no other use than to exercise the lungs and to delight our ears; it ought to come from the conscience, and not from the tongue. It is not fit that a 'prentice in his shop, among his vain and frivolous thoughts, should be permitted to pass away his time and divert himself with such sacred things. Neither is it decent to see the Holy Book of the holy mysteries of our belief tumbled up and down a hall or a kitchen; they were formerly mysteries, but are now become sports and recreations. 'Tis a book too serious and too venerable to be cursorily or slightly turned over: the reading of the Scripture ought to be a temperate and premeditated act, and to which men should always add this devout preface, *sursum corda*, preparing even the body to so humble and composed a gesture and countenance as shall evidence a particular veneration and attention. Neither is it a book for every one to fist, but the study of select men set apart for that purpose, and whom Almighty God has been pleased to call to that office and sacred function: the wicked and ignorant grow worse by it. 'Tis not a story to tell, but a history to revere, fear, and adore. Are not they then pleasant men, who think they have rendered this fit for the people's handling, by translating it into the vulgar tongue? Does the understanding of all therein contained only stick at words? Shall I venture to say further, that by coming so near to understand a little, they are much wider of the whole scope than before? A pure and simple ignorance and wholly depending upon the exposition of qualified persons, was far more learned and salutary than this vain and verbal knowledge, which has only proved the nurse of temerity and presumption.

And I do further believe that the liberty every one has taken to disperse the sacred writ into so many idioms carries with it a great deal more of danger than utility. The Jews, Mohammedans, and almost all other peoples, have reverentially espoused the language wherein their mysteries were first conceived, and have expressly, and not without color of reason, forbidden the alteration of them into any other. Are we assured that in Biscay and in Brittany there are enough competent judges of this affair to establish this translation into their own language? The universal Church has not a more difficult and solemn judgment to make. In preaching and speaking the interpretation is vague, free, mutable, and of a piece by itself; so 'tis not the same thing.

One of our Greek historians justly censures the age he lived in, because the secrets of the Christian religion were dispersed into the hands of every mechanic, to expound and argue upon, according to his own fancy, and that we ought to be much ashamed, we who by God's especial favor enjoy the pure mysteries of piety, to suffer them to be profaned by the ignorant rabble; considering that the Gentiles expressly forbade Socrates, Plato, and the other sages to inquire into or so much as to mention the things committed to the priests of

Delphi; and he says, moreover, that the factions of princes upon theological subjects are armed not with zeal but fury; that zeal springs from the divine wisdom and justice, and governs itself with prudence and moderation, but degenerates into hatred and envy, producing tares and nettles instead of corn and wine when conducted by human passions. And it was truly said by another, who, advising the Emperor Thedosius, told him, that disputes did not so much rock the schisms of the Church asleep, as it roused and animated heresies; that, therefore, all contentions and dialectic disputations were to be avoided, and men absolutely to acquiesce in the prescriptions and formulas of faith established by the ancients. And the Emperor Andronicus having overheard some great men at high words in his palace with Lapodius about a point of ours of great importance, gave them so severe a check as to threaten to cause them to be thrown into the river if they did not desist. The very women and children nowadays take upon them to lecture the oldest and most experienced men about the ecclesiastical laws; whereas the first of those of Plato forbids them to inquire so much as into the civil laws, which were to stand instead of divine ordinances; and, allowing the old men to confer among themselves or with the magistrate about those things, he adds, provided it be not in the presence of young or profane persons.

A bishop has left in writing that at the other end of the world there is an isle, by the ancients called Dioscorides, abundantly fertile in all sorts of trees and fruits, and of an exceedingly healthful air; the inhabitants of which are Christians, having churches and altars, only adorned with crosses without any other images, great observers of fasts and feasts, exact payers of their tithes to the priests, and so chaste, that none of them is permitted to have to do with more than one woman in his life; as to the rest, so content with their condition, that environed with the sea they know nothing of navigation, and so simple that they understand not one syllable of the religion they profess and wherein they are so devout: a thing incredible to such as do not know that the pagans, who are so zealous idolaters, know nothing more of their gods than their bare names and their statues. The ancient beginning of *Menalippus*, a tragedy of Euripides, ran thus,

> "O Jupiter! for that name alone
> Of what thou art to me is known."

I have also known in my time some men's writings found fault with for being purely human and philosophical, without any mixture of theology; and yet, with some show of reason, it might, on the contrary, be said that the divine doctrine, as queen and regent of the rest, better keeps her state apart, that she ought to be sovereign throughout, not subsidiary and suffragan, and that, peradventure, grammatical, rhetorical, logical examples may elsewhere be more suitably chosen, as also the material for the stage, games, and public entertainments, than from so sacred a matter; that divine reasons are considered with greater veneration and attention by themselves, and in their own proper style, than when mixed with and adapted to human discourse; that is, it is a fault much more often observed that the divines write too humanly, than that the humanists write not theologically enough. Philosophy, says St. Chrysostom, has long been banished the holy schools, as an handmaid altogether useless and thought unworthy to look, so much as in passing by the door, into the sanctuary of the holy treasures of the celestial doctrine; that the human way of speaking is of a much lower form and ought not to adopt for herself the dignity and majesty of divine eloquence. Let who will *verbis indisciplinatis* talk of fortune, destiny, accident, good and evil hap, and other such like phrases, according to his own humor; I for my part propose fancies merely human and merely my own, and that simply as human fancies, and separately considered, not as determined by any decree from heaven, incapable of doubt or dispute; matter of opinion not matter of faith; things which I discourse of according to my own notions, not as I believe, according to God; after a laical, not clerical, and yet always after a very religious manner, as children prepare their exercises, not to instruct, but to be instructed.

And might it not be said, that an edict enjoining all people but such as are public professors of divinity, to be very reserved in writing of religion, would carry with it a very good color of utility and justice— and to me, among the rest peradventure, to hold my prating? I have been told that even those who are not of our Church nevertheless among themselves expressly forbid the name of God to be used in common discourse, not so much even by way of interjection, exclamation, assertion of a truth, or comparison; and I think them in the right: upon what occasion soever we call upon God to accompany and assist us, it ought always to be done with the greatest reverence and devotion.

There is, as I remember, a passage in Xenophon where he tells us that we ought so much the more seldom to call upon God, by how much it is hard to compose our souls to such a degree of calmness, patience, and devotion as it ought to be in at such a time; otherwise our prayers are not only vain and fruitless, but vicious: "Forgive us," we say, "our trespasses, as we forgive them that trespass against us;" what do we mean by this

petition but that we present to God a soul free from all rancor and revenge? And yet we make nothing of invoking God's assistance in our
vices, and inviting Him into our unjust designs: "Which you can only
impart to the gods privately." [Persius]. The covetous man prays for the
conservation of his vain and superfluous riches; the ambitious for victory
and the good conduct of his fortune; the thief calls Him to his assistance,
to deliver him from the dangers and difficulties that obstruct his wicked
designs, or returns Him thanks for the facility he has met with in cutting
a man's throat; at the door of the house men are going to storm or break
into by force of a petard, they fall to prayers for success, their intentions
and hopes full of cruelty, avarice, and lust.

Marguerite, queen of Navarre, tells of a young prince, who,
though she does not name him, is easily enough by his great qualities
to be known, who going upon an amorous assignation to lie with an
advocate's wife of Paris, his way thither being through a church, he
never passed that holy place going to or returning from his pious
exercise, but he always kneeled down to pray. Wherein he would
employ the divine favor, his soul being full of such virtuous medita-
tions, I leave others to judge, which, nevertheless, she instances for a
testimony of singular devotion. But this is not the only proof we have
that women are not very fit to treat of theological affairs.

A true prayer and religious reconciling of ourselves to Almighty God
cannot enter into an impure soul, subject at the very time to the dominion of Satan. He who calls God to his assistance while in a course
of vice, does as if a cutpurse should call a magistrate to help him, or like
those who introduce the name of God to the attestation of a lie.

There are few men who dare publish to the world the prayers they
make to Almighty God: "'Tis not convenient for every one to bring
the prayers he mutters, out of the temple, and to give his wishes to
the public ear" [Persius]. And this is the reason why the Pythagoreans
would have them always public and heard by every one, to the end
they might not prefer indecent or unjust petitions as this man: "He
first exclaims aloud, Apollo! Then gently moving his lips, fearful to
be heard, he murmurs: Oh fair Laverna, grant me the talent to deceive and cheat; yet all the while to appear holy and just; shroud my
sins with night, and my frauds with a sable cloud" [Horace. Laverna
was the goddess of thieves].

The gods severely punished the wicked prayers of Œdipus in
granting them: he had prayed that his children might among themselves determine the succession to his throne by arms, and was so
miserable as to see himself taken at his word. We are not to pray that
all things may go as we would have them, but as most concurrent
with prudence.

We seem, in truth, to make use of our prayers as of a kind of gibberish, and as those do who employ holy words about sorceries and magical operations; and as if we reckoned the benefit we are to reap from them as depending upon the contexture, sound, and jingle of words, or upon the grave composing of the countenance. For having the soul contaminated with concupiscence, not touched with repentance, or comforted by any late reconciliation with God, we go to present Him such words as the memory suggests to the tongue, and hope from thence to obtain the remission of our sins. There is nothing so easy, so sweet, and so favorable, as the divine law: it calls and invites us to her, guilty and abominable as we are; extends her arms and receives us into her bosom, foul and polluted as we at present are, and are for the future to be. But then, in return, we are to look upon her with a respectful eye; we are to receive this pardon with all gratitude and submission, and for that instant at least, wherein we address ourselves to her, to have the soul sensible of the ills we have committed, and at enmity with those passions that seduced us to offend her; neither the gods nor good men (says Plato) will accept the present of a wicked man. Says Horace: "If a pure hand touch the altar, the pious offering of a small cake and a few grains of salt will appease the offended gods more effectually than costly sacrifices."

OF BOOKS.

I make no doubt but that I often happen to speak of things that are much better and more truly handled by those who are masters of the trade. You have here purely an essay of my natural parts, and not of those acquired; and whoever shall catch me tripping in ignorance, will not in any sort get the better of me; for I should be very unwilling to become responsible to another for my writings, who am not so to myself, nor satisfied with them. Whoever goes in quest of knowledge, let him fish for it where it is to be found; there is nothing I so little profess. These are fancies of my own, by which I do not pretend to discover things but to lay open myself; they may, peradventure, one day be known to me, or have formerly been, according as fortune has been able to bring me in place where they have been explained; but I have utterly forgotten it; and if I am a man of some reading, I am a man of no retention; so that I can promise no certainty, more than to make known to what point the knowledge I now have has risen.

Therefore, let none lay stress upon the matter I write, but upon my method in writing it. Let them observe, in what I borrow, if I have known how to choose what is proper to raise or help the invention, which is always my own. For I make others say for me, not before but after me, what either for want of language or want of sense I cannot myself so well express. I do not number my borrowings, I weigh them: and had I designed to raise their value by number, I had made them twice as many; they are all, or within a very few, so famed and ancient authors, that they seem, methinks, themselves sufficiently to tell who they are, without giving me the trouble.

In reasons, comparisons, and arguments, if I transplant any into my own soil, and confound them among my own, I purposely conceal the author, to awe the temerity of those precipitate censors who fall upon all sorts of writings, particularly the late ones, of men yet living, and in the vulgar tongue which puts every one into a capacity of criticising and which seem to convict the conception and design as vulgar also. I will have them give Plutarch a fillip on my nose, and rail against Seneca when they think they rail at me. I must shelter my own weakness under these great reputations. I shall love any one that can unplume me, that is, by clearness of understanding and judgment, and by the sole distinction of the force and beauty of the discourse. For I who, for want of memory, am at every turn at a loss to pick them out of their national livery, am yet wise enough to know, by the measure of my own abilities, that my soil is incapable of producing any of those rich flowers that I there find growing; and that all the fruits of my own growth are not worth any one of them. For this, indeed, I hold myself responsible; if I get in my own way; if there be any vanity and defect in my writings which I do not of myself perceive nor can discern, when pointed out to me by another; for many faults escape our eye, but the infirmity of judgment consists in not being able to discern them when by another laid open to us.

Knowledge and truth may be in us without judgment, and judgment also without them; but the confession of ignorance is one of the finest and surest testimonies of judgment that I know. I have no other officer to put my writings in rank and file, but only fortune. As things come into my head, I heap them one upon another; sometimes they advance in whole bodies, sometimes in single file. I would that every one should see my natural and ordinary pace, irregular as it is; I suffer myself to jog on at my own rate. Neither are these subjects which a man is not permitted to be ignorant in, or casually and at a venture, to discourse of. I could wish to have a more perfect knowledge of things, but I will not buy it so dear as it costs. My design is to pass over easily, and not laboriously, the remainder of my life; there is nothing that I will cudgel my brains about; no, not even knowledge, of what value soever.

I seek, in the reading of books, only to please myself, by an honest diversion; or, if I study, 'tis for no other science than what treats of the knowledge of myself, and instructs me how to die and how to live well. I do not bite my nails about the difficulties I meet with in my reading; after a charge or two, I give them over. Should I insist upon them, I should both lose myself and time; for I have an impatient understanding, that must be satisfied at first; what I do not discern at once, is by persistence rendered more obscure. I do nothing without gayety; continuation and a too obstinate endeavor darken, stupefy, and tire my judgment. My sight is confounded and dissipated with poring; I must withdraw it, and refer my discovery to new attempts; just as to judge rightly of the lustre of scarlet, we are taught to pass the eye lightly over it, and again to run it over at several sudden and reiterated glances. If one book does not please me, I take another; and never meddle with any, but at such times as I am weary of doing nothing. I care not much for new ones, because the old seem fuller and stronger; neither do I converse much with Greek authors, because my judgment cannot do its work with imperfect intelligence of the material.

Among books that are simply pleasant, of the moderns, Boccaccio's *Decameron*, Rabelais, and the *Basia* of Johannes Secundus (if those may be ranged under the title) are worth reading for amusement. As to *Amadis*, and such kind of stuff, they had not credit to take me, so much as in my childhood. And I will, moreover, say, whether boldly or rashly, that this old, heavy soul of mine is now no longer tickled with Ariosto, no, nor with Ovid; his facility and inventions with which I was formerly so ravished, are now of no more relish, and I can hardly have the patience to read them. I speak my opinion freely of all things, even of those that, perhaps, exceed my capacity, and that I do not conceive to be, in any wise, under my jurisdiction. And, accordingly, the judgment I deliver is to show the measure of my own sight, and not of the things I make so bold to criticise. When I find myself disgusted with Plato's *Axiochus*,[1] as with a work, with due respect to such an author be it spoken, without force, my judgment does not believe itself: it is not so arrogant as to oppose the authority of so many other famous judgments of antiquity, which it considers as its tutors and masters, and with whom it is rather content to err; in such a case, it condemns itself either to stop at the outward bark, not being able to penetrate to the heart, or to consider it by some false light. It is content with only securing itself from trouble and disorder;

---

[1] The *Axiochus* is not by Plato, as Diogenes Laertius admitted. It is attributed by some to Æschines the Socratic, and by others to Xenocrates of Chalcedon.—Le Clerc.

as to its own weakness, it frankly acknowledges and confesses it. It thinks it gives a just interpretation to the appearances by its conceptions presented to it; but they are weak and imperfect. Most of the Fables of Æsop have diverse senses and meanings of which the mythologists chose some one that quadrates well to the Fable; but, for the most part, 'tis but the first face that presents itself and is superficial only; there yet remain others more vivid, essential, and profound, into which they have not been able to penetrate; and just so 'tis with me.

But, to pursue the business of this essay, I have always thought that, in poesy, Virgil, Lucretius, Catullus, and Horace by many degrees excel the rest; and signally, Virgil in his *Georgics*, which I look upon as the most accomplished piece in poetry; and in comparison of which a man may easily discern that there are some places in his *Æneids*, to which the author would have given a little more of the file, had he had leisure: and the fifth book of his *Æneids* seems to me the most perfect. I also love Lucan, and willingly read him, not so much for his style, as for his own worth, and the truth and solidity of his opinions and judgments. As for Terence, that model of the refined elegancies and grace of the Latin tongue, I find him admirable in his vivid representation of our manners and the movements of the soul; our actions throw me at every turn upon him; and I cannot read him so often that I do not still discover some new grace and beauty. Such as lived near Virgil's time were scandalized that some should compare him with Lucretius. I am, I confess, of opinion that the comparison is, in truth, very unequal; a belief that, nevertheless, I have much ado to assure myself in, when I come upon some excellent passage in Lucretius. But if they were so angry at this comparison, what would they say to the brutish and barbarous stupidity of those who, nowadays, compare him with Ariosto? Would not Ariosto himself say, "O stupid and tasteless age!"

I think the ancients had more reason to be angry with those who compared Plautus with Terence, though much nearer the mark, than Lucretius with Virgil. It makes much for the estimation and preference of Terence, that the father of Roman eloquence has him so often, and alone of his class, in his mouth; and the opinion that the best judge of Roman poets[1] has passed upon his companion. I have often observed that those of our times, who take upon them to write comedies (in imitation of the Italians, who are happy enough in that way of writing), take three or four plots of those of Plautus or Terence to make one of their own, and crowd five or six of

---

[1] Horace.

Boccaccio's novels into one single comedy. That which makes them so load themselves with matter is the diffidence they have of being able to support themselves with their own strength. They must find out something to lean to; and not having of their own stuff wherewith to entertain us, they bring in the story to supply the defect of language.

It is quite otherwise with my author; the elegance and perfection of his way of speaking makes us lose the appetite of his plot; his refined grace and elegance of diction everywhere occupy us: he is so pleasant throughout, "Liquid, and like a crystal stream," and so possesses the soul with his graces that we forget those of his fable. This same consideration carries me further: I observe that the best of the ancient poets have avoided affectation and the hunting after, not only fantastic Spanish and Petrarchal elevations, but even the softer and more gentle touches, which are the ornament of all succeeding poesy. And yet there is no good judgment that will condemn this in the ancients, and that does not incomparably more admire the equal polish, and that perpetual sweetness and flourishing beauty of Catullus' epigrams, than all the stings with which Martial arms the tails of his. This is by the same reason that I gave before, and as Martial says of himself: "He had all the less for his wit to do that the subject itself supplied what was necessary." The first, without being moved, or without getting angry, make themselves sufficiently felt; they have matter enough of laughter throughout, they need not tickle themselves; the others have need of foreign assistance; as they have the less wit they must have the more body; they mount on horseback, because they are not able to stand on their own legs.

As in our balls, those mean fellows who teach to dance, not being able to represent the presence and dignity of our noblesse, are fain to put themselves forward with dangerous jumping, and other strange motions and tumblers' tricks; and the ladies are less put to it in dances, where there are various coupees, changes, and quick motions of body, than in some other of a more sedate kind, where they are only to move a natural pace, and to represent their ordinary grace and presence. And so I have seen good drolls, when in their own everyday clothes, and with the same face they always wear, give us all the pleasure of their art, when their apprentices, not yet arrived at such a pitch of perfection, are fain to meal their faces, put themselves into ridiculous disguises, and make a hundred grotesque faces to give us whereat to laugh. This conception of mine is nowhere more demonstrable than in comparing the *Æneid* with *Orlando Furioso*; of which we see the first, by dint of wing, flying in a brave and lofty place, and always following his point; the latter, fluttering and hopping from tale to tale, as from branch to branch, not daring to trust his wings but in very short flights, and perching at every turn, lest his breath and strength should fail; *Excursusque breves tentat*. These, then, as to this sort of subjects, are the authors that best please me.

As to what concerns my other reading, that mixes a little more profit with the pleasure, and whence I learn how to marshal my opinions and conditions, the books that serve me to this purpose are Plutarch, since he has been translated into French, and Seneca. Both of these have this notable convenience suited to my humor, that the knowledge I there seek is discoursed in loose pieces, that do not require from me any trouble of reading long, of which I am incapable. Such are the minor works of the first and the epistles of the latter, which are the best and most profiting of all their writings. 'Tis no great attempt to take one of them in hand, and I give over at pleasure; for they have no sequence or dependence upon one another. These authors, for the most part, concur in useful and true opinions; and there is this parallel between them, that fortune brought them into the world about the same century: they were both tutors to two Roman emperors: both sought out from foreign countries: both rich and both great men. Their instruction is the cream of philosophy, and delivered after a plain and pertinent manner. Plutarch is more uniform and constant; Seneca more various and waving: the last toiled and bent his whole strength to fortify virtue against weakness, fear, and vicious appetites; the other seems more to slight their power, and to disdain to alter his pace and to stand upon his guard. Plutarch's opinions are Platonic, gentle, and accommodated to civil society; those of the other are Stoical and Epicurean, more remote from the common use, but, in my opinion, more individually commodious and more firm. Seneca seems to lean a little to the tyranny of the emperors of his time, and only seems; for I take it for certain that he speaks against his judgment when he condemns the action of the generous murderers of Cæsar. Plutarch is frank throughout: Seneca abounds with brisk touches and sallies; Plutarch with things that heat and move you more; this contents and pays you better: he guides us, the other pushes us on.

As to Cicero, those of his works that are most useful to my design are they that treat of philosophy, especially moral. But boldly to confess the truth (for since one has passed the barriers of impudence, off with the bridle), his way of writing, and that of all other long-winded authors, appears to me very tedious: for his prefaces, definitions, divisions, and etymologies take up the greatest part of his work: whatever there is of life and marrow is smothered and lost in the long preparation. When I have spent an hour in reading him, which is a great deal for me, and try to recollect what I have thence extracted of juice and substance, for the most part I find nothing but wind; for he is not yet come to the arguments that serve to his purpose, and to the reasons that properly help to form the knot I seek. For me, who only desire to become more wise, not more learned or eloquent, these logical and Aristotelian dispositions of parts are of no use. I would have a man begin with the main proposition. I know well enough what death and pleasure are; let no man give himself the trouble to anatomize them to me. I look for good and solid reasons, at the first dash, to instruct me how to stand their shock, for which purpose neither grammatical subtleties nor the quaint contexture of words and argumentations are of any use at all. I am for discourses that give the first charge into the heart of the redoubt; his languish about the subject; they are proper for the schools, for the bar, and for the pulpit, where we have leisure to nod, and may awake a quarter of an hour after, time enough to find again the thread of the discourse.

It is necessary to speak after this manner to judges, whom a man has a desire to gain over, right or wrong, to children and common people, to whom a man must say all, and see what will come of it. I would not have an author make it his business to render me attentive: or that he should cry out fifty times *Oyez*, as the heralds do. The Romans, in their religious exercises, began with *Hoc age*: as we in ours do with *Sursum corda*; these are so many words lost to me: I come already fully prepared from my chamber. I need no allurement, no invitation, no sauce; I eat the meat raw, so that, instead of whetting my appetite by these preparatives, they tire and pall it. Will the license of the time excuse my sacrilegious boldness if I censure the dialogism of Plato himself as also dull and heavy, too much stifling the matter, and lament so much time lost by a man, who had so many better things to say, in so many long and needless preliminary interlocutions? My ignorance will better excuse me in that I understand not Greek so well as to discern the beauty of his language.

I generally choose books that use sciences, not such as only lead to them. The two first, and Pliny, and their like, have nothing of this *Hoc age*; they will have to do with men already instructed; or if they have, 'tis a substantial *Hoc age*, and that has a body by itself. I also delight in reading the *Epistles to Atticus*, not only because they contain a great deal of the history and affairs of his time, but much more because I therein discover much of his own private humors; for I have a singular curiosity, as I have said elsewhere, to pry into the souls and the natural and true opinions of the authors with whom I converse. A man may indeed judge of their parts, but not of their manners nor of themselves, by the writings they exhibit upon the theatre of the world. I have a thousand times lamented the loss of the treatise Brutus wrote upon virtue, for it is well to learn the theory from those who best know the practice. But seeing the matter preached and the preacher are different things, I would as willingly see Brutus in Plutarch, as in a book of his own. I would rather choose to be certainly informed of the conference he had in his tent with some particular friends of his the night before a battle, than of the harangue he made the next day to his army; and of what he did in his closet and his chamber, than what he did in the public square and in the senate.

As to Cicero, I am of the common opinion that, learning excepted, he had no great natural excellence. He was a good citizen, of an affable nature, as all fat, heavy men, such as he was, usually are; but given to ease, and had, in truth, a mighty share of vanity and ambition. Neither do I know how to excuse him for thinking his poetry fit to be published; 'tis no great imperfection to make ill verses, but it is an imperfection not to be able to judge how unworthy his verses were of the glory of his name. For what concerns his eloquence, that is totally out of all comparison, and I believe it will never be equalled. The younger Cicero, who resembled his father in nothing but in name, while commanding in Asia, had several strangers one day at his table and, among the rest, Cestius seated at the lower end, as men often intrude to the open tables of the great. Cicero asked one of his people who that man was, who presently told him his name; but he, as one who had his thoughts taken up with something else, and who had forgotten the answer made him, asking three or four times, over and over again, the same question, the fellow, to deliver himself from so many answers and to make him know him by some particular circumstance; "'Tis that Cestius," said he, "of whom it was told you, that he makes no great account of your father's eloquence in comparison of his own." At which Cicero, being suddenly nettled, commanded poor Cestius presently to be seized, and caused him to be very well whipped in his own presence; a very discourteous entertainer!

Yet even among those, who, all things considered, have reputed his eloquence incomparable, there have been some who have not stuck to observe some faults in it; as that great Brutus his friend, for example, who said it was a broken and feeble eloquence, *fractam et elumbem*. The orators also, nearest to the age wherein he lived, reprehended in him the care he had of a certain long cadence in his periods, and particularly took notice of these words, *esse videatur*, which he there so often makes use of. For my part, I more approve of a shorter style, and that comes more roundly off. He does, though, sometimes shuffle his parts more briskly together, but 'tis very seldom. I have myself taken notice of this one passage: "*Ego vero me minus diu senem mallem, quam esse senem antequam essem.*"

The historians are my right ball, for they are pleasant and easy, and where man, in general, the knowledge of whom I hunt after, appears more vividly and entire than anywhere else: the variety and truth of his internal qualities, in gross and piecemeal, the diversity of means by which he is united and knit, and the accidents that threaten him. Now those that write lives, by reason they insist more upon counsels than events, more upon what sallies from within, than upon what happens without, are the most proper for my reading: and, therefore, above all others, Plutarch is the man for me. I am very sorry we have not a dozen Laertii, or that he was not further extended; for I am equally curious to know the lives and fortunes of these great instructors of the world, as to know the diversities of their doctrines and opinions. In this kind of study of histories, a man must tumble over, without distinction, all sorts of authors, old and new, French or foreign, there to know the things of which they variously treat.

But Cæsar, in my opinion, particularly deserves to be studied, not for the knowledge of the history only, but for himself, so great an excellence and perfection he has above all the rest, though Sallust be one of the number. In earnest, I read this author with more reverence and respect than is usually allowed to human writings; one while considering him in his person, by his actions and miraculous greatness, and another in the purity and inimitable polish of his language, wherein he not only excels all other historians, as Cicero confesses, but, peradventure, even Cicero himself; speaking of his enemies with so much sincerity in his judgment, that, the false colors with which he strives to palliate his evil cause, and the ordure of his pestilent ambition excepted, I think there is no fault to be objected against him, saving this, that he speaks too sparingly of himself, seeing so many great things could not have been performed under his conduct, but that his own personal acts must necessarily have had a greater share in them than he attributes to them.

I love historians, whether of the simple sort, or of the higher order. The simple, who have nothing of their own to mix with it, and who only make it their business to collect all that comes to their knowledge, and faithfully to record all things, without choice or discrimination, leave to us the entire judgment of discerning the truth. Such, for example among others, is honest Froissart, who has proceeded in his undertaking with so frank a plainness that, having committed an error, he is not ashamed to confess, and correct it in the place where the finger has been laid, and who represents to us even the variety of rumors that were then spread abroad, and the different reports that were made to him; 'tis the naked and inform matter of history, and of which every one may make his profit, according to his understanding.

The more excellent sort of historians have judgment to pick out what is most worthy to be known; and, of two reports, to examine which is the most likely to be true: from the condition of princes and their humors, they conclude their counsels, and attribute to them words proper for the occasion; such have title to assume the authority of regulating our belief to what they themselves believe; but, certainly, this privilege belongs to very few. For the middle sort of historians, of which the most part are, they spoil all; they will chew our meat for us; they take upon them to judge of, and consequently, to incline the history to their own fancy; for if the judgment lean to one side, a man cannot avoid wresting and writhing his narrative to that bias; they undertake to select things worthy to be known, and yet often conceal from us such a word, such a private action, as would much better instruct us; omit, as incredible, such things as they do not understand, and peradventure some, because they cannot express them well in good French or Latin. Let them display their eloquence and intelligence, and judge according to their own fancy: but let them, withal, leave us something to judge of after them, and neither alter nor disguise, by their abridgments and at their own choice, anything of the substance of the matter, but deliver it to us pure and entire in all its dimensions.

For the most part, and especially in these latter ages, persons are culled out for this work from among the common people, upon the sole consideration of well-speaking, as if we were to learn grammar from them; and the men so chosen have fair reason, being hired for no other end and pretending to nothing but babble, not to be very solicitous of any part but that, and so, with a fine jingle of words, prepare us a pretty contexture of reports they pick up in the streets. The only good histories are those that have been written by the persons themselves who held command in the affairs whereof they write, or who participated in the conduct of them, or, at least, who have had the conduct of others of the same nature. Such are almost all the Greek and Roman histories: for, several eyewitnesses having written of the same subject, in the time when grandeur and learning commonly met in the same person, if there happen to be an error, it must of necessity be a very slight one, and upon a very doubtful incident. What can a man expect from a physician who writes of war, or from a mere scholar, treating of the designs of princes?

If we could take notice how scrupulous the Romans were in this, there would need but this example: Asinius Pollio found in the histories of Cæsar himself something misreported, a mistake occasioned either by reason he could not have his eye in all parts of his army at once and had given credit to some individual persons who had not delivered him a very true account; or else, for not having had too perfect notice given him by his lieutenants of what they had done in his absence. By which we may see, whether the inquisition after truth be not very delicate, when a man cannot believe the report of a battle from the knowledge of him who there commanded, nor from the soldiers who were engaged in it, unless, after the method of a judicial inquiry, the witnesses be confronted and objections considered upon the proof of the least detail of every incident.

In good earnest the knowledge we have of our own affairs is much more obscure: but that has been sufficiently handled by Bodin, and according to my own sentiment. A little to aid the weakness of my memory (so extreme that it has happened to me more than once, to take books again into my hand as new and unseen, that I had carefully read over a few years before, and scribbled with my notes) I have adopted a custom of late, to note at the end of every book (that is, of those I never intend to read again) the time when I made an end on't, and the judgment I had made of it, to the end that this might, at least, represent to me the character and general idea I had conceived of the author in reading it; and I will here transcribe some of those annotations.

I wrote this, some ten years ago, in my Guicciardini (of what language soever my books speak to me in, I always speak to them in my own): "He is a diligent historiographer, from whom, in my opinion, a man may learn the truth of the affairs of his time, as exactly as from any other; in the most of which he was himself also a personal actor, and in honorable command. There is no appearance that he disguised anything, either upon the account of hatred, favor, or vanity; of which the free censures he passes upon the great ones, and particularly those by whom he was advanced and employed in commands of great trust and honor, as Pope Clement VII, give ample testimony.

"As to that part which he thinks himself the best at, namely his digressions and discourses, he has indeed some very good, and enriched with fine features; but he is too fond of them: for, to leave nothing unsaid, having a subject so full, ample, almost infinite, he degenerates into pedantry and smacks a little of scholastic prattle. I have also observed this in him, that of so many souls and so many effects, so many motives and so many counsels as he judges, he never attributes any one to virtue, religion, or conscience, as if all these were utterly extinct in the world: and of all the actions, how brave soever in outward show they appear in themselves, he always refers the cause and motive to some vicious occasion or some prospect of profit. It is impossible to imagine but that, among such an infinite number of actions as he makes mention of, there must be some one produced by the way of honest reason. No corruption could so universally have infected men that some one would not escape the contagion: which makes me suspect that his own taste was vicious, whence it might happen that he judged other men by himself."

In my Philip de Comines, there is this written: "You will here find the language sweet and delightful, of a natural simplicity, the narration pure, with the good faith of the author conspicuous therein; free from vanity, when speaking of himself, and from affection or envy, when speaking of others: his discourses and exhortations rather accompanied with zeal and truth, than with any exquisite sufficiency; and, throughout, authority and gravity, which bespeak him a man of good extraction, and brought up in great affairs."

Upon the *Memoirs* of Monsieur du Bellay I find this: "'Tis always pleasant to read things written by those that have experienced how they ought to be carried on; but withal, it cannot be denied but there is a manifest decadence in these two lords from the freedom and liberty of writing that shine in the elder historians, such as the Sire de Joinville, the familiar companion of St. Louis; Eginhard, chancellor to Charlemagne: and of later date, Philip de Comines. What we have here is rather an apology for King Francis, against the Emperor Charles V., than history. I will not believe that they have falsified anything, as to matter of fact; but they make a common practice of twisting the judgment of events, very often contrary to reason, to our advantage, and of omitting whatsoever is ticklish to be handled in the life of their master; witness the proceedings of Messieurs de Montmorency and de Biron, which are here omitted: nay, so much as the very name of Madame d'Estampes is not here to be found.

"Secret actions an historian may conceal; but to pass over in silence what all the world knows, and things that have drawn after them public and such high consequences, is an inexcusable defect. In fine, whoever has a mind to have a perfect knowledge of King Francis and the events of his reign, let them seek it elsewhere, if my advice may prevail. The only profit a man can reap from these *Memoirs* is in the special narrative of battles and other exploits of war wherein these gentlemen were personally engaged; in some words and private actions of the princes of their time, and in the treaties and negotiations carried on by the Seigneur de Langey, where there are everywhere things worthy to be known, and discourses above the vulgar strain."

OF CRUELTY.

I fancy virtue to be something else, and something more noble, than good nature, and the mere propension to goodness, that we are born into the world withal. Well-disposed and well-descended souls pursue, indeed, the same methods, and represent in their actions the same face that virtue itself does: but the word virtue imports something more great and active than merely for a man to suffer himself by a happy disposition, to be gently and quietly drawn to the rule of reason. He who, by a natural sweetness and facility, should despise injuries received, would doubtless do a very fine and laudable thing; but he who, provoked and nettled to the quick by an offence, should fortify himself with the arms of reason against the furious appetite of revenge, and, after a great conflict, master his own passion, would certainly do a great deal more. The first would do well; the latter virtuously: one action might be called goodness, and the other virtue; for, methinks, the very name of virtue presupposes difficulty and contention, and cannot be exercised without an opponent. 'Tis for this reason, perhaps, that we call God good, mighty, liberal, and just; but we do not call him virtuous, being that all His operations are natural and without endeavor.

It has been the opinion of many philosophers, not only Stoics, but Epicureans—(and this addition I borrow from the vulgar opinion, which is false, notwithstanding the witty conceit of Arcesilaus in answer to one, who, being reproached that many scholars went from his school to the Epicurean, but never any from thence to his school, said in answer, "I believe it indeed; numbers of capons being made out of cocks, but never any cocks out of capons." For, in truth, the Epicurean sect is not at all inferior to the Stoic in steadiness, and the rigor of opinions and precepts. And a certain Stoic, showing more honesty than those disputants, who, in order to quarrel with Epicurus, and to throw the game into their hands, make him say what he never thought, putting a wrong construction upon his words, clothing his sentences, by the strict rules of grammar, with another meaning, and a different opinion from that which they knew he entertained in his mind, and in his morals, the Stoic, I say, declared that he abandoned the Epicurean sect, upon this, among other considerations, that he thought their road too lofty and inaccessible; "And those whom we call lovers of pleasure, being, in effect, lovers of honor and justice, cultivate and practise all the virtues" [Cicero])—these philosophers say that it is not enough to have the soul seated in a good place, of a good temper, and well disposed to virtue; it is not enough to have our resolutions and our reasoning fixed above all the power of fortune, but that we are, moreover, to seek occasions wherein to put them to the proof: they would seek pain, necessity, and contempt, to contend with them and to keep the soul in breath: "*Multum sibi adjicit virtus lacessita.*" 'Tis one of the reasons why Epaminondas who was yet of a third sect, refused the riches fortune presented to him by very lawful means; because, said he, "I am to contend with poverty," in which extreme he maintained himself to the last. Socrates put himself, methinks, upon a ruder trial, keeping for his exercise a confounded scolding wife; which was fighting at sharps. Metellus having of all the Roman senators alone attempted, by the power of virtue, to withstand the violence of Saturninus, tribune of the people at Rome, who would, by all means, cause an unjust law to pass in favor of the commons, and by so doing, having incurred the capital penalties that Saturninus had established against the dissentient, entertained those who, in this extremity, led him to execution with words to this effect: that it was a thing too easy and too base to do ill; and that to do well where there was no danger was a common thing; but that to do well where there was danger was the proper office of a man of virtue. These words of Metellus very clearly represent to us what I would make out, viz., that virtue refuses facility for a companion; and that the easy, smooth, and descending way by which the regular steps of a sweet disposition of nature are conducted is not that of a true virtue; she requires a rough and stormy passage; she will have either exotic difficulties to wrestle with, like that of Metellus, by means whereof fortune delights to interrupt the speed of her career, or internal difficulties, that the inordinate appetites and imperfections of our condition introduce to disturb her.

I am come thus far at my ease; but here it comes into my head that the soul of Socrates, the most perfect that ever came to my knowledge, should, by this rule, be of very little recommendation; for I cannot conceive in that person any the least motion of a vicious inclination: I cannot imagine there could be any difficulty or constraint in the course of his virtue: I know his reason to be so powerful and sovereign over him that she would never have suffered a vicious appetite so much as to spring in him. To a virtue so elevated as his, I have nothing to oppose. Methinks I see him march, with a victorious and triumphant pace, in pomp and at his ease, without opposition or disturbance.

If virtue cannot shine bright, but by the conflict of contrary appetites, shall we then say that she cannot subsist without the assistance of vice, and that it is from her that she derives her reputation and honor? What then, also, would become of that brave and generous Epicurean pleasure, which makes account that it nourishes virtue tenderly in her lap, and there makes it play and wanton, giving it for toys to play withal, shame, fevers, poverty, death, and torments? If I presuppose that a perfect virtue manifests itself in contending, in patient enduring of pain, and undergoing the uttermost extremity of the gout, without being moved in her seat; if I give her troubles and difficulty for her necessary objects: what will become of a virtue elevated to such a degree, as not only to despise pain, but, moreover, to rejoice in it, and to be tickled with the daggers of a sharp gout, such as the Epicureans have established, and of which many of them, by their actions, have given most manifest proofs? As have several others, who I find to have surpassed in effects even the very rules of their discipline; witness the younger Cato: when I see him die, and tearing out his own bowels, I am not satisfied simply to believe that he had then his soul totally exempt from all trouble and horror: I cannot think that he only maintained himself in the steadiness that the Stoical rules prescribed him: temperate, without emotion, and imperturbed.

There was, methinks, something in the virtue of this man too sprightly and fresh to stop there; I believe that, without doubt, he felt a pleasure and delight in so noble an action, and was more pleased in it than in any other of his life: "He quitted life, rejoicing that a reason for dying had arisen" [Cicero]. I believe it so thoroughly that I question whether he would have been content to have been deprived of the occasion of so brave an execution; and if the goodness that made him embrace the public concern more than his own withheld me not, I should easily fall into an opinion that he thought himself obliged to fortune for having put his virtue upon so brave a trial, and for having favored that thief[1] in treading underfoot the ancient liberty of his country. Methinks I read in this action I know not what exaltation in his soul, and an extraordinary and manly emotion of pleasure when he looked upon the generosity and height of his enterprise: "*Deliberata morte ferocior*," not stimulated with any hope of glory, as the popular and effeminate judgments of some have concluded (for that consideration was too mean and low to possess so generous, so haughty, and so determined a heart as his), but for the very beauty of the thing in itself, which he who had the handling of the springs discerned more clearly and in its perfection than we are able to do.

Philosophy has obliged me in determining that so brave an action had been indecently placed in any other life than that of Cato; and that it only appertained to his to end so; notwithstanding, and according to reason, he commanded his son and the senators who accompanied him to take another course in their affairs: "Nature having endued Cato with an incredible gravity, which he had also fortified with a perpetual constancy, without ever flagging in his resolution, he must of necessity rather die than see the face of the tyrant" [Cicero].

Every death ought to hold proportion with the life before it; we do not become others for dying. I always interpret the death by the

---

[1] Cæsar.

life preceding; and if any one tell me of a death strong and constant in appearance, annexed to a feeble life, I conclude it produced by some feeble cause, and suitable to the life before. The easiness then of this death and the facility of dying he had acquired by the vigor of his soul; shall we say that it ought to abate anything of the lustre of his virtue? And who, that has his brain never so little tinctured with the true philosophy, can be content to imagine Socrates only free from fear and passion in the accident of his prison, fetters, and condemnation? and that will not discover in him not only firmness and constancy (which was his ordinary condition), but, moreover, I know not what new satisfaction, and a frolic cheerfulness in his last words and actions? In the start he gave with the pleasure of scratching his leg when his irons were taken off, does he not discover an equal serenity and joy in his soul for being freed from past inconveniences, and at the same time to enter into the knowledge of things to come? Cato shall pardon me, if he please; his death indeed is more tragical and more lingering; but yet this is, I know not how, methinks, finer. Aristippus, to one that was lamenting this death: "The gods grant me such a one," said he. A man discerns in the soul of these two great men and their imitators (for I very much doubt whether there were ever their equals) so perfect a habitude to virtue, that it was turned to a complexion. It is no longer a laborious virtue nor the precepts of reason, to maintain which the soul is so racked, but the very essence of their soul, its natural and ordinary habit; they have rendered it such by a long practice of philosophical precepts having lit upon a rich and fine nature; the vicious passions that spring in us can find no entrance into them: the force and vigor of their soul stifle and extinguish irregular desires, so soon as they begin to move.

Now, that it is not more noble, by a high and divine resolution, to hinder the birth of temptations, and to be so formed to virtue, that the very seeds of vice are rooted out, than to hinder by main force their progress; and, having suffered ourselves to be surprised with the first motions of the passions, to arm ourselves and to stand firm to oppose their progress, and overcome them; and that this second effect is not also much more generous than to be simply endowed with a facile and affable nature, of itself disaffected to debauchery and vice, I do not think can be doubted; for this third and last sort of virtue seems to render a man innocent, but not virtuous; free from doing ill, but not apt enough to do well: considering also, that this condition is so near neighbor to imperfection and cowardice, that I know not very well how to separate the confines and distinguish them; the very names of goodness and innocence are, for this reason, in some sort grown into contempt. I very well know that several virtues, as chastity, sobriety, and temperance, may come to a man through personal defects. Constancy in danger, if it must be so called, the contempt of death, and patience in misfortunes, may ofttimes be found in men for want of well judging of such accidents, and not apprehending them for such as they are.

Want of apprehension and stupidity sometimes counterfeit virtuous effects: as I have often seen it happen, that men have been commended for what really merited blame. An Italian lord once said this, in my presence, to the disadvantage of his own nation: that the subtlety of the Italians, and the vivacity of their conceptions were so great, and they foresaw the dangers and accidents that might befall them so far off, that it was not to be thought strange, if they were often in war observed to provide for their safety, even before they had discovered the peril; that we French and the Spaniards, who were not so cunning, went on further, and that we must be made to see and feel the danger before we would take the alarm; but that even then we could not stick to it. But the Germans and Swiss, more heavy and thick-skulled, had not the sense to look about them, even when the blows were falling about their ears. Peradventure, he only talked so for mirth's sake; and yet it is most certain that in war raw soldiers rush into danger with more precipitancy than after they have been well cudgelled: "Not ignorant how hope of glory excites the young soldier in the first essay of arms" [*Æneid*]. For this reason it is that, when we judge of a particular action, we are to consider the circumstances, and the whole man by whom it is performed, before we give it a name.

To instance in myself: I have sometimes known my friends call that prudence in me, which was merely fortune; and repute that courage and patience, which was judgment and opinion; and attribute to me one title for another, sometimes to my advantage and sometimes otherwise. As to the rest, I am so far from being arrived at the first and most perfect degree of excellence, where virtue is turned into habit, that even of the second I have made no great proofs. I have not been very solicitous to curb the desires by which I have been importuned. My virtue is a virtue, or rather an innocence, casual and accidental. If I had been born of a more irregular complexion, I am afraid I should have made scurvy work; for I never observed any great stability in my soul to resist passions, if they were never so little vehement: I have not the knack of nourishing quarrels and debates in my own bosom, and, consequently, owe myself no great thanks that I am free from several vices. I owe it rather to my fortune than my reason. She has caused me to be descended of a race famous for integrity and of a very good father; I know not whether or no he has infused into me part of his humors, or whether domestic examples and the good education

of my infancy have insensibly assisted in the work, or, if I was otherwise born so; but so it is, that I have naturally a horror for most
vices.

The answer of Antisthenes to him who asked him, which was the
best apprenticeship, "to unlearn evil," seems to point at this. I have
them in horror, I say, with a detestation so natural, and so much my
own, that the same instinct and impression I brought of them with
me from my nurse, I yet retain, and no temptation whatever has had
the power to make me alter it. Not so much as my own discourses,
which in some things lashing out of the common road might seem
easily to license me to actions that my natural inclination makes me
hate. I will say a prodigious thing, but I will say it however: I find
myself in many things more under reputation by my manners than by
my opinion, and my concupiscence less debauched than my reason.

Aristippus instituted opinions so bold in favor of pleasure and riches
as set all the philosophers against him: but as to his manners, Dionysius
the tyrant, having presented three beautiful women before him, to
take his choice, he made answer, that he would choose them all, and
that Paris got himself into trouble for having preferred one before the
other two: but, having taken them home to his house, he sent them
back untouched. His servant finding himself overladen upon the way,
with the money he carried after him, he ordered him to pour out and
throw away that which troubled him. And Epicurus, whose doctrines
were so irreligious and effeminate, was in his life very laborious and
devout; he wrote to a friend of his that he lived only upon biscuit and
water, entreating him to send him a little cheese, to lie by him against
he had a mind to make a feast.

Must it be true, that to be a perfect good man, we must be so by
an occult, natural, and universal propriety, without law, reason, or
example? The debauches wherein I have been engaged, have not
been, I thank God, of the worst sort, and I have condemned them in
myself, for my judgment was never infected by them; on the contrary, I accuse them more severely in myself than in any other; but
that is all, for, as to the rest, I oppose too little resistance and suffer
myself to incline too much to the other side of the balance, excepting
that I moderate them, and prevent them from mixing with other
vices, which, for the most part will cling together, if a man have not
a care. I have contracted and curtailed mine, to make them as single
and as simple as I can: "not to carry wrong further."

For as to the opinion of the Stoics, who say, "That the wise man
when he works, works by all the virtues together though one be most
apparent, according to the nature of the action;" and herein the similitude of a human body might serve them somewhat, for the action

of anger cannot work unless all the humors assist it, though choler predominate;—if they will thence draw a like consequence, that when the wicked man does wickedly, he does it by all the vices together, I do not believe it to be so, or else I understand them not, for I by effect find the contrary. These are sharp, unsubstantial subtleties, with which philosophy sometimes amuses itself. I follow some vices, but I fly others as much as a saint would do. The Peripatetics also disown this indissoluble connection; and Aristotle is of opinion that a prudent and just man may be intemperate and inconsistent. Socrates confessed to some who had discovered a certain inclination to vice in his physiognomy, that it was, in truth, his natural propension, but that he had by discipline corrected it. And such as were familiar with the philosopher Stilpo said, that being born with addiction to wine and women, he had by study rendered himself very abstinent both from the one and the other.

What I have in me of good, I have, quite contrary, by the chance of my birth; and hold it not either by law, precept, or any other instruction: the innocence that is in me is a simple one; little vigor and no art. Among other vices, I mortally hate cruelty, both by nature and judgment as the very extreme of all vices; nay, with so much tenderness that I cannot see a chicken's neck pulled off, without trouble, and cannot, without impatience, endure the cry of a hare in my dog's teeth, though the chase be a violent pleasure. I conceive that the example of the pleasure of the chase would be more proper; wherein though the pleasure be less, there is the higher excitement of unexpected joy; giving no time for the reason, taken by surprise, to prepare itself for the encounter, when after a long quest the beast starts up on a sudden in a place where, peradventure, we least expected it; the shock and the ardor of the shouts and cries of the hunters so strike us, that it would be hard for those who love this lesser chase, to turn their thoughts, upon the instant, another way; and the poets make Diana triumph over the torch and shafts of Cupid: "Who among such delights, would not remove out of his thoughts the anxious cares of love?" asks Horace.

To return to what I was saying before, I am tenderly compassionate of others' afflictions, and should readily cry for company, if, upon any occasion whatever, I could cry at all. Nothing tempts my tears, but tears, and not only those that are real and true, but whatever they are, feigned or painted. I do not much lament the dead, and should envy them rather; but I very much lament the dying. The savages do not so much offend me, in roasting and eating the bodies of the dead, as they do who torment and persecute the living. Nay, I cannot look so much as upon the ordinary executions of justice, how reasonable soever, with a steady eye. Some one having to give testimony of Julius Cæsar's clemency; "he was," says he, "mild in his revenges. Having compelled the pirates to yield by whom he had before been taken prisoner and put to ransom; forasmuch as he had threatened them with the cross, he indeed condemned them to it, but it was after they had been first strangled. He punished his secretary Philemon, who had attempted to poison him, with no greater severity than mere death." Without naming that Latin author who thus dares to allege as a testimony of mercy the killing only of those by whom we have been offended, it is easy to guess that he was struck with the horrid and inhuman examples of cruelty practised by the Roman tyrants.

For my part, even in justice itself, all that exceeds a simple death appears to me pure cruelty; especially in us who ought, having regard to their souls, to dismiss them in a good and calm condition; which cannot be, when we have agitated them by insufferable torments. Not long since a soldier who was a prisoner, perceiving from a tower where he was shut up, that the people began to assemble to the place of execution, and that the carpenters were busy erecting a scaffold, he presently concluded that the preparation was for him; and therefore entered into a resolution to kill himself, but could find no instrument to assist him in his design except an old rusty cart-nail that fortune presented to him. With this he first gave himself two great wounds about his throat, but finding these would not do, he presently afterwards gave himself a third in the belly, where he left the nail sticking up to the head. The first of his keepers who came in found him in this condition; yet alive, but sunk down and exhausted by his wounds. To make use of time, therefore, before he should die, they made haste to read his sentence; which having done, and he hearing that he was only condemned to be beheaded, he seemed to take new courage, accepted wine which he had before refused, and thanked his judges for the unhoped-for mildness of their sentence; saying, that he had taken a resolution to despatch himself for fear of a more severe and insupportable death, having entertained an opinion, by the preparations he had seen in the place, that they were resolved to torment him with some horrible execution; and seemed to be delivered from death, in having it changed from what he apprehended.

I should advise that those examples of severity, by which 'tis designed to retain the people in their duty, might be exercised upon the dead bodies of criminals; for to see them deprived of sepulture, to see them boiled and divided into quarters, would almost work as much upon the vulgar, as the pain they make the living endure; though that in effect be little or nothing, as God himself says, "Who kill the body, and, after that, have no more that they can do;" and the poets singularly dwell upon the horrors of this picture, as something worse than death: "Alas! that the half-burned remains of these kings, and their bared bones, should be shamefully dragged through the dirt!" exclaims Cicero.

I happened to come by one day, accidentally, at Rome, just as they were executing Catena, a notorious robber: he was strangled without any emotion of the spectators, but when they came to cut him in quarters the hangman gave not a blow that the people did not follow with a doleful cry and exclamation, as if every one had lent his sense of feeling to the miserable carcass. Those inhuman excesses ought to be exercised upon the bark, and not upon the quick. Artaxerxes, in almost a like case, moderated the severity of the ancient laws of Persia, ordaining that the nobility who had committed a fault, instead of being whipped, as they were used to be, should be stripped only and their clothes whipped for them; and that whereas they were wont to tear off their hair, they should only take off their high-crowned tiara. The so devout Egyptians thought they sufficiently satisfied the divine justice by sacrificing hogs in effigy and representation; a bold invention to pay God, so essential a substance, in picture only and in show.

I live in a time wherein we abound in incredible examples of this vice, through the license of our civil wars: and we see nothing in ancient histories more extreme than what we have proof of every day, but I cannot, any the more, get used to it. I could hardly persuade myself, before I saw it with my eyes, that there could be found souls so cruel and fell, who, for the sole pleasure of murder, would commit it; would hack and lop off the limbs of others; sharpen their wits to invent unusual torments and new kinds of death, without hatred, without profit, and for no other end but only to enjoy the pleasant spectacle of the gestures and motions, the lamentable groans and cries of a man dying in anguish. For this is the utmost point to which cruelty can arrive: "*Ut homo hominem, non iratus, non timens, tantum spectaturus, occidat*" [Seneca]. For my own part I cannot without grief see so much as an innocent beast pursued and killed that has no defence; and from which we have received no offence at all; and that which frequently happens, that the stag we hunt, finding himself weak and out of breath, and seeing no other remedy, surrenders himself to us who pursue him, imploring mercy by his tears, has ever been to me a very unpleasing sight; and I hardly ever take a beast alive that I do not presently turn out again. Pythagoras bought them of fishermen and fowlers to do the same.

Those natures that are sanguinary toward beasts discover a natural propension to cruelty. After they had accustomed themselves at

Rome to spectacles of the slaughter of animals, they proceeded to those of the slaughter of men, to the gladiators. Nature has, herself, I fear, imprinted in man a kind of instinct to inhumanity; nobody takes pleasure in seeing beasts play with and caress one another, but every one is delighted with seeing them dismember, and tear one another to pieces. And that I may not be laughed at for the sympathy I have with them, theology itself enjoins us some favor in their behalf; and considering that one and the same master has lodged us together in this palace for his service, and that they, as well as we, are of his family, it has reason to enjoin us some affection and regard to them. Pythagoras borrowed the metempsychosis from the Egyptians; but it has since been received by several nations, and particularly by our Druids: "Souls never die, but, having left one seat, are received into new houses," says Ovid.

The religion of our ancient Gauls maintained that souls, being eternal, never ceased to remove and shift their places from one body to another; mixing moreover with this fancy some consideration of divine justice; for according to the deportments of the soul, while it had been in Alexander, they said that God assigned it another body to inhabit, more or less painful, and proper for its condition. If it had been valiant, he lodged it in the body of a lion; if voluptuous, in that of a hog; if timorous, in that of a hart or hare; if malicious, in that of a fox, and so of the rest, till having purified it by this chastisement, it again entered into the body of some other man: "For I myself remember that in the days of the Trojan war, I was Euphorbus, son of Pantheus," cites Ovid.

As to the relationship between us and beasts, I do not much admit of it; nor of that which several nations, and those among the most ancient and most noble, have practised, who have not only received brutes into their society and companionship, but have given them a rank infinitely above themselves, esteeming them one while familiars and favorites of the gods, and having them in more than human reverence and respect; others acknowledge no other god or divinity than they. Cicero says, "The barbarians consecrated beasts for their good qualities;" and Juvenal: "This place adores the crocodile; another dreads the ibis, feeder on serpents: here you may behold the statue of a monkey shining in gold: here men venerate a river fish; there whole towns worship a dog."

And the very interpretation that Plutarch gives to this error, which is very well conceived, is advantageous to them: for he says that it was not the cat or the ox, for example, that the Egyptians adored: but that they, in those beasts, adored some image of the divine faculties: in this, patience and utility; in that vivacity, or, as with our neighbors the Burgundians and all the Germans, impatience to see themselves shut up; by which they represented liberty, which they loved and adored above all other godlike attributes, and so of the rest. But when, among the more moderate opinions, I meet with arguments that endeavor to demonstrate the near resemblance between us and animals, how large a share they have in our greatest privileges, and with how much probability they compare us together, truly I abate a great deal of our presumption, and willingly resign that imaginary sovereignty that is attributed to us over other creatures.

But supposing all this were not true, there is, nevertheless, a certain respect, a general duty of humanity, not only to beasts that have life and sense, but even to trees and plants. We owe justice to men, and graciousness and benignity to other creatures that are capable of it; there is a certain commerce and mutual obligation between them and us. Nor shall I be afraid to confess the tenderness of my nature so childish, that I cannot well refuse to play with my dog, when he the most unseasonably importunes me so to do. The Turks have alms and hospitals for beasts. The Romans had public care to the nourishment of geese, by whose vigilance their Capitol had been preserved. The Athenians made a decree that the mules and moyls which had served at the building of the temple called Hecatompedon should be free and suffered to pasture at their own choice, without hindrance. The Agrigentines had a common use solemnly to inter the beasts they had a kindness for, as horses of some rare quality, dogs, and useful birds, and even those that had only been kept to divert their children; and the magnificence that was ordinary with them in all other things, also particularly appeared in the sumptuosity and numbers of monuments erected to this end, and which remained in their beauty several ages after. The Egyptians buried wolves, bears, crocodiles, dogs, and cats in sacred places, embalmed their bodies, and put on mourning at their death. Cimon gave an honorable sepulture to the mares with which he had three times gained the prize of the course at the Olympic Games. The ancient Xantippus caused his dog to be interred on an eminence near the sea, which has ever since retained the name, and Plutarch says, that he had a scruple about selling for a small profit to the slaughterer an ox that had been long in his service.

OF THE INCONSTANCY OF OUR ACTIONS.

Such as make it their business to oversee human actions, do not find themselves in anything so much perplexed as to reconcile them and bring them into the world's eye with the same lustre and reputation; for they commonly so strangely contradict one another that it seems impossible they should proceed from one and the same person. We find the younger Marius one while a son of Mars, and another, a son of Venus. Pope Boniface VIII. entered, it is said, into his papacy like a fox, behaved himself in it like a lion and died like a dog; and who could believe it to be the same Nero, the perfect image of all cruelty, who, having the sentence of a condemned man brought to him to sign, as was the custom, cried out, "O, that I had never been taught to write!" so much it went to his heart to condemn a man to death. All story is full of such examples, and every man is able to produce so many to himself, or out of his own practice or observation, that I sometimes wonder to see men of understanding give themselves the trouble of sorting these pieces, considering that irresolution appears to me to be the most common and manifest vice of our nature; witness the famous verse of the player Publius, "*Malum consilium est, quod mutari non potest.*"

There seems some reason in forming a judgment of a man from the most usual methods of his life; but, considering the natural instability of our manners and opinions, I have often thought even the best authors a little out in so obstinately endeavoring to make of us any constant and solid contexture; they choose a general air of a man, and according to that interpret all his actions, of which, if they cannot bend some to a uniformity with the rest, they are presently imputed to dissimulation. Augustus has escaped them, for there was in him so apparent, sudden, and continual variety of actions all the whole course of his life, that he has slipped away clear and undecided from the most daring critics. I can more hardly believe a man's constancy than any other virtue, and believe nothing sooner than the contrary. He that would judge of a man in detail and distinctly, bit by bit, would oftener be able to speak the truth. It is a hard matter, from all antiquity, to pick out a dozen men who have formed their lives to one certain and constant course, which is the principal design of wisdom; for to comprise it all in one word, says one of the ancients,[1] and to contract all the rules of human life into one, "it is to will, and not to will, always one and the same thing: I will not vouchsafe," says he, "to add, provided the will be just, for if it be not just, it is impossible it should be always one."

I have indeed formerly learned that vice is nothing but irregularity and want of measure, and therefore 'tis impossible to fix constancy to it. 'Tis a saying of Demosthenes, "that the beginning of all virtue is consultation and deliberation; the end and perfection, constancy." If we would resolve on any certain course by reason, we should pitch upon the best, but nobody has thought on't. "That which he sought

---

[1] Seneca.

he despises; what he has lost, he seeks. He fluctuates, and flies from that to this; his whole life a contradiction" [Horace].

Our ordinary practice is to follow the inclinations of our appetite, be it to the left or right, upward or downward, according as we are wafted by the breath of occasion. We never meditate what we would have till the instant we have a mind to have it; and change like that little creature which receives its color from what it is laid upon. What we but just now proposed to ourselves we immediately alter, and presently return again to it; 'tis nothing but shifting and inconstancy: "We are turned about as tops turn with the thong," says Horace.

We do not go, we are driven; like things that float, now leisurely, then with violence, according to the gentleness or rapidity of the current: "Do we not see them, uncertain what they would have, and always asking for something new, and to get rid of a burthen?" asks Lucretius. Every day a new whimsy, and our humors keep motion with the time. Says Cicero: "Such are the minds of men, that they change as the days that father Jupiter sends on the earth."

We fluctuate between various inclinations; we will nothing freely, nothing absolutely, nothing constantly. In any one who had prescribed and established determinate laws and rules in his head for his own conduct, we should perceive an equality of manners, an order and an infallible relation of one thing or action to another, shine through his whole life; Empedocles observed this discrepancy in the Agrigentines, that they gave themselves up to delights, as if every day were their last, and built as if they had been to live forever. The judgment would not be hard to make, as is very evident in the younger Cato; he who therein has found one step, it will lead them to all the rest. 'Tis a harmony of very according sounds, that cannot jar. But with us 'tis quite contrary; every particular action requires a particular judgment. The surest way to steer, in my opinion, would be to take our measures from the nearest allied circumstances, without engaging in a longer inquisition, or without concluding any other consequence.

Antigonus, having taken one of his soldiers into a great degree of favor and esteem for his virtue and valor, gave his physicians strict charge to cure him of a long and inward disease under which he had a great while languished, and observing that, after his cure, he went much more coldly to work than before, he asked him what had so altered and cowed him: "Yourself, sir," replied the other, "by having eased me of the pains that made me weary of my life." Lucullus' soldier having been rifled by the enemy, performed upon them in revenge a brave exploit, by which having made himself a gainer, Lucullus, who had conceived a good opinion of him from that action, went about to engage him in some enterprise of very great danger, with all the plausible persuasions and promises he could think of: "Words which would have inspired the greatest coward" [Horace]. "Pray employ," answered he, "some miserable plundered soldier in that affair;" and flatly refused to go.

When we read that Mohammed having furiously rated Chasan, Bassa of the Janizaries, because he had seen the Hungarians break into his squadrons, and himself behave very ill in the business, and that Chasan, instead of any other answer, rushed furiously alone, scimitar in hand, into the first body of the enemy where he was presently cut to pieces, we are not to look upon that action, peradventure, so much as vindication as a turn of mind not so much proceeding from natural valor as from a sudden despite. The man you saw yesterday so adventurous and brave, you must not think it strange to see him as great a poltroon the next: anger, necessity, company, wine, or the sound of the trumpet had roused his spirits; this is no valor formed and established by reason, but accidentally created by such circumstances, and therefore it is no wonder, if by contrary circumstances it appear quite another thing.

These supple variations and contradictions so manifest in us, have given occasion to some to believe that man has two souls; other two distinct powers that always accompany and incline us, the one toward good and the other toward ill, according to their own nature and propension; so abrupt a variety not being imaginable to flow from one and the same source.

For my part, the puff of every accident not only carries me along with it according to its own proclivity, but moreover I discompose and trouble myself by the instability of my own posture; and whoever will look narrowly into his own bosom, will hardly find himself twice in the same condition. I give to my soul sometimes one face and sometimes another, according to the side I turn her to. If I speak variously of myself, it is because I consider myself variously; all the contrarieties are there to be found in one corner or another, after one fashion or another: bashful, insolent; chaste, lustful; prating, silent; laborious, delicate; ingenious, heavy; melancholic, pleasant; lying, true; knowing, ignorant; liberal, covetous, and prodigal. I find all this in myself, more or less, according as I turn myself about; and whoever will sift himself to the bottom, will find in himself and even in his own judgment, this volubility and discordance. I have nothing to say of myself entirely, simply, and solidly without mixture and confusion. *Distinguo* is the most universal member of my logic. Though I always intend to speak well of good things, and rather to interpret such things as fall out in the best sense than otherwise, yet such is the strangeness of our condition, that we are often pushed on to do well even by vice itself, if well-doing were not judged by the intention only.

One gallant action, therefore, ought not to conclude a man valiant; if a man were brave indeed, he would be always so, and upon all occasions. If it were a habit of valor and not a sally, it would render a man equally resolute in all accidents; the same alone as in company; the same in lists as in a battle: for, let them say what they will, there is not one valor for the pavement and another for the field; he would bear a sickness in his bed as bravely as a wound in the field; and no more fear death in his own house than at an assault. We should not then see the same man charge into a breach with a brave assurance, and afterward torment himself like a woman for the loss of a trial at law or the death of a child; when, being an infamous coward, he is firm in the necessities of poverty; when he shrinks at the sight of a barber's razor and rushes fearless upon the swords of the enemy, the action is commendable, not the man.

Many of the Greeks, says Cicero, cannot endure the sight of an enemy, and yet are courageous in sickness; the Cimbrians and Celtiberians quite contrary; "*nihil enim potest esse æquabile, quod non a certâ ratione proficiscatur.*" No valor can be more extreme in its kind than that of Alexander: but it is of but one kind nor full enough throughout, nor universal. Incomparable as it is, it has yet some blemishes; of which his being so often at his wits' end upon every light suspicion of his captains, conspiring against his life, and the carrying himself in that inquisition with so much vehemence and indiscreet injustice, and with a fear that subverted his natural reason, is one pregnant instance. The superstition also, with which he was so much tainted, carries along with it some image of pusillanimity; and the excess of his penitence for the murder of Clytus is also a testimony of the unevenness of his courage.

All we perform is no other than a cento, as a man may say, of several pieces, and we would acquire honor by a false title. Virtue cannot be followed but for herself, and if one sometimes borrows her mask to some other purpose, she presently pulls it away again. 'Tis a vivid and strong tincture which, when the soul has once thoroughly imbibed it, will not out but with the piece. And, therefore, to make a right judgment of a man, we are long and very observingly to follow his trace: if constancy does not there stand firm upon her own proper base, "*cui vivendi via considerata atque provisa est*" if the variety of occurrences makes him alter his pace (his path, I mean, for the pace may be faster or slower) let him go; such a one runs before the wind, "*Avau le vent*" as the motto of our Talebot has it.

'Tis no wonder, says one of the ancients, that chance has so great a dominion over us, since it is by chance we live. It is not possible for any one who has not designed his life for some certain end, to dispose his particular actions; it is impossible for any one to arrange the pieces, who has not the whole form already contrived in his imagination. Of what use are colors to him that knows not what he is to paint? No one lays down a certain design for his life, and we only deliberate thereof by pieces. The archer ought first to know at what he is to aim, and then accommodate his arm, bow, string, shaft, and motion to it; our counsels deviate and wander, because not levelled to any determinate end. No wind serves him who addresses his voyage to no certain port. I cannot acquiesce in the judgment given by one in the behalf of Sophocles, who concluded him capable of the management of domestic affairs, against the accusation of his son, from having read one of his tragedies.

Neither do I allow of the conjecture of the Parians, sent to regulate the Milesians, sufficient for such a consequence, as they from thence derived: coming to visit the island, they took notice of such grounds as were best husbanded, and such country-houses as were best governed; and having taken the names of the owners, when they had assembled the citizens, they appointed these farmers for new governors and magistrates; concluding that they, who had been so provident in their own private concerns, would be so of the public too. We are all lumps, and of so various and inform a contexture, that every piece plays, every moment, its own game, and there is as much difference between us and ourselves as between us and others; "*magnam rem puta, unum hominem agere.*" Since ambition can teach men valor, temperance, and liberality, and even justice too; seeing that avarice can inspire the courage of a shop-boy, bred and nursed up in obscurity and ease, with the assurance to expose himself so far from the fireside to the mercy of the waves and angry Neptune in a frail boat; that she further teaches discretion and prudence; and that even Venus can inflate boys under the discipline of the rod with boldness and resolution, and infuse masculine courage into the heart of tender virgins in their mothers' arms: 'tis not all the understanding has to do, simply to judge us by our outward actions; it must penetrate the very soul, and there discover by what springs the motion is guided. But that being a high and hazardous undertaking, I could wish that fewer would attempt it.

USE MAKES PERFECT.

'Tis not to be expected that argument and instruction, though we never so voluntarily surrender our belief to what is read to us, should be of force to lead us on so far as to action, if we do not, over and above, exercise and form the soul by experience to the course for which we design it; it will, otherwise, doubtless find itself at a loss when it comes to the pinch of the business. This is the reason, why those among the philosophers who were ambitious to attain to a greater excellence, were not contented to await the severities of fortune in the retirement and repose of their own habitations, lest she should have surprised them raw and inexpert in the combat, but sallied out to meet her, and purposely threw themselves into the proof and difficulties. Some of them abandoned riches to exercise themselves in a voluntary poverty; others sought out labor and an austerity of life, to inure them to hardships and inconveniences; others have deprived themselves of their dearest members, as of sight, and of the instruments of generation, lest their too delightful and effeminate service should soften and debauch the stability of their souls.

But in dying, which is the greatest work we have to do, practice can give us no assistance at all. A man may by custom fortify himself against pain, shame, necessity, and such like accidents, but, as to death, we can experiment it but once, and are all apprentices when we come to it. There have, anciently, been men so excellent managers of their time that they have tried, even in death itself, to relish and taste it, and who have bent their utmost faculties of mind to discover what this passage is, but they are none of them come back to tell us the news: "No one was ever known to wake who has once fallen into the cold sleep of death" [Lucretius].

Canius Julius, a noble Roman of singular constancy and virtue, having been condemned to die by that scoundrel Caligula, besides many marvellous testimonies that he gave of his resolution, as he was just going to receive the stroke of the executioner, was asked by a philosopher, a friend of his: "Well, Canius, where-about is your soul now? what is she doing? What are you thinking of?" "I was thinking," replied the other, "to keep myself ready, and the faculties of my mind full settled and fixed, to try if in this short and quick instant of death, I could perceive the motion of the soul when she parts from the body, and whether she has any sentiment at the separation, that I may after come again, if I can, to acquaint my friends with it." This man philosophizes not unto death only, but in death itself. What a strange assurance was this, and what bravery of courage, to desire his death should be a lesson to him, and to have leisure to think of other things in so great an affair!

And yet I fancy, there is a certain way of making it familiar to us, and in some sort of making trial what it is. We may gain experience, if not entire and perfect, yet such, at least, as shall not be totally useless to us, and that may render us more confident and more assured. If we cannot overtake it, we may approach it and view it, and if we do not advance so far as the fort, we may at least discover and make ourselves acquainted with the avenues. It is not without reason that we are taught to consider sleep as a resemblance of death; with how great facility do we pass from waking to sleeping, and with how little concern do we lose the knowledge of light and of ourselves. Peradventure, the faculty of sleeping would seem useless and contrary to nature, since it deprives us of all action and sentiment, were it not that by it nature instructs us that she has equally made us to die as to live; and in life presents to us the eternal state she reserves for us after it, to accustom us to it and to take from us the fear of it. But such as have by some violent accident fallen into a swoon, and in it have lost all sense, these, methinks, have been very near seeing the true and natural face of death; for as to the moment of the passage, it is not to be feared that it brings with it any pain or displeasure, forasmuch as we can have no feeling without leisure; our sufferings require time, which in death is so short and so precipitous, that it must necessarily be insensible. They are the approaches that we are to fear, and these may fall within the limits of experience.

Many things seem greater by imagination than they are in effect; I have passed a good part of my life in a perfect and entire health; I say, not only entire, but, moreover, sprightly and wanton. This state, so full of verdure, jollity, and vigor, made the consideration of sickness so formidable to me, that when I came to experience it, I found the attacks faint and easy in comparison with what I had apprehended. Of this I have daily experience; if I am under the shelter of a warm room, in a stormy and tempestuous night, I wonder how people can live abroad, and am afflicted for those who are out in the fields; if I am there myself, I do not wish to be anywhere else. This one thing of being always shut up in a chamber I fancied insupportable; but I was presently inured to be so imprisoned a week, nay a month together, in a very weak, disordered, and sad condition: and I have found that, in the time of my health, I much more pitied the sick, than I think myself to be pitied when I am so, and that the force of my imagination enhances near one-half of the essence and reality of the thing. I hope that when I come to die, I shall find it the same, and that, after all, it is not worth the pains I take, so much preparation and so much assistance as I call in, to undergo the stroke. But at all events, we cannot give ourselves too much advantage.

In the time of our third, or second troubles (I do not well remember which), going one day abroad to take the air, about a league from my own house, which is seated in the very centre of all the bustle and mischief of the late civil wars in France; thinking myself in all security and so near to my retreat that I stood in need of no better equipage, I had taken a horse that went very easy upon his pace, but was not very strong. Being upon my return home, a sudden occasion falling out to make use of this horse in a kind of service that he was not accustomed to, one of my train, a lusty, tall fellow, mounted upon a strong German horse that had a very ill mouth, fresh and vigorous, to play the brave and set on ahead of his fellows, comes thundering full speed in the very track where I was, rushing like a Colossus upon the little man and the little horse, with such a career of strength and weight, that he turned us both over and over, topsy-turvy with our heels in the air; so that there lay the horse overthrown and stunned with the fall, and I ten or twelve paces from him stretched out at length, with my face all battered and broken, my sword which I had had in my hand, above ten paces beyond that, and my belt broken all to pieces, without motion or sense any more than a stock. 'Twas the only swoon I was ever in till that hour in my life. Those who were with me, after having used all the means they could to bring me to myself, concluding me dead, took me up in their arms, and carried me with very much difficulty home to my house, which was about half a French league from thence. On the way, having been for more than two hours given over for a dead man, I began to move and to fetch my breath; for so great abundance of blood was fallen into my stomach, that nature had need to rouse her forces to discharge it. They then raised me upon my feet, where I threw off a whole bucket of clots of blood, as this I did also several times by the way. This gave me so much ease, that I began to recover a little life, but so leisurely and by so small advances, that my first sentiments were much nearer the approaches of death than life: "For the soul doubtful as to its return, could not compose itself" [Tasso].

The remembrance of this accident, which is very well imprinted in my memory, so naturally representing to me the image and idea of death, has in some sort reconciled me to that untoward adventure. When I first began to open my eyes, it was with so perplexed, so weak and dead a sight, that I could yet distinguish nothing but only discern the light. "A man now opening, now shutting his eyes, between sleep and waking" [Tasso].

As to the functions of the soul, they advanced with the same pace and measure with those of the body. I saw myself all bloody, my doublet being stained all over with the blood I had vomited. The first thought that came into my mind was, that I had a harquebus shot in my head, and indeed, at the time there were a great many fired round about us. Methought my life but just hung upon my lips: and I shut my eyes, to help, methought, to thrust it out, and took a pleasure in languishing and letting myself go. It was an imagination that only superficially floated upon my soul, as tender and weak as all the rest,

but really not only exempt from anything displeasing, but mixed with
that sweetness that people feel when they glide into a slumber.

I believe it is the very same condition those people are in, whom
we see swoon with weakness in the agony of death; I am of opinion
that we pity them without cause, supposing them agitated with grievous dolors, or that their souls suffer under painful thoughts. It has ever
been my belief, contrary to the opinion of many, and particularly of
La Boetie, that those whom we see so subdued and stupefied at the
approaches of their end, or oppressed with the length of the disease,
or by accident of an apoplexy of falling sickness,—"Compelled by the
force of disease, we often see men as thunderstruck, fall, groan, and
foam, tremble, stretch, writhe, breathe short, and in strugglings tire
out their strength" [Lucretius]; or hurt in the head, whom we hear to
mutter, and by fits to utter grievous groans; though we gather from
these signs by which it seems as if they had some remains of con-
sciousness, and that there are movements of the body,—I have always
believed, I say, both the body and the soul benumbed and asleep, and
could not believe that in so great a stupefaction of the members and
so great a defection of the senses, the soul could maintain any force
within to take cognizance of herself, and that, therefore, they had no
tormenting reflections to make them consider and be sensible of the
misery of their condition, and consequently were not much to be
pitied.

I can, for my part, think of no state so insupportable and dreadful,
as to have the soul vivid and afflicted, without means to declare itself;
as one should say of such as are sent to execution with their tongues
first cut out (were it not that in this kind of dying, the most silent
seems to me the most graceful, if accompanied with a grave and constant countenance); or of those miserable prisoners, who fall into the
hands of the base hangman soldiers of this age, by whom they are
tormented with all sorts of inhuman usage to compel them to some
excessive and impossible ransom; kept, in the meantime, in such condition and place, where they have no means of expressing or signify-
ing their thoughts and their misery. The poets have feigned some
gods who favor the deliverance of such as suffer under a languishing
death; "I by command offer to Pluto this, and from that body dismiss
the soul" [Æneid]; both the interrupted words, and the short and irregular answers one gets from them sometimes, by bawling and keeping a clutter about them; or the motions which seem to yield some
consent to what we would have them do, are no testimony, nevertheless, that they live an entire life at least. So it happens to us in the
yawning of sleep, before it has fully possessed us, to perceive, as in a
dream, what is done about us, and to follow the last things that are

said with a perplexed and uncertain hearing which seems but to touch upon the borders of the soul; and make answers to the last words that have been spoken to us, which have more in them of chance than sense.

Now seeing I have in effect tried it, I have no doubt but I have hitherto made a right judgment; for first, being in a swoon, I labored to rip open the buttons of my doublet with my nails, for my sword was gone; and yet I felt nothing in my imagination that hurt me; for we have many motions in us that do not proceed from our direction. "Half-dead fingers grope about, and seek to grasp again the sword" [*Æneid*]; so falling people extend their arms before them by a natural impulse, which prompts our limbs to offices and motions without any commission from our reason. "They tell how limbs by scythe-bearing chariots are lopped off, but yet move and tremble on the ground; and yet the mind of him from whom the limb is taken, by the swiftness of the blow feels no pain" [Lucretius].

My stomach was so oppressed with the coagulated blood, that my hands moved to that part, of their own voluntary motion, as they frequently do to the part that itches, without being directed by our will. There are several animals, and even men, in whom one may perceive the muscles to stir and tremble after they are dead. Every one experimentally knows that there are some members which grow stiff and flag without his leave. Now, those passions which only touch the outward bark of us cannot be said to be ours: to make them so, there must be a concurrence of the whole man; and the pains which are felt by the hand or the foot while we are sleeping are none of ours.

As I drew near my own house, where the alarm of my fall was already got before me, and that my family were come out to meet me, with the hubbub usual in such cases, not only did I make some little answer to some questions which were asked me, but they moreover tell me, that I was sufficiently collected to order them to bring a horse to my wife whom I saw struggling and tiring herself on the road, which is hilly and rugged. This consideration should seem to proceed from a soul that retained its functions; but it was nothing so with me. I knew not what I said or did, and they were nothing but idle thoughts in the clouds, that were stirred up by the senses of the eyes and ears, and proceeded not from me. I knew not for all that, whence I came or whither I went, neither was I capable to weigh and consider what was said to me: these were light effects, that the senses produced of themselves as of custom; what the soul contributed was in a dream, lightly touched, licked and bedewed by the soft impression of the senses. Notwithstanding, my condition was, in truth, very easy and quiet; I had no affliction upon me, either for others or myself; it was an extreme languor and weakness, without any manner of pain. I saw my own house, but knew it not.

When they had put me to bed I found an inexpressible sweetness in that repose; for I had been desperately tugged and lugged by those poor people who had taken the pains to carry me upon their arms a very great and a very rough way, and had in so doing all quite tired out themselves, twice or thrice one after another. They offered me several remedies, but I would take none, certainly believing that I was mortally wounded in the head. And, in earnest, it had been a very happy death, for the weakness of my understanding deprived me of the faculty of discerning, and that of my body of the sense of feeling; I was suffering myself to glide away so sweetly and after so soft and easy a manner, that I scarce find any other action less troublesome than that was. But when I came again to myself and to resume my faculties, which was two or three hours after, I felt myself on a sudden involved in terrible pain, having my limbs battered and ground with my fall, and was so ill for two or three nights after, that I thought I was once more dying again, but a more painful death, having concluded myself as good as dead before, and to this hour am sensible of the bruises of that terrible shock.

I will not here omit, that the last thing I could make them beat into my head was the memory of this accident, and I had it over and over again repeated to me, whither I was going, from whence I came, and at what time of the day this mischance befell me, before I could comprehend it. As to the manner of my fall, that was concealed from me in favor to him who had been the occasion, and other flim-flams were invented. But a long time after, and the very next day that my memory began to return and to represent to me the state wherein I was, at the instant that I perceived this horse coming full drive upon me (for I had seen him at my heels, and gave myself for gone, but this thought had been so sudden, that fear had had no leisure to introduce itself) it seemed to me like a flash of lightning that had pierced my soul, and that I came from the other world.

This long story of so light an accident would appear vain enough, were it not for the knowledge I have gained by it for my own use; for I do really find, that to get acquainted with death needs no more but nearly to approach it. Every one, as Pliny says, is a good doctrine to himself, provided he be capable of discovering himself near at hand. Here, this is not my doctrine, 'tis my study; and is not the lesson of another, but my own; and if I communicate it, it ought not to be ill taken, for that which is of use to me, may also, peradventure, be useful to another. As to the rest, I spoil nothing, I make use of nothing but my own; and if I play the fool, 'tis at my own expense and nobody else is concerned in't; for 'tis a folly that will die with me, and that no one is to inherit. We hear but two or three of the ancients, who have beaten this road, and yet I cannot say if it was after this manner, knowing no more of them but their names. No one since has followed the track; 'tis a rugged road, more so than it seems, to follow a pace so rambling and uncertain, as that of the soul; to penetrate the dark profundities of its intricate internal windings; to choose and lay hold of so many little nimble motions; 'tis a new and extraordinary undertaking, and that withdraws us from the common and most recommended employments of the world.

'Tis now many years since that my thoughts have had no other aim and level than myself, and that I have only pried into and studied myself: or, if I study any other thing, 'tis to apply it to or rather in myself. And yet I do not think it a fault, if, as others do by other much less profitable sciences, I communicate what I have learned in this, though I am not very well pleased with my own progress. There is no description so difficult, nor doubtless of so great utility, as that of a man's self, and withal a man must curl his hair and set out and adjust himself, to appear in public; now I am perpetually tricking myself out, for I am eternally upon my own description. Custom has made all speaking of a man's self vicious, and positively interdicts it, in hatred to the boasting that seems inseparable from the testimony men give of themselves: "The avoiding a mere fault often leads us into a greater," says Horace.

Instead of blowing the child's nose, this is to take his nose off altogether. I think the remedy worse than the disease. But, allowing it to be true that it must of necessity be presumption to entertain people with discourses of one's self, I ought not, pursuing my general design, to forbear an action that publishes this infirmity of mine, nor conceal the fault which I not only practise but profess. Notwithstanding, to speak my thought freely, I think that the custom of condemning wine, because some people will be drunk, is itself to be condemned; a man cannot abuse anything but what is good in itself; and I believe that this rule has only regard to the popular vice. They are bits for calves, with which neither the saints whom we hear speak so highly of themselves, nor the philosophers, nor the divines, will be curbed; neither will I, who am as little the one as the other. If they do not write of it expressly, at all events, when the occasions arise, they don't hesitate to put themselves on the public highway. Of what does Socrates treat more largely than of himself? To what does he more direct and address the discourses of his disciples, than to speak of themselves, not of the lesson in their book, but of the essence and motion of their souls? We confess ourselves religiously to God and

our confessor; as our neighbors do to all the people. But some will
answer that we there speak nothing but accusation against ourselves;
why then, we say all; for our very virtue itself is faulty and penit-
able.

My trade and art is to live; he that forbids me to speak according
to my own sense, experience, and practice, may as well enjoin an
architect not to speak of building according to his own knowledge,
but according to that of his neighbor; according to the knowledge of
another, and not according to his own. If it be vainglory for a man
to publish his own virtues, why does not Cicero prefer the eloquence of Hortensius, and Hortensius that of Cicero? Peradventure
they mean that I should give testimony of myself by works and
effects, not barely by words. I chiefly paint my thoughts, a subject
void of form and incapable of operative production; 'tis all that I can
do to couch it in this airy body of the voice; the wisest and devout-
est men have lived in the greatest care to avoid all apparent effects.
Effects would more speak of fortune than of me; they manifest their
own office and not mine, but uncertainly and by conjecture; patterns
of some one particular virtue. I expose myself entire; 'tis a body
where, at one view, the veins, muscles, and tendons are apparent,
every one of them in its proper place; here the effect of a cold; there
of the heart beating, very dubiously. I do not write my own acts, but
myself and my essence.

I am of opinion that a man must be very cautious how he values
himself, and equally conscientious to give a true report, be it better
or worse, impartially. If I thought myself perfectly good and wise, I
would rattle it out to some purpose. To speak less of one's self than
what one really is, is folly, not modesty; and to take that for current
pay, which is under a man's value, is pusillanimity and cowardice,
according to Aristotle. No virtue assists itself with falsehood; truth is
never a matter of error. To speak more of one's self than is really true,
is not always mere presumption; 'tis, moreover, very often folly; to be
immeasurably pleased with what one is, and to fall into an indiscreet
self-love, is in my opinion the substance of this vice. The most sovereign remedy to cure it, is to do quite contrary to what these people
direct who, in forbidding men to speak of themselves, consequently,
at the same time, interdict thinking of themselves too. Pride dwells in
the thought; the tongue can have but a very little share in it.

They fancy that to think of one's self is to be delighted with one's
self; to frequent and converse with one's self, to be over-indulgent;
but this excess springs only in those who take but a superficial view
of themselves, and dedicate their main inspection in their affairs; who
call it mere revery and idleness to occupy one's self with one's self and

the building one's self up a mere building of castles in the air; who look upon themselves as a third person only, a stranger. If any one be in rapture with his own knowledge looking only on those below him, let him but turn his eye upward toward past ages, and his pride will be abated, when he shall there find so many thousand wits that trample him under foot. If he enter into a flattering presumption of his personal valor, let him but recollect the lives of Scipio, Epaminondas; so many armies, so many nations, that leave him so far behind them. No particular quality can make any one proud, that will at the same time put the many other weak and imperfect ones he has in the other scale, and the nothingness of human condition to make up the weight. Because Socrates had alone digested to purpose the precept of his god, "to know himself," and by that study arrived at the perfection of setting himself at naught, he only was reputed worthy the title of a sage. Whosoever shall so know himself, let him boldly speak it out.

OF GLORY.

There is the name and the thing; the name is a voice which denotes and signifies the thing; the name is no part of the thing, nor of the substance; 'tis a foreign piece joined to the thing, and outside it.

God, who is all fulness in Himself and the height of all perfection, cannot augment or add anything to Himself within; but His name may be augmented and increased by the blessing and praise we attribute to His exterior works: which praise seeing we cannot incorporate it in Him, forasmuch as He can have no accession of good, we attribute to His name, which is the part out of Him that is nearest to us. Thus is it that to God alone glory and honor appertain; and there is nothing so remote from reason as that we should go in quest of it for ourselves; for, being indigent and necessitous within, our essence being imperfect, and having continual need of amelioration, 'tis to that we ought to employ all our endeavor. We are all hollow and empty; 'tis not with wind and voice that we are to fill ourselves; we want a more solid substance to repair us: a man starving with hunger would be very simple to seek rather to provide himself with a gay garment than with a good meal: we are to look after that whereof we have most need. As we have it in our ordinary prayers, "*Gloria in excelsis Deo, et in terra pax hominibus.*" We are in want of beauty, health, wisdom, virtue, and such like essential qualities: exterior ornaments should be looked after when we have made provision for necessary things. Divinity treats amply and more pertinently of this subject, but I am not much versed in it.

Chrysippus and Diogenes were the earliest and firmest advocates of the contempt of glory; and maintained that among all pleasures, there was none more dangerous nor more to be avoided, than that which proceeds from the approbation of others. And, in truth, experience makes us sensible of many very hurtful treasons in it. There is nothing that so poisons princes as flattery, nor anything whereby wicked men more easily obtain credit and favor with them; nor panderism so apt and so usually made use of to corrupt the chastity of women as to wheedle and entertain them with their own praises. The first charm, says Homer, that the Syrens made use of to allure Ulysses is of this nature: "Come hither to us, oh admirable Ulysses, come hither, thou greatest ornament and pride of Greece."

These philosophers said that all the glory of the world was not worth an understanding man's holding out his finger to obtain it. I say for it alone; for it often brings several commodities along with it, for which it may justly be desired: it acquires us good will, and renders us less subject and exposed to insult and offence from others, and the like. It was also one of the principal doctrines of Epicurus; for this precept of his sect, Conceal thy life, that forbids men to encumber themselves with public negotiations and offices, also necessarily presupposes a contempt of glory, which is the world's approbation of those actions we produce in public. He that bids us conceal ourselves, and to have no other concern but for ourselves, and who will not have us known to others, would much less have us honored and glorified; and so advises Idomeneus not in any sort to regulate his actions by the common reputation or opinion, except so as to avoid the other accidental inconveniences that the contempt of men might bring upon him.

Those discourses are, in my opinion, very true and rational; but we are, I know not how, double in ourselves, which is the cause that what we believe we do not believe, and cannot disengage ourselves from what we condemn. Let us see the last and dying words of Epicurus; they are grand, and worthy of such a philosopher, and yet they carry some touches of the recommendation of his name and of that humor he had decried by his precepts. Here is a letter that he dictated a little before his last gasp:[1]

"EPICURUS to HERMACHUS, greeting

"While I was passing over the happy and last day of my life, I write this, but at the same time, afflicted with such pain in my bladder and bowels that nothing can be greater, but it was recompensed with the

---

[1] Cicero.

pleasure the remembrance of my inventions and doctrines brought to
my soul. Now, as the affection thou hast ever from thy infancy borne
toward me and philosophy requires, take upon thee the protection of
Metrodorus' children."

This is the letter. And that which makes me interpret that the pleasure he says he had in his soul concerning his inventions, has some
reference to the reputation he hoped for thence after his death, is the
manner of his will in which he gives order that Amynomachus and
Timocrates, his heirs should, every January, defray the expense of the
celebration of his birthday as Hermachus should appoint: and also the
expense that should be made the twentieth of every moon in entertaining the philosophers, his friends, who should assemble in honor
of the memory of him and of Metrodorus.

Carneades was head of the contrary opinion, and maintained that
glory was to be desired for itself, even as we embrace our posthumous
issue for themselves, having no knowledge nor enjoyment of them.
This opinion has not failed to be the more universally followed, as
those commonly are that are most suitable to our inclinations.
Aristotle gives it the first place among external goods; and avoids, as
too extreme vices, the immoderate either seeking or evading it. I
believe that, if we had the books Cicero wrote upon this subject, we
should there find pretty stories; for he was so possessed with this passion, that, if he had dared, I think he could willingly have fallen into
the excess that others did, that virtue itself was not to be coveted, but
upon the account of the honor that always attends it: "Virtue concealed little differs from dead sloth," says Horace, which is an opinion
so false, that I am vexed it could ever enter into the understanding of
a man that was honored with the name of philosopher.

If this were true, men need not be virtuous but in public; and we
should be no further concerned to keep the operations of the soul,
which is the true seat of virtue, regular and in order, than as they are
to arrive at the knowledge of others. Is there no more in it, then, but
only slyly and with circumspection to do ill? "If thou knowest," says
Carneades, "of a serpent lurking in a place where, without suspicion,
a person is going to sit down, by whose death thou expectest an advantage, thou dost ill if thou dost not give him caution of his danger;
and so much the more because the action is to be known by none but
thyself." If we do not take up of ourselves the rule of well-doing, if
impunity pass with us for justice, to how many sorts of wickedness
shall we every day abandon ourselves? I do not find what Sextus
Peduceus did, in faithfully restoring the treasure that C. Plotius had
committed to his sole secrecy and trust, a thing that I had often done
myself, so commendable, as I should think it an execrable baseness

had we done otherwise; and I think it of good use in our days to recall the example of P. Sextilius Rufus, whom Cicero accuses to have entered upon an inheritance contrary to his conscience, not only not against law, but even by the determination of the laws themselves; and M. Crassus and Q. Hortensius, who, by reason of their authority and power, having been called in by a stranger to share in the succession of a forged will, that so he might secure his own part, satisfied themselves with having no hand in the forgery, and refused not to make their advantage and to come in for a share: secure enough, if they could shroud themselves from accusations, witnesses, and the cognizance of the laws: "Let them consider they have God to witness, that is (as I interpret it) their own consciences," says Cicero.

Virtue is a very vain and frivolous thing, if it derive its recommendation from glory; and 'tis to no purpose that we endeavor to give it a station by itself, and separate it from fortune; for what is more accidental than reputation? "Fortune rules in all things, and advances and depresses things more out of her own will than of right and justice" [Sallust]. So to order it that actions may be known and seen is purely the work of fortune; 'tis chance that helps us to glory, according to its own temerity. I have often seen her go before merit, and often very much outstrip it. He who first likened glory to a shadow did better than he was aware of; they are both of them things preeminently vain: glory also, like a shadow, goes sometimes before the body, and sometimes in length infinitely exceeds it. They who instruct gentlemen only to employ their valor for the obtaining of honor, "*quasi non sit honestum, quod nobilitatum non sit;*" what do they intend by that but to instruct them never to hazard themselves if they are not seen, and to observe well if there be witnesses present who may carry news of their valor, whereas a thousand occasions of welldoing present themselves which cannot be taken notice of? How many brave individual actions are buried in the crowd of a battle? Whoever shall take upon him to watch another's behavior in such a confusion is not very busy himself, and the testimony he shall give of his companion's deportment will be evidence against himself. Says Cicero "The true and wise magnanimity judges that the bravery which most follows nature more consists in act than glory."

All the glory that I pretend to derive from my life is that I have lived it in quiet; in quiet, not according to Metrodorus, or Arcesilaus, or Aristippus, but according to myself. For seeing philosophy has not been able to find out any way to tranquillity that is good in common, let every one seek it in particular.

To what do Cæsar and Alexander owe the infinite grandeur of their renown but to fortune? How many men has she extinguished in the beginning of their progress, of whom we have no knowledge, who brought as much courage to the work as they, if their adverse hap had not cut them off in the first sally of their arms? Among so many and so great dangers I do not remember I have anywhere read that Cæsar was ever wounded; a thousand have fallen in less dangers than the least of those he went through. An infinite number of brave actions must be performed without witness and lost, before one turns to account. A man is not always on the top of a breach, or at the head of an army, in the sight of his general, as upon a scaffold; a man is often surprised between the hedge and the ditch; he must run the hazard of his life against a henroost; he must dislodge four rascally musketeers out of a barn; he must prick out single from his party, and alone make some attempts, according as necessity will have it. And whoever will observe will, I believe, find it experimentally true that occasions of the least lustre are ever the most dangerous; and that in the wars of our own times there have more brave men been lost in occasions of little moment, and in the dispute about some little paltry fort, than in places of greatest importance, and where their valor might have been more honorably employed.

Who thinks his death unworthy of him if he do not fall in some signal occasion, instead of illustrating his death, wilfully obscures his life, suffering in the meantime many very just occasions of hazarding himself to slip out of his hands; and every just one is illustrious enough, every man's conscience being a sufficient trumpet to him. "*Gloria nostra est testimonium conscientiæ nostræ.*" He who is only a good man that men may know it, and that he may be the better esteemed when 'tis known: who will not do well but upon condition that his virtue may be known to men: is one from whom much service is not to be expected. "The rest of the winter, I presume, was spent in actions worthy of narration, but they were done so secretly that if I do not tell them I am not to blame, for Orlando was more bent to do great acts than to boast of them, so that no deeds of his were ever known but those that had witnesses "[Ariosto].

A man must go to the war upon the account of duty, and expect the recompense that never fails brave and worthy actions, how private soever, or even virtuous thoughts — the satisfaction that a well-disposed conscience receives in itself in doing well. A man must be valiant for himself, and upon account of the advantage it is to him to have his courage seated in a firm and secure place against the assaults of fortune. Says Horace: "Virtue, repudiating all base repulse, shines in taintless honors, nor takes nor leaves dignities at the mere will of the vulgar."

It is not for outward show that the soul is to play its part, but for ourselves within, where no eyes can pierce but our own; there she defends us from the fear of death, of pain, of shame itself; there she arms us against the loss of our children, friends, and fortunes; and when opportunity presents itself, she leads us on to the hazards of war, "*non emolumento aliquot, sed ipsius honestatis decore.*" This profit is of much greater advantage, and more worthy to be coveted and hoped for, than honor and glory, which are no other than a favorable judgment given of us.

A dozen men must be called out of a whole nation to judge about an acre of land; and the judgment of our inclinations and actions, the most difficult and most important matter that is, we refer to the voice and determination of the rabble, the mother of ignorance, injustice, and inconstancy. Is it reasonable that the life of a wise man should depend upon the judgment of fools? "Can anything be more foolish than to think that those you despise single can be any other when joined together?" asks Cicero. He that makes it his business to please them, will have enough to do and never have done; 'tis a mark that can never be aimed at or hit: "*Nil tam næstimabile est, quam animi multitudinis.*" Demetrius pleasantly said of the voice of the people, that he made no more account of that which came from above than of that which came from below. Cicero says more: "I am of opinion, that though a thing be not foul in itself, yet it cannot but become so when commended by the multitude." No art, no activity of wit, could conduct our steps so as to follow so wandering and so irregular a guide; in this windy confusion of the noise of vulgar reports and opinions that drive us on, no way worth anything can be chosen.

Let us not propose to ourselves so floating and wavering an end; let us follow constantly after reason; let the public approbation follow us there, if it will; and as it wholly depends upon fortune, we have no reason sooner to expect it by any other way than that. Even though I would not follow the right way because it is right, I should, however, follow it as having experimentally found that, at the end of the reckoning, 'tis commonly the most happy and of greatest utility: "This gift Providence has given to men, that honest things should be the most useful" [Quintilian]. The mariner of old said thus to Neptune, in a great tempest: "Oh, God, thou mayest save me if thou wilt, and if thou wilt, thou mayest destroy me; but, however, I will steer my rudder true." I have seen in my time a thousand men supple, mongrel, ambiguous, whom no one doubted to be more worldly wise than I, destroy themselves, where I have saved myself.

Paulus Æmilius, going on the glorious expedition of Macedonia, above all things charged the people of Rome not to speak of his actions during his absence. Oh, the license of judgments is a great disturbance to great affairs! forasmuch as every one has not the firmness of Fabius against common, adverse, and injurious tongues, who rather suffered his authority to be dissected by the vain fancies of men, than to do less well in his charge with a favorable reputation and the popular applause.

There is I know not what natural sweetness in hearing one's self commended; but we are a great deal too fond of it. Says Persius: "I don't dislike being praised, for my heart is not made of horn; but I deny that 'excellent — admirably done,' are the terms and final aim of virtue."

I care not so much what I am in the opinion of others, as what I am in my own; I would be rich of myself, and not by borrowing. Strangers see nothing but events and outward appearances; everybody can set a good face on the matter, when they have trembling and terror within; they do not see my heart, they see but my countenance. 'Tis with good reason that men decry the hypocrisy that is in war; for what is more easy to an old soldier than to shift in a time of danger, and to counterfeit the brave when he has no more heart than a chicken? There are so many ways to avoid hazarding a man's own person, that we have deceived the world a thousand times before we come to be engaged in a real danger: and even then, finding ourselves in an inevitable necessity of doing something, we can make shift for that time to conceal our apprehensions by setting a good face on the business, though the heart beats within; and whoever had the use of the Platonic ring, which renders those invisible that wear it, if turned inward toward the palm of the hand, a great many would very often hide themselves when they ought most to appear, and would repent being placed in so honorable a post, when necessity must make them bold. Horace says: "False honor pleases, and calumny affrights, the guilty and the liar."

Thus we see how all the judgments that are founded upon external appearances, are marvellously uncertain and doubtful; and that there is no so certain testimony as every one is to himself. In these, how many soldier's boys are companions of our glory? he who stands firm in an open trench, what does he in that more than fifty poor pioneers, who open to him the way and cover it with their own bodies for fivepence a day pay, do before him? "Do not, if turbid Rome should disparage anything, agree with it, nor correct a false balance by that scale; seek not thyself out of thyself," says Persius.

The dispersing and scattering our names into many mouths, we call making them more great; we will have them there well received, and that this increase turn to their advantage, which is all that can be excusable in this design. But the excess of this disease proceeds so far that many covet to have a name, be it what it will. Trogus Pompeius says of Herostratus, and Titus Livius of Manlius Capitolinus, that they were more ambitious of a great reputation than of a good one. This is very common; we are more solicitous that men speak of us, than how they speak: and it is enough for us that our names are often mentioned, be it after what manner it will. It should seem that to be known, is in some sort to have a man's life and its duration in others' keeping.

I, for my part, hold that I am not, but in myself; and of that other life of mine which lies in the knowledge of my friends, to consider it naked and simply in itself, I know very well that I am sensible of no fruit nor enjoyment from it but by the vanity of a fantastic opinion; and when I shall be dead, I shall be still and much less sensible of it; and shall, withal, absolutely lose the use of those real advantages that sometimes accidentally follow it. I shall have no more handle whereby to take hold of reputation, neither shall it have any whereby to take hold of or to cleave to me; for to expect that my name should be advanced by it, in the first place, I have no name that is enough my own; of two that I have, one is common to all my race, and, indeed, to others also; there are two families at Paris and Montpellier, whose surname is Montaigne, another in Brittany, and one in Xaintonge, De La Montaigne. The transposition of one syllable only would suffice so to ravel our affairs that I shall share in their glory, and they, peradventure, shall partake of my shame: and, moreover, my ancestors have formerly been surnamed Eyquem, a name wherein a family well known in England is at this day concerned.

As to my other name, every one may take it that will, and so, perhaps, I may honor a porter in my own stead. And, besides, though I had a particular distinction by myself, what can it distinguish when I am no more? Can it point out and favor inanity? "The tomb will not press with less weight upon my bones. Posterity may praise: what then? not from my manes, not from the tomb, not from the ashes, will violets grow" [Persius]: but of this I have spoken elsewhere. As to what remains, in a great battle where ten thousand men are maimed or killed, there are not fifteen who are taken notice of; it must be some very eminent greatness, or some consequence of great importance that fortune has added to it, that signalizes a private action, not of a harquebuser only, but of a great captain; for to kill a man, or two, or ten: to expose a man's self bravely to the utmost peril of death, is, indeed, something in every one of us, because we there hazard all; but for the world's concern, they are things so ordinary, and so many of them are every day seen, and there must of necessity be so many of the same kind to produce any notable effect, that we cannot expect any particular renown from it; "The accident is known to many, and now trite; and drawn from the amidst of Fortune's heap" [Juvenal].

Of so many thousands of valiant men who have died within these fifteen hundred years in France with their swords in their hands, not a hundred have come to our knowledge. The memory, not of the commanders only, but of battles and victories, is buried and gone; the fortunes of above half of the world, for want of a record, stir not from their place, and vanish without duration. If I had unknown events in my possession, I should think with great ease to outdo those that are recorded, in all sorts of examples. Is it not strange that even of the Greeks and Romans, with so many writers and witnesses, and so many rare and noble exploits, so few are arrived at our knowledge? It will be much, if a hundred years hence, it be remembered in gross that in our times there were civil wars in France. The Lacedæmonians, entering into battle, sacrificed to the Muses, to the end that their actions might be well and worthily written, looking upon it as a divine and no common favor, that brave acts should find witnesses that could give them life and memory. Do we expect that at every musket shot we receive, and at every hazard we run, there must be a register ready to record it? and, besides, a hundred registers may enroll them whose commentaries will not last above three days, and will never come to the sight of any one.

We have not the thousandth part of ancient writings; 'tis fortune that gives them a shorter or longer life, according to her favor; and 'tis permissible to doubt whether those we have be not the worst, not having seen the rest. Men do not write histories of things of so little moment: a man must have been general in the conquest of an empire or a kingdom; he must have won two-and-fifty set battles, and always the weaker in number, as Cæsar did: ten thousand brave fellows and many great captains lost their lives valiantly in his service, whose names lasted no longer than their wives and children lived: "*Quos fama obscura recondit.*" Even those we see behave themselves the best, three months or three years after they have been knocked on the head, are no more spoken of than if they had never been. Whoever will justly consider, and with due proportion, of what kind of men and of what sort of actions the glory sustains itself in the records of history, will find that there are very few actions and very few persons of our times who can there pretend any right. How many worthy men have we known to survive their own reputation, who have seen and suffered the honor and glory most justly acquired in their youth, extinguished in their own presence? And for three years of this fantastic and imaginary life we must go and throw away our true and essential life, and engage ourselves in a perpetual death!

The sages propose to themselves a nobler and more just end in so important an enterprise. Says Seneca: "The reward of a good deed is the deed itself." It were, peradventure, excusable in a painter or other artisan, or in a rhetorician or a grammarian, to endeavor to raise himself a name by his works; but the actions of virtue are too noble in themselves to seek any other reward than from their own value, and especially to seek it in the vanity of human judgments.

If this false opinion, nevertheless, be of such use to the public as to keep men in their duty; if the people are thereby stirred up to virtue; if princes are touched to see the world bless the memory of Trajan, and abominate that of Nero; if it moves them to see the name of that great beast, once so terrible and feared, so freely cursed and reviled by every schoolboy, let it by all means increase, and be as much as possible nursed up and cherished among us; and Plato, bending his whole endeavor to make his citizens virtuous, also advises them not to despise the good repute and esteem of the people; and says it falls out, by a certain divine inspiration, that even the wicked themselves ofttimes, as well by word as opinion, can rightly distinguish the virtuous from the wicked. This person and his tutor are both marvellous and bold artificers everywhere to add divine operations and revelations where human force is wanting. "As tragic poets fly to some god, when they cannot explain the trend of their argument," says Cicero: and, peradventure, for this reason it was that Timon, railing at him, called him the great forger of miracles. Seeing that men by their insufficiency cannot pay themselves well enough with current money, let the counterfeit be superadded. 'Tis a way that has been practised by all the legislators; and there is no government that has not some mixture either of ceremonial vanity or of false opinion, that serves for a curb to keep the people in their duty.

'Tis for this that most of them have their originals and beginnings fabulous, and enriched with supernatural mysteries; 'tis this that has given credit to bastard religions, and caused them to be countenanced by men of understanding; and for this, that Numa and Sertorius, to possess their men with a better opinion of them, fed them with this foppery; one, that the nymph Egeria, the other that his white hind, brought them all their counsels from the gods. And the authority that Numa gave to his laws, under the title of the patronage of this goddess, Zoroaster, legislator of the Bactrians and Persians, gave to his under the name of the god Oromazis; Trismegistus, legislator of the Egyptians, under that of Mercury; Xamolxis, legislator of the Scythians, under that of Vesta; Charondas, legislator of the Chalcidians, under that of Saturn; Minos, legislator of the Candiots, under that of Jupiter; Lycurgus, legislator of the Lacedæmonians, under that of

Apollo; and Draco and Solon, legislators of the Athenians, under that of Minerva. And every government has a god at the head of it; the others falsely, that truly, which Moses set over the Jews at their departure out of Egypt. The religion of the Bedouins, as the Sire de Joinville reports, among other things, enjoined a belief that the soul of him among them who died for his prince, went into another body more happy, more beautiful, and more robust than the former, by which means they much more willingly ventured their lives: "Men invite the steel and seek death: 'tis base to save a life that is to return" [Lucan]. This is a very comfortable belief, however erroneous. Every nation has many such examples of its own; but this subject would require a treatise by itself.

To add one word more to my former discourse, I would advise the ladies no longer to call that honor which is but their duty; "According to the vulgar notion, which only approves that as honorable that is glorious by the public voice" [Cicero]; their duty is the mark, their honor but the outward rind. Neither would I advise them to give this excuse for payment of their denial: for I presuppose that their intentions, their desire, and will, which are things wherein their honor is not at all concerned, forasmuch as nothing thereof appears without, are much better regulated than the effects: "*Quæ, quia non liceat, non facit, illa facit.*"

The offence, both toward God and in the conscience, would be as great to desire as to do it: and, besides, they are actions so private and secret of themselves, as would be easily enough kept from the knowledge of others, wherein the honor consists, if they had not another respect to their duty, and the affection they bear to chastity, for itself. Every woman of honor will much rather choose to lose her honor, than to hurt her conscience.

OF PRESUMPTION.

There is another sort of glory, which is the having too good an opinion of our own worth. 'Tis an inconsiderate affection with which we flatter ourselves, and that represents us to ourselves other than we truly are; like the passion of love, and that lends beauties and graces to the object, and makes those who are caught by it, with a depraved and corrupt judgment, consider the thing which they love other and more perfect than it is.

I would not, nevertheless, for fear of failing on this side, that a man should not know himself aright, or think himself less than he is; the judgment ought in all things to maintain its rights; 'tis all the reason in the world he should discern in himself, as well as in others, what truth sets before him; if it be Cæsar, let him boldly think himself the greatest captain in the world. We are nothing but ceremony; ceremony carries us away, and we leave the substance of things; we hold by the branches, and quit the trunk and the body; we have taught the ladies to blush when they hear that but named which they are not at all afraid to do; we dare not call our members by their right names, yet are not afraid to employ them in all sorts of debauchery; ceremony forbids us to express by words things that are lawful and natural, and we obey it: reason forbids us to do things unlawful and ill, and nobody obeys it. I find myself here fettered by the laws of ceremony; for it neither permits a man to speak well of himself, nor ill; we will leave it there for this time.

They whom fortune (call it good or ill) has made to pass their lives in some eminent degree, may by their public actions manifest what they are; but they whom she has only employed in the crowd, and of whom nobody will say a word unless they speak themselves, are to be excused if they take the boldness to speak of themselves to such as are interested to know them; by the example of Lucilius, "He confided his secret thoughts to his writings, as to a tried friend, and for good and evil, sought no other confidant; hence it came to pass, that the old man's life is there all seen as on a votive tablet" [Horace]; he always committed to paper his actions and thoughts, and there portrayed himself such as he found himself to be; "Nor were Rutilius or Scaurus misbelieved or condemned for writing their memoirs" [Tacitus].

I remember, then, that from my infancy there was observed in me I know not what kind of carriage and behavior, that seemed to relish of pride and arrogance. I will say this, by the way, that it is not unreasonable to suppose that we have qualities and inclinations so much our own, and so incorporate in us, that we have not the means to feel and recognize them; and of such natural inclinations the body will retain a certain bent, without our knowledge or consent. It was an affectation conformable with his beauty, that made Alexander carry his head on one side, and caused Alcibiades to lisp; Julius Cæsar scratched his head with one finger, which is the fashion of a man full of troublesome thoughts; and Cicero, as I remember, was wont to pucker up his nose, a sign of a man given to scoffing; such motions as these may imperceptibly happen in us. There are other artificial ones which I meddle not with, as salutations and congees, by which men acquire, for the most part unjustly, the reputation of being humble and courteous; one may be humble out of pride.

I am prodigal enough of my hat, especially in summer, and never am so saluted but that I pay it again from persons of what quality

soever, unless they be in my own service. I should make it my request
to some princes whom I know, that they would be more sparing of
that ceremony, and bestow that courtesy where it is more due; for
being so indiscreetly and indifferently conferred on all, it is thrown
away to no purpose; if it be without respect of persons, it loses its
effect. Among irregular deportment, let us not forget that haughty
one of the Emperor Constantius, who always in public held his head
upright and stiff, without bending or turning on either side, not so
much as to look upon those who saluted him on one side, planting
his body in a rigid immovable posture, without suffering it to yield to
the motion of his coach, not daring so much as to spit, blow his nose,
or wipe his face before people. I know not whether the gestures that
were observed in me were of this first quality, and whether I had
really any occult propension to this vice, as it might well be; and I
cannot be responsible for the motions of the body; but as to the motions of the soul, I must here confess what I think of the matter.

This glory consists of two parts; the one in setting too great a value
upon ourselves, and the other in setting too little a value upon others.
As to the one, methinks these considerations ought, in the first place,
to be of some force; I feel myself importuned by an error of the soul
that displeases me, both as it is unjust, and still more as it is troublesome; I attempt to correct it, but I cannot root it out: and this is, that
I lessen the just value of things that I possess, and overvalue things,
because they are foreign, absent, and none of mine; this humor
spreads very far. As the prerogative of the authority makes husbands
look upon their own wives with a vicious disdain, and many fathers
their children; so I, between two equal merits should always be
swayed against my own; not so much that the jealousy of my advancement and bettering troubles my judgment, and hinders me from
satisfying myself, as that of itself possession begets a contempt of what
it holds and rules.

Foreign governments, manners, and languages, insinuate themselves into my esteem; and I am sensible that Latin allures me by the
favor of its dignity to value it above its due, as it does with children,
and the common sort of people: the domestic government, house,
horse, of my neighbor, though no better than my own, I prize above
my own, because they are not mine. Besides that I am very ignorant
in my own affairs, I am struck by the assurance that every one has of
himself: whereas, there is scarcely anything that I am sure I know, or
that I dare be responsible to myself that I can do: I have not my means
of doing anything in condition and ready, and am only instructed
therein after the effect; as doubtful of my own force as I am of another's. Whence it comes to pass that if I happen to do anything

commendable, I attribute it more to my fortune than industry, forasmuch as I design everything by chance and in fear. I have this, also, in general, that of all the opinions antiquity has held of men in gross, I most willingly embrace and adhere to those that most contemn and undervalue us, and most push us to naught; methinks, philosophy has never so fair a game to play as when it falls upon our vanity and presumption; when it most lays open our irresolution, weakness, and ignorance.

I look upon the too good opinion that man has of himself to be the nursing mother of all the most false opinions, both public and private. Those people who ride astride upon the epicycle of Mercury, who see so far into the heavens, are worse to me than a tooth-drawer that comes to draw my teeth; for in my study, the subject of which is man, finding so great a variety of judgments, so profound a labyrinth of difficulties, one upon another, so great diversity and uncertainty, even in the school of wisdom itself, you may judge, seeing these people could not resolve upon the knowledge of themselves and their own condition, which is continually before their eyes, and within them, seeing they do not know how that moves, which they themselves move, nor how to give us a description of the springs they themselves govern and make use of, how can I believe them about the ebbing and flowing of the Nile. The curiosity of knowing things has been given to man for a scourge, says the holy Scripture.

But to return to what concerns myself; I think it would be very difficult for any other man to have a meaner opinion of himself; nay, for any other to have a meaner opinion of me than I have of myself: I look upon myself as one of the common sort, saving in this, that I have no better an opinion of myself; guilty of the meanest and most popular defects, but not disowning or excusing them; and I do not value myself upon any other account than because I know my own value. If there be any vanity in the case, 'tis superficially infused into me by the treachery of my complexion, and has no body that my judgment can discern: I am sprinkled, but not dyed. For in truth, as to the effects of the mind, there is no part of me, be it what it will, with which I am satisfied; and the approbation of others makes me not think the better of myself. My judgment is tender and nice, especially in things that concern myself; I ever repudiate myself, and feel myself float and waver by reason of my weakness. I have nothing of my own that satisfies my judgment. My sight is clear and regular enough, but, at working, it is apt to dazzle; as I most manifestly find in poetry: I love it infinitely, and am able to give a tolerable judgment of other men's works; but, in good earnest, when I apply myself to it, I play the child, and am not able to endure myself. A man may play the fool in everything else, but not in poetry; "Neither men, nor gods, nor the pillars [on which the poets offered their writings], permit mediocrity in poets," says Horace.

I would to God this sentence from Martial were written over the doors of all our printers, to forbid the entrance of so many rhymesters! "The truth is, that nothing is more confident than a bad poet."

Why have not we such people? Dionysius the father valued himself upon nothing so much as his poetry; at the Olympic games, with chariots surpassing all the others in magnificence, he sent also poets and musicians to present his verses, with tent and pavilions royally gilt and hung with tapestry. When his verses came to be recited, the excellence of the delivery at first attracted the attention of the people; but when they afterwards came to poise the meanness of the composition, they first entered into disdain, and continuing to nettle their judgments, presently proceeded to fury, and ran to pull down and tear to pieces all his pavilions: and, that his chariots neither performed anything to purpose in the race, and that the ship which brought back his people failed of making Sicily, and was by the tempest driven and wrecked upon the coast of Tarentum, they certainly believed was through the anger of the gods, incensed, as they themselves were, against that paltry poem; and even the mariners who escaped from the wreck seconded this opinion of the people: to which also the oracle that foretold his death seemed to subscribe; which was, "that Dionysius should be near his end, when he should have overcome those who were better than himself," which he interpreted of the Carthaginians, who surpassed him in power; and having war with them, often declined the victory, not to incur the sense of this prediction, but he understood it ill; for the god indicated the time of the advantage, that by favor and injustice he obtained at Athens over the tragic poets, better than himself, having caused his own play called the *Leneians* to be acted in emulation; presently after which victory he died, and partly of the excessive joy he conceived at the success.

What I find tolerable of mine, is not so really and in itself, but in comparison of other worse things, that I see well enough received. I envy the happiness of those who can please and hug themselves in what they do; for 'tis an easy thing to be so pleased, because a man extracts that pleasure from himself, especially if he be constant in his self-conceit. I know a poet, against whom the intelligent and the ignorant, abroad and at home, both heaven and earth exclaim that he has but very little notion of it; and yet for all that he has never a whit the worse opinion of himself; but is always falling upon some new piece, always contriving some new invention, and still persists in his opinion, by so much the more obstinately, as it only concerns him to maintain it.

My works are so far from pleasing me, that as often as I review them, they disgust me: "When I re-peruse, I blush at what I have written; I ever see one passage after another that I the author, being the judge, consider should be erased" [Ovid]. I have always an idea in my soul, and a sort of disturbed image which presents me as in a dream with a better form than that I have made use of; but I cannot catch it nor fit it to my purpose; and even that idea is but of the meaner sort. Hence I conclude that the productions of those great and rich souls of former times are very much beyond the utmost stretch of my imagination or my wish: their writings do not only satisfy and fill me, but they astound me, and ravish me with admiration; I judge of their beauty; I see it, if not to the utmost, yet so far at least as 'tis possible for me to aspire. Whatever I undertake, I owe a sacrifice to the Graces, as Plutarch says of some one, to conciliate their favor: "If anything please that I write, if it infuse delight into men's minds, all is due to the charming Graces."

They abandon me throughout; all I write is rude; polish and beauty are wanting: I cannot set things off to any advantage; my handling adds nothing to the matter; for which reason I must have it forcible, very full, and that has lustre of its own. If I pitch upon subjects that are popular and gay, 'tis to follow my own inclination, who do not affect a grave and ceremonious wisdom, as the world does; and to make myself more sprightly, but not my style more wanton, which would rather have them grave and severe; at least, if I may call that a style, which is an inform and irregular way of speaking, a popular jargon, a proceeding without definition, division, conclusion, perplexed like that Amafanius and Rabirius. I can neither please nor delight, nor even tickle my readers: the best story in the world is spoiled by my handling, and becomes flat; I cannot speak but in rough earnest, and am totally unprovided of that facility which I observe in many of my acquaintance, of entertaining the first comers and keeping a whole company in breath, or taking up the ear of a prince with all sorts of discourse without wearying themselves: they never want matter by reason of the faculty and grace they have in taking hold of the first thing that starts up, and accommodating it to the humor and capacity of those with whom they have to do.

Princes do not much affect solid discourses, nor I to tell stories. The first and easiest reasons, which are commonly the best taken, I know not how to employ: I am an ill orator to the common sort. I am apt of everything to say the extremest that I know. Cicero is of opinion that in treatises of philosophy the exordium is the hardest part; if this be true, I am wise in sticking to the conclusion. And yet we are to know how to wind the string to all notes, and the sharpest is that which is the most seldom touched. There is at least as much perfection in elevating an empty as in supporting a weighty thing. A man must sometimes superficially handle things, and sometimes push them home. I know very well that most men keep themselves in this lower form from not conceiving things otherwise than by this outward bark; but I likewise know that the greatest masters, and Xenophon and Plato are often seen to stoop to this low and popular manner of speaking and treating of things, but supporting it with graces which never fail them.

Further, my language has nothing in it that is facile and polished; 'tis rough, free, and irregular, and as such pleases, if not my judgment, at all events my inclination, but I very well perceive that I sometimes give myself too much rein, and that by endeavoring to avoid art and affectation I fall into the other inconvenience: "Endeavoring to be brief, I become obscure."

Plato says that the long or the short are not properties that either take away or give value to language. Should I attempt to follow the other more moderate, united, and regular style, I should never attain to it; and though the short round periods of Sallust best suit with my humor, yet I find Cæsar much grander and harder to imitate; and though my inclination would rather prompt me to imitate Seneca's way of writing, yet I do, nevertheless, more esteem that of Plutarch. Both in doing and speaking I simply follow my own natural way; whence, peradventure, it falls out that I am better at speaking than writing. Motion and action animate words, especially in those who lay about them briskly, as I do, and grow hot. The comportment, the countenance, the voice, the robe, the place, will set off some things that of themselves would appear no better than prating. Massalla complains in Tacitus of the straightness of some garments in his time, and of the fashion of the benches where the orators were to declaim, that were a disadvantage to their eloquence.

My French tongue is corrupted, both in the pronunciation and otherwise, by the barbarism of my country. I never saw a man who was a native of any of the provinces on his side of the kingdom who had not a twang of his place of birth, and that was not offensive to ears that were purely French. And yet it is not that I am so perfect in my Perigordin: for I can no more speak it than High Dutch, nor do I much care. 'Tis a language (as the rest about me on every side, of Poitou, Xaintonge, Angoumousin, Limosin, Auvergne), a poor, drawling, scurvy language. There is, indeed, above us toward the mountains a sort of Gascon spoken, that I am mightily taken with:

blunt, brief, significant, and in truth a more manly and military language than any other I am acquainted with, as sinewy, powerful, and pertinent as the French is graceful, neat, and luxuriant.

As to the Latin, which was given me for my mother tongue, I have, by discontinuance, lost the use of speaking it, and, indeed, of writing it too, wherein I formerly had a particular reputation, by which you may see how inconsiderable I am on that side.

Beauty is a thing of great recommendation in the correspondence among men; 'tis the first means of acquiring the favor and good liking of one another, and no man is so barbarous and morose as not to perceive himself in some sort struck with its attraction. The body has a great share in our being, has an eminent place there, and therefore its structure and composition are of very just consideration. They who go about to disunite and separate our two principal parts from one another are to blame; we must, on the contrary, reunite and rejoin them. We must command the soul not to withdraw and entertain itself apart, not to despise and abandon the body (neither can she do it but by some apish counterfeit), but to unite herself close to it, to embrace, cherish, assist, govern, and advise it, and to bring it back and set it into the true way when it wanders; in sum, to espouse and be a husband to it, so that their effects may not appear to be diverse and contrary, but uniform and concurring.

Christians have a particular instruction concerning this connection, for they know that the Divine justice embraces this society and juncture of body and soul, even to the making the body capable of eternal rewards; and that God has an eye to the whole man's ways, and wills that he receive entire chastisement or reward according to his demerits or merits. The sect of the Peripatetics, of all sects the most sociable, attribute to wisdom this sole care equally to provide for the good of these two associate parts: and the other sects, in not sufficiently applying themselves to the consideration of this mixture, show themselves to be divided, one for the body and the other for the soul, with equal error, and to have lost sight of their subject, which is Man, and their guide, which they generally confess to be Nature. The first distinction that ever was among men, and the first consideration that gave some pre-eminence over others, 'tis likely was the advantage of beauty: "They distributed and conferred the lands to every man according to his beauty, strength, or understanding, for beauty and strength had first influence," says Lucretius.

Now I am of something lower than the middle stature, a defect that not only borders upon deformity, but carries withal a great deal of inconvenience along with it, especially for those who are in office and command; for the authority which a graceful presence and a majestic mien beget, is wanting. C. Marius did not willingly enlist any soldiers who were not six feet high. The courtier has, indeed, reason to desire a moderate stature in the gentlemen he is setting forth, rather than any other, and to reject all strangeness that should make him be pointed at. But if I were to choose whether this medium must be rather below than above the common standard, I would not have it so in a soldier. Little men, says Aristotle, are pretty but not handsome; and greatness of soul is discovered in a great body, as beauty is in a conspicuous stature: the Ethiopians and Indians, says he, in choosing their kings and magistrates, had regard to the beauty and stature of their persons. They had reason; for it creates respect in those who follow them, and is a terror to the enemy to see a leader of a brave and goodly stature march at the head of a battalion. "In the first rank marched Turnus, brandishing his weapon, taller by a head than all the rest," says Virgil.

Our holy and heavenly King, of whom every circumstance is most carefully and with the greatest religion and reverence to be observed, has not himself rejected bodily recommendation, "*Speciosus forma præ filiis hominum.*" And Plato, together with temperance and fortitude, requires beauty in the conservators of his republic. It would vex you that a man should apply himself to you among your servants to inquire where Monsieur is, and that you should only have the remainder of the compliment of the hat that is made to your barber or your secretary; as it happened to poor Philopœmen, who arriving the first of all his company at an inn where he was expected, the hostess who knew him not, and saw him an unsightly fellow, employed him to go help her maids a little to draw water, and make a fire against Philopœmen's coming: the gentlemen of his train arriving presently after, and surprised to see him busy in this fine employment, for he failed not to obey his landlady's command, asked him what he was doing there. "I am," said he, "paying the penalty of my ugliness." The other beauties belong to women; the beauty of stature is the only beauty of men.

Where there is a contemptible stature, neither the largeness and roundness of the forehead, nor the whiteness and sweetness of the eyes, nor the moderate proportion of the nose, nor the littleness of the ears and mouth, nor the evenness and whiteness of the teeth, nor the thickness of a well-set brown beard, shining like the husk of a chestnut, nor curled hair, nor the just proportion of the head, nor a fresh complexion, nor a pleasing air of a face, nor a body without any offensive scent, nor the just proportion of limbs, can make a handsome man. I am, as to the rest, strong and well knit; my face is not puffed, but full, and my complexion between jovial and melancholic,

moderately sanguine and hot, my health vigorous and sprightly, even
to a well advanced age, and rarely troubled with sickness. Such I was,
for I do not now make any account of myself, now that I am engaged
in the avenues of old age, being already past forty: what shall be from
this time forward, will be but a half-being, and no more me. I every
day escape and steal away from myself. "Of the fleeting years each
steals something from me" [Horace]. Agility and address I never had,
and yet am the son of a very active and sprightly father, who continued to be so to an extreme old age. I have scarce known any man of
his condition, his equal in all bodily exercises: as I have seldom met
with any who have not excelled me, except in running, at which I
was pretty good. In music or singing, for which I have a very unfit
voice, or to play on any sort of instrument, they could never teach
me anything. In dancing, tennis, or wrestling, I could never arrive to
more than an ordinary pitch; in swimming, fencing, vaulting, and
leaping, to none at all. My hands are so clumsy that I cannot even
write so as to read it myself, so that I had rather do what I have
scribbled over again, than take upon me the trouble to make it out. I
do not read much better than I write, and feel that I weary my audi-
tors: otherwise, not a bad clerk. I cannot decently fold up a letter, nor
could ever make a pen, or carve at table worth a pin, nor saddle a
horse, nor carry a hawk and fly her, nor hunt the dogs, nor lure a
hawk, nor speak to a horse.

In fine, my bodily qualities are very well suited to those of my soul;
there is nothing sprightly, only a full and firm vigor: I am patient
enough of labor and pains, but it is only when I go voluntary to work,
and only so long as my own desire prompts me to it; otherwise, if I
am not allured with some pleasure, or have other guide than my own
pure and free inclination, I am good for nothing: for I am of a humor
that, life and health excepted, there is nothing for which I will bite
my nails, and that I will purchase at the price of torment of mind and
constraint: "I would not buy rich Tagus sands so dear, nor all the gold
that lies in the sea" [Juvenal]. Extremely idle, extremely given up to
my own inclination both by nature and art, I would as willingly lend
a man my blood as my pains. I have a soul free and entirely its own,
and accustomed to guide itself after its own fashion; having hitherto
never had either master or governor imposed upon me; I have walked
as far as I would, and at the pace that best pleased myself; that is it that
has rendered me unfit for the service of others, and has made me of
no use to any one but myself.

Nor was there any need of forcing my heavy and lazy disposition;
for being born to such a fortune as I had reason to be contented with
(a reason, nevertheless, that a thousand others of my acquaintance

would have rather made use of for a plank upon which to pass over in search of higher fortune, to tumult and disquiet), and with as much intelligence as I required, I sought for no more, and also got no more: "The northern wind does not agitate my sails; nor Auster trouble my course with storms. In strength, talent, figure, virtue, honor, wealth, I am short of the foremost, but before the last" [Horace]. I had only need of what was sufficient to content me: which nevertheless is a government of soul, to take it right, equally difficult in all sorts of conditions, and that, of custom, we see more easily found in want than in abundance: forasmuch, peradventure, as according to the course of our other passions, the desire of riches is more sharpened by their use than by the need of them: and the virtue of moderation more rare than that of patience; and I never had anything to desire, but happily to enjoy the estate that God by His bounty had put into my hands. I have never known anything of trouble, and have had little to do in anything but the management of my own affairs: or, if I have, it has been upon condition to do it at my own leisure and after my own method; committed to my trust by such as had a confidence in me, who did not importune me, and who knew my humor; for good horsemen will make shift to get service out of a rusty and broken-winded jade.

Even my infancy was trained up after a gentle and free manner, and exempt from any rigorous subjection. All this has helped me to a complexion delicate and incapable of solicitude, even to that degree that I love to have my losses and the disorders wherein I am concerned, concealed from me. In the account of my expenses, I put down what my negligence costs me in feeding and maintaining it; "That overplus, which the owner knows not of, but which benefits the thieves" [Horace].

I love not to know what I have, that I may be less sensible of my loss; I entreat those who serve me, where affection and integrity are absent, to deceive me with something like a decent appearance. For want of constancy enough to support the shock of adverse accidents to which we are subject, and of patience seriously to apply myself to the management of my affairs, I nourish as much as I can this in myself, wholly leaving all to fortune "to take all things at the worst, and to resolve to bear that worst with temper and patience;" that is the only thing I aim at, and to which I apply my whole meditation. In a danger, I do not so much consider how I shall escape it, as of how little importance it is, whether I escape it or no; should I be left dead upon the place, what matter? Not being able to govern events, I govern myself, and apply myself to them, if they will not apply themselves to me. I have no great art to evade, escape from, or force fortune, and by prudence to guide and incline things to my own bias. I have still less patience to undergo the troublesome and painful care therein required; and the most uneasy condition for me is to be suspended on urgent occasions, and to be agitated between hope and fear.

Deliberation, even in things of lightest moment, is very troublesome to me; and I find my mind more put to it to undergo the various tumblings and tossings of doubt and consultation, than to set up its rest and to acquiesce in whatever shall happen after the die is thrown. Few passions break my sleep, but of deliberations, the least will do it. As in roads, I preferably avoid those that are sloping and slippery, and put myself into the beaten track how dirty or deep soever, where I can fall no lower, and there seek my safety; so I love misfortunes that are purely so, that do not torment and tease me with the uncertainty of their growing better; but that at the first push plunge me directly into the worst that can be expected: — for, says Seneca, "Doubtful ills plague us worst."

In events, I carry myself like a man; in the conduct, like a child. The fear of the fall more fevers me than the fall itself. The game is not worth the candle. The covetous man fares worse with his passion than the poor, and the jealous man than the cuckold; and a man ofttimes loses more by defending his vineyard than if he gave it up. The lowest walk is the safest; 'tis the seat of constancy; you have there need of no one but yourself; 'tis there founded and wholly stands upon its own basis. Has not this example of a gentleman very well known, some air of philosophy in it? He married, being well advanced in years, having spent his youth in good fellowship, a great talker and a great jeerer, calling to mind how much the subject of cuckoldry had given him occasion to talk and scoff at others. To prevent them from paying him in his own coin he married a wife from a place where any one may have flesh for his money; "Good-morrow, strumpet;" "good-morrow, cuckold;" and there was not anything wherewith he more commonly and openly entertained those who came to see him, than with this design of his, by which he stopped the private chattering of mockers, and blunted all the point from this reproach.

As to ambition, which is neighbor, or rather daughter to presumption, fortune, to advance me, must have come and taken me by the hand; for to trouble myself for an uncertain hope, and to have submitted myself to all the difficulties that accompany those who endeavor to bring themselves into credit in the beginning of their progress, I could never have done it. Terence puts it: "I will not purchase hope with ready money."

I apply myself to what I see and to what I have in my hand, and go not very far from the shore; "One oar plunging into the sea, the other raking the sands" [Propertius]: and besides, a man rarely arrives to these advancements but in first hazarding what he has of his own; and I am of opinion, that if a man have sufficient to maintain him in the condition wherein he was born and brought up, 'tis a great folly to hazard that upon the uncertainty of augmenting it.

He to whom fortune has denied whereon to set his foot, and to settle a quiet and composed way of living, is to be excused if he venture what he has, because, happen what will, necessity puts him upon shifting for himself. "A desperate case must have a desperate course" says Seneca: and I rather excuse a younger brother for exposing what his friends have left him to the courtesy of fortune, than him with whom the honor of his family is intrusted, who cannot be necessitous but by his own fault. I have found a much shorter and more easy way, by the advice of the good friends I had in my younger days, to free myself from any such ambition, and to sit still; "What more agreeable condition, than to have gained the palm without the dust of the course" [Horace]; judging rightly enough of my own strength, that it was not capable of any great matters; and calling to mind the saying of the late Chancellor Olivier, that the French were like monkeys that swarm up a tree from branch to branch, and never stop till they come to the highest, and there show their breech. Propertius says: "It is a shame to load the head so that it cannot bear the burthen, and the knees give way."

I should find the best qualities I have useless in that age; the facility of my manners would have been called weakness and negligence; my faith and conscience, scrupulosity and superstition; my liberty and freedom would have been reputed troublesome, inconsiderate, and rash. Ill luck is good for something. It is good to be born in a very depraved age; for so, in comparison of others, you shall be reputed virtuous cheaply; he who in our days is but a parricide and a sacrilegious person, is an honest man and a man of honor. Juvenal says of the times, "Nowadays, if a friend does not deny his trust, but restores the old purse with all its rusty coin untouched, 'tis a prodigious faith, that ought to be enrolled in gold, among the Tuscan annals, and a crowned lamb should be sacrificed to such exemplary integrity": and never was time or place wherein princes might propose to themselves more assured or greater rewards for virtue and justice.

The first who shall make it his business to get himself into favor and esteem by those ways, I am much deceived if he do not and by the best title outstrip his competitors: force and violence can do something, but not always all. We see merchants, country justices, and artisans, go cheek by jowl with the best gentry in valor and military knowledge: they perform honorable actions, both in public engagements and private quarrels; they fight duels, they defend towns in our present wars; a prince stifles his special recommendation, renown, in this crowd; let him shine bright in humanity, truth, loyalty, temperance, and especially in justice; marks rare, unknown, and exiled; 'tis by no other means but by the sole good will of the people that he can do his business; and no other qualities can attract their good will like those, as being of the greatest utility to them: *"Nil est tam populare, quam donitas."*

By this standard, I had been great and rare, just as I find myself now pygmy and vulgar by the standard of some past ages, wherein, if no other better qualities concurred, it was ordinary and common to see a man moderate in his revenges, gentle in resenting injuries, religious of his word, neither double nor supple, nor accommodating his faith to the will of others, or the turns of the times: I would rather see all affairs go to wreck and ruin than falsify my faith to secure them. For as to this new virtue of feigning and dissimulation, which is now in so great credit, I mortally hate it; and of all vices find none that evidences so much baseness and meanness of spirit. 'Tis a cowardly and servile humor to hide and disguise a man's self under a visor, and not to dare to show himself what he is; 'tis by this our servants are trained up to treachery; being brought up to speak what is not true, they make no conscience of a lie. A generous heart ought not to belie its own thoughts; it will make itself seen within; all there is good, or at least, human.

Aristotle reputes it the office of magnanimity openly and professedly to love and hate; to judge and speak with all freedom; and not to value the approbation or dislike of others in comparison of truth. Apollonius said, it was for slaves to lie, and for freemen to speak truth: 'tis the chief and fundamental part of virtue; we must love it for itself. He who speaks truth because he is obliged so to do, and because it serves him, and who is not afraid to lie when it signifies nothing to anybody, is not sufficiently true. My soul naturally abominates lying, and hates the very thought of it. I have an inward shame and a sharp remorse, if sometimes a lie escape me; as sometimes it does, being surprised by occasions that allow me no premeditation. A man must not always tell all, for that were folly: but what a man says should be what he thinks, otherwise 'tis knavery.

I do not know what advantage men pretend to by eternally counterfeiting and dissembling, if not, never to be believed when they speak the truth; it may once or twice pass with men; but to profess the concealing their thought, and to brag, as some of our princes have done, that they would burn their shirts if they knew their true intentions, which was a saying of the ancient Metellus of Macedon; and that they who know not how to dissemble know not how to rule, is to give warning to all who have anything to do with them, that all they say is nothing but lying and deceit. "By how much any one is more subtle and cunning, by so much is he hated and suspected, the opinion of his integrity being lost and gone" says Cicero. It were a great simplicity in any one to lay any stress either on the countenance or word of a man, who has put on a resolution to be always another thing without than he is within, as Tiberius did; and I cannot conceive what part such persons can have in conversation with men, seeing they produce nothing that is received as true: whoever is disloyal to truth, is the same to falsehood also.

Those of our time, who have considered in the establishment of the duty of a prince, the good of his affairs only, and have preferred that to the care of his faith and conscience, might have something to say to a prince whose affairs fortune had put into such a posture that he might forever establish them by only once breaking his word: but it will not go so; they often buy in the same market; they make more than one peace and enter into more than one treaty in their lives. Gain tempts to the first breach of faith, and almost always presents itself, as in all other ill acts, sacrileges, murders, rebellions, treasons, as being undertaken for some kind of advantage; but this first gain has infinite mischievous consequences, throwing this prince out of all correspondence and negotiation, by this example of infidelity. Soliman, of the Ottoman race, a race not very solicitous of keeping their words or compacts, when, in my infancy he made his army land at Otranto, being informed that Mercurino de' Gratinare, and the inhabitants of Castro were detained prisoners, after having surrendered the place, contrary to the articles of their capitulation, sent orders to have them set at liberty, saying that having other great enterprises in hand in those parts, the disloyalty, though it carried a show of present utility, would for the future bring on him a disrepute and distrust of infinite prejudice.

Now, for my part, I had rather be troublesome and indiscreet, than a flatterer and a dissembler. I confess that there may be some mixture of pride and obstinacy in keeping myself so upright and open as I do without any consideration of others; and methinks I am a little too free, where I ought least to be so, and that I grow hot by the opposition of respect; and it may be, also, that I suffer myself to follow the propension of my own nature for want of art; using the same liberty, speech, and countenance toward great persons, that I bring with me from my own house: I am sensible how much it declines toward incivility and indiscretion: but, besides that I am so bred, I have not a wit supple enough to evade a sudden question and to escape by some evasion, nor to feign a truth, nor memory enough to retain it so feigned; nor, truly, assurance enough to maintain it, and so play the brave out of weakness. And therefore it is that I abandon myself to candor, always to speak as I think, both by complexion and design leaving the event to fortune. Aristippus was wont to say that the principal benefit he had extracted from philosophy was that he spoke freely and openly to all.

Memory is a faculty of wonderful use, and without which the judgment can very hardly perform its office; for my part I have none at all. What any one will propound to me, he must do it piecemeal, for to answer a speech consisting of several heads I am not able. I could not receive a commission by word of mouth, without a note-book. And when I have a speech of consequence to make, if it be long, I am reduced to the miserable necessity of getting by heart, word for word, what I am to say; I should otherwise have neither method nor assurance, being in fear that my memory would play me a slippery trick. But this way is no less difficult to me than the other; I must have three hours to learn three verses. And besides, in a work of a man's own, the liberty and authority of altering the order, of changing a word, incessantly varying the matter, makes it harder to stick in the memory of the author. The more I mistrust it the worse it is; it serves me best by chance; I must solicit it negligently; for if I press it, 'tis confused, and after it once begins to stagger, the more I sound it, the more it is perplexed; it serves me at its own hour, not at mine.

And the same defect I find in my memory, I find also in several other parts. I fly command, obligation, and constraint; that which I can otherwise naturally and easily do, if I impose it upon myself by an express and strict injunction, I cannot do it. Even the members of my body, which have a more particular jurisdiction of their own, sometimes refuse to obey me, if I enjoin them a necessary service at a certain hour. This tyrannical and compulsive appointment baffles them; they shrink up either through fear or spite, and fall into a trance. Being once in a place where it is looked upon as the greatest discourtesy imaginable not to pledge those who drink to you, though I had there all liberty allowed me, I tried to play the good fellow, out of respect to the ladies who were there, according to the custom of the country; but there was sport enough; for this threatening and preparation, that I was to force myself contrary to my custom and inclination, so stopped my throat that I could not swallow one drop, and was deprived of drinking so much as with my meat; I found myself gorged, and my thirst quenched by the quantity of drink that my imagination had swallowed. This effect is most manifest in such as have the most vehement and powerful imagination; but it is natural, notwithstanding, and there is no one who does not in some measure feel it. They offered an excellent archer, condemned to die, to save his life, if he would show some notable proof of his art, but he refused to try, fearing lest the too great contention of his will should make him shoot wide, and that instead of saving his life, he should also lose the reputation he had got of being a good marksman. A man who thinks of something else, will not fail to take over and over again the same number and measure of steps, even to an inch, in the place where he walks; but if he make it his business to measure and count them, he will find that what he did by nature and accident, he cannot so exactly do by design.

My library, which is of the best sort of country libraries, is situated in a corner of my house; if anything comes into my head that I have a mind to look at or to write there, lest I should forget it in but going across the court, I am fain to commit it to the memory of some other. If I venture in speaking to digress never so little from my subject, I am infallibly lost, which is the reason that I keep myself, in discourse, strictly close. I am forced to call the men who serve me either by the names of their offices or their country; for names are very hard for me to remember. I can tell, indeed, that there are three syllables, that it has a harsh sound, and that it begins or ends with such a letter, but that's all: and if I should live long, I do not doubt but I should forget my own name, as some others have done. Messala Corvinus was two years without any trace of memory, which is also said of Georgius Trapezuntius. For my own interest, I often meditate what a kind of life theirs was, and if, without this faculty, I should have enough left to support me with any manner of ease; and prying narrowly into it, I fear that this privation, if absolute, destroys all the other functions of the soul: "*Plenus rimarum sum, hac atque illac perfluo.*"

It has befallen me more than once to forget the watchword I had three hours before given or received, and to forget where I had hidden my purse; whatever Cicero is pleased to say, I help myself to lose what I have a particular care to lock safe up. "It is certain that memory contains not only philosophy, but all the arts and all that appertain to the use of life." Memory is the receptacle and case of science: and therefore mine being so treacherous, if I know little, I cannot much complain. I know, in general, the names of the arts, and of what they treat, but nothing more. I turn over books; I do not study them. What I retain I no longer recognize as another's; 'tis only what my judgment has made its advantage of, the discourses and imaginations in which it has been instructed: the author, place, words, and other circumstances, I immediately forget; and I am so excellent at forgetting, that I no less forget my own writings and compositions than the rest. I am very often quoted to myself and am not aware of it. Whoever should inquire of me where I had the verses and examples that I have here huddled together, would puzzle me to tell him, and yet I have not borrowed them but from famous and known authors, not contenting myself that they were rich, if I, moreover, had them not from rich and honorable hands, where there is a concurrence of authority with reason. It is no great wonder if my book run the same fortune that other books do, and if my memory lose what I have written as well as what I have read, and what I give as well as what I receive.

Besides the defect of memory, I have others which very much contribute to my ignorance; I have a slow and heavy wit, the least cloud stops its progress, so that, for example, I never proposed to it any never so easy a riddle that it could find out; there is not the least idle subtlety that will not gravel me; in games, where wit is required, as chess, draughts, and the like, I understand no more than the common movements. I have a slow and perplexed apprehension, but what it once apprehends, it apprehends well, for the time it retains it. My sight is perfect, entire, and discovers at a very great distance, but is soon weary and heavy at work, which occasions that I cannot read long, but am forced to have one to read to me. The younger Pliny can inform such as have not experimented it themselves, what, and how important, an impediment this is to those who addict themselves to study.

There is no so wretched and coarse a soul, wherein some particular faculty is not seen to shine; no soul so buried in sloth and ignorance, but it will sally at one end or another; and how it comes to pass that a man blind and asleep to everything else, shall be found sprightly, clear, and excellent in some one particular effect, we are to inquire of our masters: but the beautiful souls are they that are universal, open, and ready for all things; if not instructed, at least capable of being so; which I say to accuse my own; for whether it be through infirmity or negligence (and to neglect that which lies at our feet, which we have in our hands, and what nearest concerns the use of life, is far from my doctrine) there is not a soul in the world so awkward as mine, and so ignorant of many common things, and such as a man cannot without shame fail to know. I must give some examples.

I was born and bred up in the country, and among husbandmen; I have had business and husbandry in my own hands ever since my predecessors, who were lords of the estate I now enjoy, left me to succeed them; and yet I can neither cast accounts, nor reckon my counters; most of our current money I do not know, nor the difference between one grain and another, either growing or in the barn, if it be not too apparent; and scarcely can distinguish between the cabbage and lettuce in my garden. I do not so much as understand the names of the chief instruments of husbandry, nor the most ordinary elements of agriculture, which the very children know; much less the mechanic arts, traffic, merchandise, the variety and nature of fruits, wines, and viands, nor how to make a hawk fly, nor to physic a horse or a dog. And, since I must publish my whole shame, 'tis not above a month ago, that I was trapped in my ignorance of the use of leaven to make bread, or to what end it was to keep wine in the vat. They conjectured of old at Athens an aptitude for the mathematics in him they saw ingeniously bavin up a burthen of brushwood. In earnest, they would draw a quite contrary conclusion from me, for give me the whole provision and necessaries of a kitchen, I should starve.

By these features of my confession men may imagine others to my prejudice: but whatever I deliver myself to be, provided it be such as I really am, I have my end; neither will I make any excuse for committing to paper such mean and frivolous things as these; the meanness of the subject compels me to it. They may, if they please, accuse my project, but not my progress; so it is, that without anybody's needing to tell me, I sufficiently see of how little weight and value all this is, and the folly of my design: 'tis enough that my judgment does not contradict itself, of which these are the essays. I am not obliged to refrain from uttering absurdities, provided I am not deceived in them and know them to be such; and to trip knowingly, is so ordinary with me, that I seldom do it otherwise, and rarely trip by chance. 'Tis no great matter to add ridiculous actions to the temerity of my humor, since I cannot ordinarily help supplying it with those that are vicious.

I was present one day at Barleduc, when King Francis II., for a memorial of René, king of Sicily, was presented with a portrait he had drawn of himself; why is it not, in like manner, lawful for every one to draw himself with a pen as he did with a crayon? I will not therefore omit this blemish, though very unfit to be published, which is irresolution; a very great defect, and very incommodious in the negotiations of the affairs of the world; in doubtful enterprises, I know not which to choose: "My heart does not tell me either yes or no."

I can maintain an opinion, but I cannot choose one. By reason that in human things, to what sect soever we incline, many appearances present themselves that confirm us in it (and the philosopher Chrysippus said, that he would of Zeno and Cleanthes, his masters, learn their doctrines only; for, as to proofs and reasons, he should find enough of his own), which way soever I turn, I still furnish myself with causes,

and likelihood enough to fix me there; which makes me detain doubt
and the liberty of choosing, till occasion presses; and then, to confess
the truth, I, for the most part, throw the feather into the wind, as the
saying is, and commit myself to the mercy of fortune; a very light inclination and circumstance carries me along with it: "The mind being
in doubt, in short time is driven this way and that" [Terence].

The uncertainty of my judgment is so equally balanced in most
occurrences, that I could willingly refer it to be decided by the chance
of a die: and I observe, with great consideration of our human infirmity, the examples that the divine history itself has left us of this
custom of referring to fortune and chance the determination of election in doubtful things: "*Sors cecidit super Matthiam.*" Human reason is
a two-edged and dangerous sword: observe in the hands of Socrates,
her most intimate and familiar friend, how many several points it has.
I am thus good for nothing but to follow and suffer myself to be easily carried away with the crowd; I have not confidence enough in my
own strength to take upon me to command and lead; I am very glad
to find the way beaten before me by others. If I must run the hazard
of an uncertain choice, I am rather willing to have it under such a one
as is more confident in his opinions than I am in mine, whose ground
and foundation I find to be very slippery and unsure.

Yet, I do not easily change, by reason that I discern the same weakness in contrary opinions. "The very custom of assenting seems dangerous," Cicero says. Especially in political affairs there is a large field
open for changes and contestation: "As a just balance pressed with
equal weight, neither dips nor rises on either side" [Tubullus].
Machiavelli's writings, for example, were solid enough for the subject, yet were they easy enough to be controverted; and they who
have taken up the cudgels against him, have left as great a facility of
controverting theirs; there was never wanting, in that kind of argument, replies and replies upon replies, and as infinite a contexture of
debates, as our wrangling lawyers have extended in favor of long suits.
"It is a fight wherein we exhaust each other by mutual wounds" says
Horace; the reasons having little other foundation than experience,
and the variety of human events presenting us with infinite examples
of all sorts of forms.

An understanding person of our times says: That whoever would,
in contradiction to our almanacs, write cold where they say hot, and
wet where they say dry, and always put the contrary to what they
foretell; if he were to lay a wager, he would not care which side he
took, excepting where no uncertainty could fall out, as to promise
excessive heats at Christmas, or extremity of cold at midsummer. I
have the same opinion of these political controversies; be on which

side you will, you have as fair a game to play as your adversary, provided you do not proceed so far as to jostle principles that are too manifest to be disputed. And yet, in my conceit, in public affairs, there is no government so ill, provided it be ancient and has been constant, that is not better than change and alteration. Our manners are infinitely corrupt, and wonderfully incline to the worse; of our laws and customs there are many that are barbarous and monstrous: nevertheless, by reason of the difficulty of reformation, and the danger of stirring things, if I could put something under to stop the wheel, and keep it where it is, I would do it with all my heart: "The examples we produce, are not so shameful and foul but that far worse remain behind," remarks Juvenal.

The worst thing I find in our state is instability, and that our laws, no more than our clothes, cannot settle in any certain form. It is very easy to accuse a government of imperfection, for all mortal things are full of it: it is very easy to beget in a people a contempt of ancient observances; never any man undertook it but he did it; but to establish a better regimen in the stead of that which a man has overthrown, many who have attempted it have foundered. I very little consult my prudence in my conduct; I am willing to let it be guided by the public rule. Happy the people who do what they are commanded, better than they who command, without tormenting themselves as to the causes; who suffer themselves gently to roll after the celestial revolution! Obedience is never pure nor calm in him who reasons and disputes.

In fine, to return to myself: the only thing by which I esteem myself to be something, is that wherein never any man thought himself to be defective; my recommendation is vulgar and common, for who ever thought he wanted sense? It would be a proposition that would imply a contradiction in itself; 'tis a disease that never is where it is discerned; 'tis tenacious and strong, but what the first ray of the patient's sight nevertheless pierces through and disperses, as the beams of the sun do thick and obscure mists: to accuse one's self would be to excuse in this case, and to condemn, to absolve. There never was porter or the silliest girl, that did not think they had sense enough to do their business. We easily enough confess in others an advantage of courage, strength, experience, activity, and beauty; but an advantage in judgment we yield to none; and the reasons that proceed simply from the natural conclusions of others, we think, if we had but turned our thoughts that way, we should ourselves have found out as well as they.

Knowledge, style, and such parts as we see in others' works, we are soon aware of, if they excel our own: but for the simple products of the understanding, every one thinks he could have found out the like in himself, and is hardly sensible of the weight and difficulty, if not (and then with much ado), in an extreme and incomparable distance. And whoever should be able clearly to discern the height of another's judgment, would be also able to raise his own to the same pitch. So that it is a sort of exercise, from which a man is to expect very little praise; a kind of composition of small repute. And, besides, for whom do you write? The learned, to whom the authority appertains of judging books, know no other value but that of learning, and allow of no other proceeding of wit but that of erudition and art: if you have mistaken one of the Scipios for another, what is all the rest you have to say worth? Whoever is ignorant of Aristotle, according to their rule, is in some sort ignorant of himself; vulgar souls cannot discern the grace and force of a lofty and delicate style. Now these two sorts of men take up the world. The third sort into whose hands you fall, of souls that are regular and strong of themselves, is so rare, that it justly has neither name nor place among us; and 'tis so much time lost to aspire unto it, or to endeavor to please it.

'Tis commonly said that the justest portion nature has given us of her favors, is that of sense; for there is no one who is not contented with his share: is it not reason? whoever should see beyond that, would see beyond his sight. I think my opinions are good and sound, but who does not think the same of his own? One of the best proofs I have that mine are so, is the small esteem I have of myself; for had they not been very well assured, they would easily have suffered themselves to have been deceived by the peculiar affection I have to myself, as one that places it almost wholly in myself, and does not let much run out. All that others distribute among an infinite number of friends and acquaintance, to their glory and grandeur, I dedicate to the repose of my own mind and to myself; that which escapes thence is not properly by my direction: "*Mihi nempe valere et vivere doctus.*"

Now I find my opinions very bold and constant in condemning my own imperfection. And, to say the truth, 'tis a subject upon which I exercise my judgment, as much as upon any other. The world looks always opposite; I turn my sight inward, and there fix and employ it. I have no other business but myself, I am eternally meditating upon myself, considering and tasting myself. Other men's thoughts are ever wandering abroad, if they will but see it; they are still going forward; "*Nemo in sese tentat descendere;*" for my part, I circulate in myself. This capacity of trying the truth, whatever it be, in myself, and this free humor of not over easily subjecting my belief, I owe principally to myself; for the strongest and most general imaginations I have are those that, as a man may say, were born with me; they are natural and entirely my own. I produced them crude and simple, with a strong and bold production, but a little troubled and imperfect; I have since established and fortified them with the authority of others and the sound examples of the ancients, whom I have found of the same judgment; they have given me faster hold, and a more manifest fruition and possession of that I had before embraced. The reputation that every one pretends to of vivacity and promptness of wit, I seek in regularity; the glory they pretend to from a striking and signal action, or some particular excellence, I claim from order, correspondence, and tranquillity of opinions and manners: "If anything be entirely decorous, nothing certainly can be more so than an equability in the whole life, and in every particular action of it; which thou canst not possibly observe and keep, if imitating other men's natures thou layest aside thy own," says Cicero.

Here, then, you see to what degree I find myself guilty of this first part, that I said was the vice of presumption. As to the second, which consists in not having a sufficient esteem for others, I know not whether or no I can so well excuse myself; but whatever comes on't I am resolved to speak the truth. And whether, peradventure, it be that the continual fréquentation I have had with the humors of the ancients, and the idea of those great souls of past ages, put me out of taste both with others and myself, or that, in truth, the age we live in produces but very indifferent things, yet so it is that I see nothing worthy of any great admiration. Neither, indeed, have I so great an intimacy with many men as is requisite to make a right judgment of them; and those with whom my condition makes me the most frequent, are, for the most part, men who have little care of the culture of the soul, but that look upon honor as the sum of all blessings, and valor as the height of all perfection.

What I see that is fine in others I very readily commend and esteem: nay, I often say more in their commendation than I think they really deserve, and give me myself so far leave to lie, for I cannot invent a false subject: my testimony is never wanting to my friends in what I conceive deserves praise, and where a foot is due I am willing to give them a foot and a half; but to attribute to them qualities that they have not, I cannot do it, nor openly defend their imperfections. Nay, I frankly give my very enemies their due testimony of honor; my affection alters, my judgment does not, and I never confound my animosity with other circumstances that are foreign to it; and I am so jealous of the liberty of my judgment that I can very hardly part with it for any passion whatever. I do myself a greater injury in lying than I do him of whom I tell a lie. This commendable and generous custom is observed of the Persian nation, that they spoke of their mortal enemies and with whom they were at deadly war, as honorably and justly as their virtues deserved.

I know men enough that have several fine parts; one wit, another courage, another address, another conscience, another language, one, one science, another, another; but a generally great man, and who has all these brave parts together, or any one of them to such a degree of excellence that we should admire him or compare him with those we honor of times past, my fortune never brought me acquainted with; and the greatest I ever knew, I mean for the natural parts of the soul, was Etienne De la Boetie; his was a full soul indeed, and that had every way a beautiful aspect: a soul of the old stamp, and that had produced great effects had his fortune been so pleased, having added much to those great natural parts by learning and study.

But how it comes to pass I know not, and yet it is certainly so, there is as much vanity and weakness of judgment in those who profess the greatest abilities, who take upon them learned callings and bookish employments as in any other sort of men whatever; either because more is required and expected from them, and that common defects are excusable in them, or because the opinion they have of their own learning makes them more bold to expose and lay themselves too open, by which they lose and betray themselves. As an artificer more manifests his want of skill in a rich matter he has in hand, if he disgrace the work by ill handling and contrary to the rules required, than in a matter of less value; and men are more displeased at a disproportion in a statue of gold than in one of plaster; so do these when they advance things that in themselves and in their place would be good; for they make use of them without discretion, honoring their memories at the expense of their understandings, and making themselves ridiculous by honoring Cicero, Galen, Ulpian, and St. Jerome alike.

I willingly fall again into the discourse of the vanity of our education, the end of which is not to render us good and wise, but learned, and she has obtained it. She has not taught us to follow and embrace virtue and prudence, but she has imprinted in us their derivation and etymology; we know how to decline virtue, if we know not how to love it: if we do not know what prudence is really and in effect, and by experience, we have it, however, by jargon and heart: we are not content to know the extraction, kindred, and alliances of our neighbors; we desire, moreover, to have them our friends and to establish a correspondence and intelligence with them; but this education of ours has taught us definitions, divisions, and partitions of virtue, as so many surnames and branches of a genealogy, without any further care of establishing any familiarity or intimacy between her and us. It has culled out for our initiatory instruction not such books as contain the soundest and truest opinions, but those that speak the best Greek and

Latin, and by their fine words has instilled into our fancy the vainest humors of antiquity.

A good education alters the judgment and manners; as it happened to Polemon, a lewd and debauched young Greek, who going by chance to hear one of Xenocrates' lectures, did not only observe the eloquence and learning of the reader, and not only brought away the knowledge of some fine matter, but a more manifest and a more solid profit, which was the sudden change and reformation of his former life. Whoever found such an effect of our discipline? That seems to me to be the least contemptible condition of men, which by its plainness and simplicity is seated in the lowest degree, and invites us to a more regular course. I find the rude manners and language of country people commonly better suited to the rule and prescription of true philosophy, than those of our philosophers themselves: The vulgar are so much the wiser, because they only know essentials.

The most remarkable men, as I have judged by outward appearance (for to judge of them according to my own method, I must penetrate a great deal deeper) for soldiers and military conduct, were the duke of Guise, who died at Orleans, and the late Marshal Strozzi; and for men of great ability and no common virtue, Olivier, and De l'Hospital, chancellors of France. Poetry, too, in my opinion, has flourished in this age of ours; we have abundance of very good artificers in the trade; D'Aurat, Beza, Buchanan, L'Hospital, Montdoré, Turnebus: as to the French poets, I believe they raised their art to the highest pitch to which it can ever arrive; and in those parts of it wherein Ronsard and du Bellay excel, I find them little inferior to the ancient perfection. Adrian Turnebus knew more and, what he did know, better than any man of his time, or long before him. The lives of the last duke of Alva, and of our Constable de Montmorency, were both of them great and noble, and that had many rare resemblances of fortune; but the beauty and glory of the death of the last, in the sight of Paris and of his king, in their service, against his nearest relations, at the head of an army through his conduct victorious, and by a sudden stroke, in so extreme old age, merits methinks to be recorded among the most remarkable events of our times. As also the constant goodness, sweetness of manners, and conscientious facility of Monsieur de la Noue, in so great an injustice of armed parties (the true school of treason, inhumanity, and robbery), wherein he always kept up the reputation of a great and experienced captain.

I have taken a delight to publish in several places the hopes I have of Marie de Gournay le Jars, my adopted daughter, and certainly beloved by me with more than a paternal love, and enveloped in my solitude and retirement as one of the best parts of my own being;

I have no longer regard to anything in this world but her. And if a
man may presage from her youth, her soul will one day be capable of
very great things; and among others, of the perfection of that sacred
friendship, to which we do not read that any of her sex could ever
yet arrive; the sincerity and solidity of her manners are already sufficient for it, and her affection towards me more than superabundant,
and such, in short, as that there is nothing more to be wished, if not
that the apprehension she has of my end, being now five and fifty
years old, might not so much afflict her. The judgment she made of
my first Essays, being a woman, so young, and in this age, and alone
in her own country; and the famous vehemence wherewith she loved
me, and desired my acquaintance solely from the esteem she had
thence of me, before she ever saw my face, is an incident very worthy
of consideration.

Other virtues have had little or no credit in this age; but valor is
become popular by our civil wars; and in this, we have souls brave
even to perfection, and in so great number that the choice is impossible to be made.

This is all of extraordinary and not common grandeur that has
hitherto arrived at my knowledge.

OF GIVING THE LIE.

Well, but some one will say to me, this design of making a man's
self the subject of his writing were indeed excusable in rare and famous men, who by their reputation had given others a curiosity to be
fully informed of them. It is most true, I confess and know very well,
that a mechanic will scarce lift his eye from his work to look at an
ordinary man, whereas a man will forsake his business and his shop to
stare at an eminent person when he comes into a town. It misbe-
comes any other to give his own character, but him who has qualities
worthy of imitation, and whose life and opinions may serve for example: Cæsar and Xenophon had a just and solid foundation whereon
to found their narrations, in the greatness of their own performances;
and it were to be wished that we had the journals of Alexander the
Great, the commentaries that Augustus, Cato, Sylla, Brutus, and others left of their actions; of such persons men love and contemplate the
very statues even in copper and marble.

This remonstrance is very true; but it very little concerns me.
Horace says: "I repeat my poems only to my friends, and when asked
to do so; not before every one, and everywhere; there are plenty of
reciters in the open market-place and at the baths." I do not here
form a statue to erect in the great square of a city, in a church, or any

public place: "I study not to make my pages swell with empty trifles; you and I are talking in private" [Persius]: 'tis for some corner of a library, or to entertain a neighbor, a kinsman, a friend, who has a mind to renew his acquaintance and familiarity with me in this image of myself. Others have been encouraged to speak of themselves, because they found the subject worthy and rich; I, on the contrary, am the bolder, by reason the subject is so poor and sterile that I cannot be suspected of ostentation. I judge freely of the actions of others; I give little of my own to judge of, because they are nothing: I do not find so much good in myself, that I cannot tell it without blushing.

What contentment would it not be to me to hear any one thus relate to me the manners, faces, countenances, the ordinary words and fortunes of my ancestors? how attentively should I listen to it! In earnest, it would be evil nature to despise so much as the pictures of our friends and predecessors, the fashion of their clothes and arms. I preserve their writing, seal, and a particular sword they wore, and have not thrown the long staves my father used to carry in his hand out of my closet: "A father's garment and ring is by so much dearer to his posterity, as they had the greater affection toward him." If my posterity, nevertheless, shall be of another mind, I shall be revenged on them; for they cannot care less for me, than I shall then do for them. All the traffic that I have in this with the public, is that I borrow their utensils of writing, which are more easy and most at hand; and in recompense shall, peradventure, keep a pound of butter in the market from melting in the sun.

And though nobody should read me, have I lost my time in entertaining myself so many idle hours, in so pleasing and useful thoughts? In moulding this figure upon myself, I have been so often constrained to temper and compose myself in a right posture that the copy is truly taken, and has in some sort formed itself; painting myself for others, I represent myself in a better coloring than my own natural complexion. I have no more made my book, than my book has made me: 'tis a book consubstantial with the author, of a peculiar design, a member of my life, and whose business is not designed for others, as that of all other books is. In giving myself so continual and so exact an account of myself, have I lost my time? For they who sometimes cursorily survey themselves only, do not so strictly examine themselves, nor penetrate so deep, as he who makes it his business, his study, and his employment, who intends a lasting record, with all his fidelity, and with all his force.

The most delicious pleasures digested within, avoid leaving any trace of themselves, and avoid the sight not only of the people, but of any other person. How often has this work diverted me from

troublesome thoughts? and all that are frivolous should be reputed so.
Nature has presented us with a large faculty of entertaining ourselves
alone; and often calls us to it, to teach us that we owe ourselves in
part to society, but chiefly and mostly to ourselves. That I may ha-
bituate my fancy even to meditate in some method and to some end,
and to keep it from losing itself and roving at random, 'tis but to give
to body and to record all the little thoughts that present themselves to
it, I give ear to my whimsies, because I am to record them. It often
falls out, that being displeased at some action that civility and reason
will not permit me openly to reprove, I here disgorge myself, not
without design of public instruction: and also these poetical lashes:

> "Zon sus l'œil, zon sur le groin,
> Zon sur le dos du sagoin,"

imprint themselves better upon paper than upon the flesh. What if I
listen to books a little more attentively than ordinary, since I watch if
I can purloin anything that may adorn or support my own? I have not
at all studied to make a book, but I have in some sort studied because
I had made it; if it be studying to scratch and pinch now one author,
and then another, either by the head or foot, not with any design to
form opinions from them, but to assist, second, and fortify those I
already have embraced.

But whom shall we believe in the report he makes of himself in so
corrupt an age? considering there are so few, if any at all, whom we
can believe when speaking of others, where there is less interest to lie.
The first thing done in the corruption of manners is banishing truth;
for, as Pindar says, to be true is the beginning of a great virtue, and
the first article that Plato requires in the governor of his Republic.
The truth of these days is not that which really is, but what every man
persuades another man to believe; as we generally give the name of
money not only to pieces of the just alloy, but even to the false also,
if they will pass. Our nation has long been reproached with this vice;
for Salvianus Massiliensis, who lived in the time of the Emperor
Valentinian, says that lying and forswearing themselves is with the
French not a vice, but a way of speaking. He who would enhance this
testimony, might say that it is now a virtue in them; men form and
fashion themselves to it as to an exercise of honor; for dissimulation
is one of the most notable qualities of this age.

I have often considered whence this custom that we so religiously
observe should spring, of being more highly offended with the reproach of a vice so familiar to us than with any other, and that it should
be the highest insult that can in words be done us to reproach us with

a lie. Upon examination, I find that it is natural most to defend the defects with which we are most tainted. It seems as if by resenting and being moved at the accusation, we in some sort acquit ourselves of the fault; though we have it in effect, we condemn it in outward appearance. May it not also be that this reproach seems to imply cowardice and feebleness of heart? of which can there be a more manifest sign than to eat a man's own words — nay, to lie against a man's own knowledge? Lying is a base vice; a vice that one of the ancients[1] portrays in the most odious colors when he says, "that it is to manifest a contempt of God, and withal a fear of men." It is not possible more fully to represent the horror, baseness, and irregularity of it; for what can a man imagine more hateful and contemptible than to be a coward toward men, and valiant against his Maker?

Our intelligence being by no other way communicable to one another but by a particular word, he who falsifies that betrays public society. 'Tis the only way by which we communicate our thoughts and wills; 'tis the interpreter of the soul, and if it deceives us, we no longer know nor have further tie upon one another; if that deceive us, it breaks all our correspondence, and dissolves all the ties of government. Certain nations of the newly discovered Indies (I need not give them names, seeing they are no more; for, by wonderful and unheard-of example, the desolation of that conquest has extended to the utter abolition of names and the ancient knowledge of places) offered to their gods human blood, but only such as was drawn from the tongue and ears, to expiate for the sin of lying, as well heard as pronounced. The good fellow of Greece[1] was wont to say that children were amused with toys and men with words.

As to the diverse usage of giving the lie, and the laws of honor in that case, and the alterations they have received, I shall defer saying what I know of them to another time, and shall learn, if I can, in the meanwhile, at what time the custom took beginning of so exactly weighing and measuring words, and of making our honor so interested in them; for it is easy to judge that it was not anciently among the Greeks and Romans; and I have often thought it strange to see them rail at and give one another the lie without any further quarrel. Their laws of duty steered some other course than ours. Cæsar is sometimes called thief, and sometimes drunkard, to his teeth. We see the liberty of invectives they practised upon one another, I mean the greatest chiefs of war of both nations, where words are only revenged with words, and never proceed any farther.

---

[1] Lysander.

OF LIBERTY OF CONSCIENCE.

'Tis usual to see good intentions, if carried on without moderation, push men on to very vicious effects. In this dispute which has at this time engaged France in a civil war, the better and the soundest cause, no doubt, is that which maintains the ancient religion and government of the kingdom. Nevertheless, among the good men of that party (for I do not speak of those who only make a pretence of it, either to execute their own particular revenges or to gratify their avarice, or to conciliate the favor of princes, but of those who engage in the quarrel out of true zeal to religion and a holy desire to maintain the peace and government of their country), of these I say, we see many whom passion transports beyond the bounds of reason, and sometimes inspires with counsels that are unjust and violent, and, moreover, rash.

It is certain that in those first times, when our religion began to gain authority with the laws, zeal armed many against all sorts of pagan books, by which the learned suffered an exceeding great loss, a disorder that I conceive to have done more prejudice to letters than all the flames of the barbarians. Of this Cornelius Tacitus is a very good testimony; for though the Emperor Tacitus, his kinsman, had, by express order, furnished all the libraries in the world with it, nevertheless one entire copy could not escape the curious examination of those who desired to abolish it for only five or six idle clauses that were contrary to our belief.

They had also the trick easily to lend undue praises to all the emperors who did anything for us, and universally to condemn all the actions of those who were our adversaries as is evidently manifest in the Emperor Julian, surnamed the Apostate, who was, in truth, a very great and rare man, a man in whose soul philosophy was imprinted in the best characters, by which he professed to govern all his actions; and, in truth, there is no sort of virtue of which he has not left behind him very notable examples; in chastity (of which the whole of his life gave manifest proof) we read the same of him, that was said of Alexander and Scipio, that being in the flower of his age, for he was slain by the Parthians at one and thirty, of a great many very beautiful captives, he would not so much as look upon one. As to his justice, he took himself the pains to hear the parties, and although he would out of curiosity inquire what religion they were of, nevertheless, the hatred he had to ours never gave any counterpoise to the balance. He made himself several good laws, and cut off a great part of the subsidies and taxes imposed and levied by his predecessors.

We have two good historians who were eye-witnesses of his actions; one of whom, Marcellinus, in several places of his history, sharply reproves an edict of his whereby he interdicted all Christians, rhetoricians, and grammarians to keep school, or to teach, and says he could wish that act of his had been buried in silence: it is probable that, had he done any more severe thing against us, he, so affectionate as he was to our party, would not have passed it over in silence. He was, indeed, sharp against us; but yet no cruel enemy; for our own people tell this story of him, that one day, walking about the city of Chalcedon, Maris, bishop of the place, was so bold as to tell him that he was impious, and an enemy to Christ, at which, say they, therein affecting a philosophical patience, he was no further moved than to reply, "Go, poor wretch, and lament the loss of thy eyes;" to which the bishop replied again, "I thank Jesus Christ for taking away my sight, that I may not see thy impudent face." But this action of his savors nothing of the cruelty that he is said to have exercised toward us.

"He was," says Eutropius, my other witness, "an enemy to Christianity, but without putting his hand to blood." And, to return to his justice, there is nothing in that whereof he can be accused, the severity excepted he practised in the beginning of his reign against those who had followed the party of Constantius, his predecessor. As to his sobriety, he lived always a soldier's kind of life; and kept a table in the most profound peace, like one that prepared and inured himself to the austerities of war. His vigilance was such, that he divided the night into three or four parts, of which the least was dedicated to sleep; the rest was spent either in visiting the state of his army and guards, in person, or in study; for among other rare qualities, he was very excellent in all sorts of learning.

'Tis said of Alexander the Great, that being in bed, for fear lest sleep should divert him from his thoughts and studies, he had always a basin set by his bedside, and held one of his hands out with a ball of copper in it, to the end that, beginning to fall asleep, and his fingers leaving their hold, the ball, by falling into the basin, might awake him. But the other had his soul so bent upon what he had a mind to do, and so little disturbed with fumes by reason of his singular abstinence, that he had no need of any such invention. As to his military experience, he was excellent in all the qualities of a great captain, as it was likely he should, being almost all his life in a continual exercise of war, and most of that time with us in France, against the Germans and Franks: we hardly read of any man who ever saw more dangers, or who made more frequent proofs of his personal valor.

His death has something in it parallel with that of Epaminondas, for he was wounded with an arrow, and tried to pull it out, and had done so, but that, being edged, it cut and disabled his hand. He incessantly called out, that they should carry him again into the heat of the battle to encourage his soldiers, who very bravely disputed the fight without him, till night parted the armies. He stood obliged to his philosophy for the singular contempt he had for his life, and all human things. He had a firm belief of the immortality of the soul.

In matter of religion, he was wrong throughout; and was surnamed the Apostate for having relinquished ours; though, methinks, 'tis more likely that he had never thoroughly embraced it, but had dissembled out of obedience to the laws, till he came to the empire. He was in his own so superstitious, that he was laughed at for it by those of his own time, of the same opinion, who jeeringly said, that had he got the victory over the Parthians, he had destroyed the breed of oxen in the world to supply his sacrifices. He was, moreover, besotted with the art of divination, and gave authority to all sorts of predictions. He said, among other things, at his death, that he was obliged to the gods, and thanked them, in that they would not cut him off by surprise, having long before advertised him of the place and hour of his death, nor by a mean and unmanly death, more becoming lazy and delicate people; nor by a death that was languishing, long, and painful; and that they had thought him worthy to die after that noble manner, in the progress of his victories, in the flower of his glory. He had a vision like that of Marcus Brutus, that first threatened him in Gaul, and afterward appeared to him in Persia just before his death. These words that some make him say when he felt himself wounded: "Thou hast overcome, Nazarene;" or as others, "Content thyself, Nazarene;" would hardly have been omitted, had they been believed, by my witnesses who, being present in the army, have set down to the least motions and words of his end; no more than certain other miracles that are reported about it.

And to return to my subject, he long nourished, says Marcellinus, paganism in his heart; but all his army being Christians, he dared not own it. But in the end, seeing himself strong enough to dare to discover himself, he caused the temples of the gods to be thrown open, and did his utmost to set on foot and to encourage idolatry. Which the better to effect, having at Constantinople found the people disunited, and also the prelates of the Church divided among themselves, having convened them all before him, he earnestly admonished them to calm those civil dissensions, and that every one might freely, and without fear, follow his own religion. Which he the more sedulously solicited, in hope that this license would augment the schisms and factions of their division, and hinder the people from reuniting, and consequently fortifying themselves against him by their unanimous intelligence and concord; having experience by the cruelty of some Christians, that there is no beast in the world so much to be feared by man as man; these are very nearly his words.

Therein this is very worthy of consideration, that the Emperor Julian made use of the same receipt of liberty of conscience to inflame the civil dissensions, that our kings do to extinguish them. So that a man may say on one side, that to give the people the reins to entertain every man his own opinion, is to scatter and sow division, and, as it were, to lend a hand to augment it, there being no legal impediment or restraint to stop or hinder their career; but, on the other side, a man may also say, that to give the people the reins to entertain every man his own opinion, is to mollify and appease them by facility and toleration, and to dull the point which is whetted and made sharper by singularity, novelty, and difficulty: and I think it is better for the honor of the devotion of our kings, that not having been able to do what they would, they have made a show of being willing to do what they could.

OF VIRTUE.

I find by experience, that there is a vast difference between the starts and sallies of the soul, and a resolute and constant habit; and very well perceive that there is nothing we may not do, nay, even to the surpassing the Divinity itself, says a certain person, forasmuch as it is more to render a man's self impassible by his own study and industry, than to be so by his natural condition; and even to be able to conjoin to man's imbecility and frailty a God-like resolution and assurance; but it is by fits and starts; and in the lives of those heroes of times past there are sometimes miraculous sallies, and that seem infinitely to exceed our natural force; but they are indeed only sallies and 'tis hard to believe, that these so elevated qualities in a man can so thoroughly tinct and imbue the soul that they should become ordinary, and, as it were, natural in him.

It accidentally happens even to us, who are but abortive births of men, sometimes to dart out our souls, when roused by the discourses or example of others, much beyond their ordinary stretch; but 'tis a kind of passion which pushes and pricks them on, and in some sort ravishes them from themselves: but, this whirlwind once blown over, we see that they insensibly flag and slacken of themselves, if not to the lowest degree, at least so as to be no more the same; insomuch as that upon every trivial occasion, the losing of a hawk, or the breaking of a glass, we suffer ourselves to be moved little less than one of the common people. I am of opinion that, order, moderation, and constancy excepted, all things are to be done by a man that is very imperfect and defective in general. Therefore it is, say the Sages, that to make a right judgment of a man, you are chiefly to pry into his common actions, and surprise him in his everyday habit.

Pyrrho, he who erected so pleasant a knowledge upon ignorance, endeavored, as all the rest who were really philosophers did, to make his life correspond with his doctrine. And because he maintained the imbecility of human judgment to be so extreme as to be incapable of any choice or inclination, and would have it perpetually wavering and suspended, considering and receiving all things as indifferent, 'tis said, that he always comported himself after the same manner and countenance: if he had begun a discourse, he would always end what he had to say, though the person he was speaking to had gone away: if he walked, he never stopped for any impediment that stood in his way, being preserved from precipices, the jostle of carts, and other like accidents, by the care of his friends: for, to fear or to avoid anything, had been to shock his own propositions, which deprived the senses themselves of all election and certainty. Sometimes he suffered incision and cauteries with so great constancy, as never to be seen so much as to wince.

'Tis something to bring the soul to these imaginations; 'tis more to join the effects, and yet not impossible; but to conjoin them with such perseverance and constancy as to make them habitual, is certainly, in attempts so remote from the common usage, almost incredible to be done. Therefore it was, that being one day taken in his house terribly scolding with his sister, and being reproached that he therein transgressed his own rules of indifference: "What!" said he, "must this foolish woman also serve for a testimony to my rules?" Another time, being seen to defend himself against a dog: "It is," said he, "very hard totally to put off man; and we must endeavor and force ourselves to resist and encounter things, first by effects, but at least by reason and argument."

A few days since, at Bergerac, within five leagues of my house, up the river Dordogne, a woman having overnight been beaten and abused by her husband, a choleric ill-conditioned fellow, resolved to escape from his ill-usage at the price of her life; and going so soon as she was up the next morning to visit her neighbors, as she was wont to do, and having let some words fall in recommendation of her affairs, she took a sister of hers by the hand, and led her to the bridge; whither being come, and having taken leave of her in jest as it were, without any manner of alteration in her countenance, she threw herself headlong from the top into the river, and was there drowned. That which is the most remarkable in this is, that this resolution was a whole night forming in her head.

But is quite another thing with the Indian women; for it being the custom there for the men to have many wives, and the best beloved of them to kill herself at her husband's decease, every one of them makes it the business of her whole life to obtain this privilege and gain this advantage over her companions; and the good offices they do their husbands aim at no other recompense but to be preferred in accompanying him in death.

A certain author of our times reports that he has seen in those oriental nations this custom in practice, that not only the wives bury themselves with their husbands, but even the slaves he has enjoyed also; which is done after this manner: the husband being dead, the widow may if she will (but few will), demand two or three months' respite wherein to order her affairs. The day being come, she mounts on horseback, dressed as fine as at her wedding, and with a cheerful countenance says she is going to sleep with her spouse, holding a looking-glass in her left hand and an arrow in the other. Being thus conducted in pomp, accompanied with her kindred and friends and a great concourse of people in great joy, she is at last brought to the public place appointed for such spectacles: this is a great space, in the midst of which is a pit full of wood, and adjoining to it a mount raised four or five steps, upon which she is brought and served with a magnificent repast: which being done, she falls to dancing and singing, and gives order, when she thinks fit, to kindle the fire. This being done, she descends, and taking the nearest of her husband's relations by the hand, they walk to the river close by, where she strips herself stark naked, and having distributed her clothes and jewels to her friends plunges herself into the water, as if there to cleanse herself from her sins; coming out thence, she wraps herself in a yellow linen of five-and-twenty ells long, and again giving her hand to this kinsman of her husband's, they return back to the mount, where she makes a speech to the people, and recommends her children to them, if she have any. Between the pit and the mount there is commonly a curtain drawn to screen the burning furnace from their sight, which some of them, to manifest the greater courage, forbid. Having ended what she has to say, a woman presents her with a vessel of oil, wherewith to anoint her head and her whole body, which when done with she throws into the fire, and in an instant precipitates herself after. Immediately, the people throw a great many billets and logs upon her that she may not be long in dying, and convert all their joy into sorrow and mourning.

If they are persons of meaner condition, the body of the defunct is carried to the place of sepulture, and there placed sitting, the widow kneeling before him, embracing the dead body; and they continue in this posture while the people build a wall about them, which so soon as it is raised to the height of the woman's shoulders, one of her relations comes behind her, and taking hold of her head, twists her neck; so soon as she is dead, the wall is presently raised up, and closed, and there they remain entombed.

There was, in this same country, something like this in their gymnosophists; for not by constraint of others nor by the impetuosity of a sudden humor, but by the express profession of their order, their custom was, as soon as they arrived at a certain age, or that they saw themselves threatened by any disease, to cause a funeral pile to be erected for them, and on the top a stately bed, where, after having joyfully feasted their friends and acquaintance, they laid them down with so great resolution, that fire being applied to it, they were never seen to stir either hand or foot; and after this manner, one of them, Calanus by name, expired in the presence of the whole army of Alexander the Great. And he was neither reputed holy nor happy among them, who did not thus destroy himself, dismissing his soul purged and purified by the fire, after having consumed all that was earthly and mortal. This constant premeditation of the whole life is that which makes the wonder.

Among our other controversies, that of *Fatum* has also crept in; and to tie things to come, and even our own wills, to a certain and inevitable necessity, we are yet upon this argument of time past; "Since God foresees that all things shall so fall out, as doubtless He does, it must then necessarily follow, that they must so fall out;" to which our masters reply: "that the seeing anything come to pass as we do, and as God Himself also does (for all things being present with Him, He rather sees, than foresees) is not to compel an event: that is, we see because things do fall out, but things do not fall out because we see: events cause knowledge, but knowledge does not cause events. That which we see happen, does happen; but it might have happened otherwise: and God, in the catalogue of the causes of events which He has in his prescience, has also those which we call accidental and voluntary, depending upon the liberty. He has given our free will, and knows that we do amiss because we would do so."

I have seen a great many commanders encourage their soldiers with this fatal necessity: for if our time be limited to a certain hour, neither the enemies' shot, nor our own boldness, nor our flight and cowardice, can either shorten or prolong our lives. This is easily said, but see who will be so persuaded; and if it be so that a strong and lively faith draws along with it actions of the same kind, certainly this faith we so much brag of, is very light in this age of ours, unless the contempt it has of works makes it disdain their company.

So it is, that to this very purpose the Sire de Joinville, as credible a witness as any other whatever, tells us of the Bedouins, a nation among the Saracens, with whom the king St. Louis had to do in the Holy Land, that they, in their religion, so firmly believe the number of every man's days to be from all eternity prefixed and set down by an inevitable decree, that they went naked to the wars, excepting a Turkish sword, and their bodies only covered with a white linen cloth: and for the greatest curse they could invent when they were angry, this was always in their mouths: "Accursed be thou, as he that arms himself for fear of death." This is a testimony of faith very much beyond ours. And of this sort is that also that two friars of Florence gave in our fathers' days. Being engaged in some controversy of learning, they agreed to go both of them into the fire in the sight of all the people, each for the verification of his argument, and all things were already prepared, and the thing just upon the point of execution, when it was interrupted by an unexpected accident.

A young Turkish lord, having performed a notable exploit in his own person in the sight of both armies, that of Amurath and that of Huniades, ready to join battle, being asked by Amurath, what in such tender and inexperienced years (for it was his first sally into arms) had inspired him with so brave a courage, replied, that his chief tutor for valor was a hare. "For being," said he, "one day a-hunting, I found a hare sitting, and though I had a brace of excellent greyhounds with me, yet methought it would be best for sureness to make use of my bow; for she sat very fair. I then fell to letting fly my arrows, and shot forty that I had in my quiver, not only without hurting, but without starting her from her form. At last I slipped my dogs after her, but to no more purpose than I had shot: by which I understood that she had been secured by her destiny; and that neither darts nor swords can wound without the permission of fate, which we can neither hasten nor defer." This story may serve, by the way, to let us see how flexible our reason is to all sorts of images.

A person of great years, name, dignity, and learning, boasted to me that he had been induced to a certain very important change in his faith by a strange and whimsical incitation, and one otherwise so inadequate, that I thought it much stronger, taken the contrary way: he called it a miracle, and so I look upon it, but in a different sense. The Turkish historians say, that the persuasion those of their nation have imprinted in them of the fatal and unalterable prescription of their days, manifestly conduces to the giving them great assurance in dangers. And I know a great prince who makes very fortunate use of it, whether it may be that he really believes it, or that he makes it his excuse for so wonderfully hazarding himself: let us hope Fortune may not be too soon weary of her favor to him.

There has not happened in our memory a more admirable effect of resolution, than in those two who conspired the death of the Prince of Orange. 'Tis marvellous how the second who executed it, could ever be persuaded into an attempt, wherein his companion, who had done his utmost, had had so ill success; and after the same method, and with the same arms, to go attack a lord, armed with so recent a late lesson of distrust, powerful in followers and bodily strength, in his own hall, amid his guards, and in a city wholly at his devotion. Assuredly, he employed a very resolute arm and a courage inflamed with furious passion. A poniard is surer for striking home, but by reason that more motion and force of hand is required than with a pistol, the blow is more subject to be put by or hindered. That this man did not run to a certain death, I make no great doubt; for the hopes any one could flatter him withal, could not find place in any sober understanding, and the conduct of his exploit sufficiently manifests that he had no want of that, no more than of courage.

The motives of so powerful a persuasion may be diverse, for our fancy does what it will, both with itself and us. The execution that was done near Orleans was nothing like this; there was in this more of chance than vigor; the wound was not mortal, if fortune had not made it so, and to attempt to shoot on horseback, and at a great distance, by one whose body was in motion from the motion of his horse, was the attempt of a man who had rather miss his blow than fail of saving himself. This was apparent from what followed; for he was so astonished and stupefied with the thought of so high an execution, that he totally lost his judgment both to find his way to flight and to govern his tongue. What needed he to have done more than to fly back to his friends across a river? 'Tis what I have done in less dangers, and that I think of very little hazard, how broad soever the river may be, provided your horse have easy going in, and that you see on the other side easy landing according to the stream. The other, when they pronounced his dreadful sentence, "I was prepared for this," said he, "beforehand, and I will make you wonder at my patience."

The Assassins, a nation bordering upon Phœnicia, are reputed among the Mohammedans a people of very great devotion, and purity of manners. They hold that the nearest way to gain paradise is to kill some one of a contrary religion; which is the reason they have often been seen, being but one or two, and without armor, to attempt against powerful enemies at the price of a certain death and without any consideration of their own danger. So was our Count Raymond of Tripoli assassinated (which word is derived from their name) in the heart of his city, during our enterprises of the Holy War: and likewise Conrad, marquis of Monserrat, the murderers at their execution bearing themselves with great pride and glory that they had performed so brave an exploit.

OF ANGER.

Plutarch is admirable throughout, but especially where he judges of human actions. What fine things does he say in the comparison of Lycurgus and Numa upon the subject of our great folly in abandoning children to the care and government of their fathers? The most of our civil governments, as Aristotle says, leave, after the manner of the Cyclops, to every one the ordering of their wives and children, according to their own foolish and indiscreet fancy; and the Lacedæmonian and Cretan are almost the only governments that have committed the education of children to the laws. Who does not see that in a state all depends upon their nurture and bringing up? and yet they are left to the mercy of parents, let them be as foolish and ill-conditioned as they may, without any manner of discretion.

Among other things, how often have I, as I have passed along our streets, had a good mind to get up a farce, to revenge the poor boys whom I have seen flayed, knocked down, and miserably beaten by some father or mother, when in their fury, and mad with rage? You shall see them come out with fire and fury sparkling in their eyes — or, as Juvenal says, "Borne headlong with burning fury as great stones torn from the mountains, by which the steep sides are left naked and bare" (and according to Hippocrates, the most dangerous maladies are they that disfigure the countenance) — with a roaring and terrible voice, very often against those that are but newly come from nurse, and there they are lamed and spoiled with blows, while our justice takes no cognizance of it, as if these maims and dislocations were not executed upon members of our commonwealth. "It is well when to thy country and the people thou hast given a citizen, provided thou make him fit for his country's service; useful to till the earth, useful in affairs of war and peace."

There is no passion that so much transports men from their right judgment as anger. No one would demur upon punishing a judge with death who should condemn a criminal on the account of his own choler; why, then, should fathers and pedagogues be any more allowed to whip and chastise children in their anger? 'Tis then no longer correction, but revenge. Chastisement is instead of physic to children; and should we endure a physician who should be animated against and enraged at his patient?

We ourselves, to do well, should never lay a hand upon our servants while our anger lasts. When the pulse beats, and we feel emotion in ourselves, let us defer the business; things will indeed appear otherwise to us when we are calm and cool. 'Tis passion that then commands, 'tis passion that speaks, and not we. Faults seen through passion appear much greater to us than they really are, as bodies do when seen through a mist. He who is hungry uses meat; but he who will make use of chastisement should have neither hunger nor thirst to it. And moreover, chastisements that are inflicted with weight and discretion, are much better received and with greater benefit by him who suffers; otherwise, he will not think himself justly condemned by a man transported with anger and fury, and will allege his master's excessive passion, his inflamed countenance, his unwonted oaths, his emotion and precipitous rashness, for his own justification: "Their faces swell, their veins grow black with rage, and their eyes sparkle with Gorgonian fire" [Ovid].

Suetonius reports that Caius Rabirius having been condemned by Caesar, the thing that most prevailed upon the people (to whom he had appealed) to determine the cause in his favor, was the animosity and vehemence that Caesar had manifested in that sentence.

Saying is one thing and doing is another; we are to consider the sermon and the preacher distinctly and apart. Though men have had a pretty business in hand, who in our times have attempted to shake the truth of our Church by the vices of her ministers, she extracts her testimony elsewhere; for 'tis a foolish way of arguing and that would throw all things into confusion. A man, whose morals are good, may have false opinions, and a wicked man may preach truth, even though he believe it not himself. 'Tis doubtless a fine harmony when doing and saying go together; and I will not deny but that saying, when the actions follow, is not of greater authority and efficacy, as Eudamidas said, hearing a philosopher talk of military affairs: "These things are finely said, but he who speaks them is not to be believed, for his ears have never been used to the sound of the trumpet." And Cleomenes, hearing an orator declaiming upon valor, burst out into laughter, at which the other being angry: "I should," said he to him, "do the same if it were a swallow that spoke of this subject; but if it were an eagle I should willingly hear him."

I perceive, methinks, in the writings of the ancients, that he who speaks what he thinks, strikes much more home than he who only feigns. Hear Cicero speak of the love of liberty; hear Brutus speak of it, the mere written words of this man sound as if he would purchase it at the price of his life. Let Cicero, the father of eloquence, treat of the contempt of death; let Seneca do the same; the first languishingly drawls it out, so that you perceive he would make you resolve upon a thing on which he is not resolved himself; he inspires you not with courage, for he himself has none; the other animates and inflames you. I never read an author, even of those who treat of virtue and of actions, that I do not curiously inquire what kind of a man he was himself; for the Ephori at Sparta, seeing a dissolute fellow propose a wholesome advice to the people, commanded him to hold his peace, and entreated a virtuous man to attribute to himself the invention, and to propose it.

Plutarch's writings, if well understood, sufficiently bespeak their author, and so that I think I know him even into his soul; and yet I could wish that we had some fuller account of his life. And I am thus far wandered from my subject, upon the account of the obligation I have to Aulus Gellius, for having left us in writing this story of his manners, that brings me back to my subject of anger.

A slave of his, a vicious, ill-conditioned fellow, but who had the precepts of philosophy often ringing in his ears, having for some offence of his been stripped by Plutarch's command, while he was being whipped, muttered at first, that it was without cause and that he had done nothing to deserve it; but at last falling in good earnest to exclaim against and rail at his master, he reproached him that he was no philosopher, as he had boasted himself to be: that he had often heard him say it was indecent to be angry, nay, had written a book to that purpose; and that the causing him to be so cruelly beaten, in the height of his rage, totally gave the lie to all his writings, to which Plutarch calmly and coldly answered: "How, ruffian," said he, "by what dost thou judge that I am now angry? Does either my face, my color, or my voice give any manifestation of my being moved? I do not think my eyes look fierce, that my countenance appears troubled, or that my voice is dreadful; am I red, do I foam, does any word escape my lips I ought to repent? Do I start? Do I tremble with fury? For those, I tell thee, are the true signs of anger." And so turning to the fellow that was whipping him, "Ply on thy work," said he, "while this gentleman and I dispute." This is the story.

Archytas Tarentinus, returning from a war wherein he had been captain-general, found all things in his house in very great disorder, and his lands quite out of tillage, through the ill husbandry of his receiver, and having caused him to be called to him: "Go," said he, "if I were not in anger I would soundly drub your sides." Plato likewise, being highly offended with one of his slaves, gave Speusippus order to chastise him, excusing himself from doing it because he was in anger. And Carillus, a Lacedaemonian, to a Helot, who carried himself insolently toward him: "By the gods," said he, "if I was not angry, I would immediately cause thee to be put to death."

'Tis a passion that is pleased with and flatters itself. How often, being moved under a false cause, if the person offending makes a good defence and presents us with a just excuse, are we angry against truth and innocence itself? In proof of which, I remember a marvellous example of antiquity.

Piso, otherwise a man of very eminent virtue, being moved against a soldier of his, for that returning alone from forage he could give him no account where he had left a companion of his, took it for granted that he had killed him, and presently condemned him to death. He was no sooner mounted upon the gibbet, but behold his wandering companion arrives, at which all the army were exceedingly glad, and after many embraces of the two comrades, the hangman carried both the one and the other into Piso's presence, all those present believing it would be a great pleasure even to himself; but it proved quite contrary; for through shame and spite, his fury, which was not yet cool, redoubled; and by a subtlety which his passion suddenly suggested to him, he made three criminal for having found one innocent, and caused them all to be despatched: the first soldier, because sentence had passed upon him; the second, who had lost his way because he was the cause of his companion's death; and the hangman, for not having obeyed the order which had been given him.

Such as have had to do with testy and obstinate women, may have experimented into what a rage it puts them, to oppose silence and coldness to their fury, and that a man disdains to nourish their anger. The orator Celius was wonderfully choleric by nature; and to one who supped in his company, a man of a gentle and sweet conversation, and who, that he might not move him, approved and consented to all he said; he, impatient that his ill humor should thus spend itself without ailment: "For the love of the gods deny me something," said he, "that we may be two." Women, in like manner, are only angry, that others may be angry again, in imitation of the laws of love. Phocion, to one who interrupted his speaking by injurious and very opprobrious words, made no other return than silence, and to give him full liberty and leisure to vent his spleen; which he having accordingly done, and the storm blown over without any mention of this disturbance, he proceeded in his discourse where he had left off before. No answer can nettle a man like such a contempt.

Of the most choleric man in France (anger is always an imperfection, but more excusable in a soldier, for in that trade it cannot sometimes be avoided) I often say, that he is the most patient man that I know, and the most discreet in bridling his passions; which rise in him with so great violence and fury, — "When with loud crackling noise, a fire of sticks is applied to the boiling caldron's side, by the heat in frisky bells the liquor dances: but within the water rages and high the smoky fluid in foam overflows. Nor can the wave now contain itself: in pitchy steam it flies all abroad " [*Æneid*], — that he must of necessity cruelly constrain himself to moderate it. And for my part, I know no passion which I could with so much violence to myself attempt to cover and conceal: I would not set wisdom at so high a price; and do not so much consider what a man does, as how much it costs him to do no worse.

Another boasted himself to me of the regularity and sweetness of his manners, which are in truth very singular; to whom I replied, that it was indeed something, especially in persons of so eminent a quality as himself, upon whom every one had their eyes, to present himself always well-tempered to the world; but that the principal thing was to make provision for within and for himself; and that it was not, in my opinion, very well to order his business inwardly to grate himself, which I was afraid he did in putting on and outwardly maintaining this visor and regular appearance.

A man incorporates anger by concealing it, as Diogenes told Demosthenes, who, for fear of being seen in a tavern, withdrew himself the more retiredly into it: "The more you retire, the farther you enter in." I would rather advise that a man should give his servant a box of the ear a little unseasonably, than rack his fancy to present this grave and composed countenance; and had rather discover my passions than brood over them at my own expense; they grow less in venting and manifesting themselves; and 'tis much better their point should wound others without, than be turned toward ourselves within. "All vices are less dangerous when open to be seen, and then most pernicious when they lurk under a dissembled good nature," says Seneca.

I admonish all those who have authority to be angry in my family, in the first place to manage their anger and not to lavish it upon every occasion, for that both lessens the value and hinders the effect: rash and incessant scolding runs into custom, and renders itself despised; and what you lay out upon a servant for a theft, is not felt, because it is the same he has seen you a hundred times employ against him for having ill washed a glass, or set a stool out of place. Secondly, that they be not angry to no purpose, but make sure that their reprehension reach him with whom they are offended; for, ordinarily, they rail and bawl before he comes into their presence, and continue scolding an age after he is gone; "*Et secum petulans amentia certat:*" they attack his shadow, and drive the storm in a place where no one is either chastised or concerned, but in the clamor of their voice. I likewise in quarrels condemn those who huff and vapor without an enemy; those rodomontades should be reserved to discharge upon the offending party: "As when a bull to usher in the fight makes dreadful bellowings, and whets his horns against the trunk of a tree, with blows he beats the air, and preludes to the fight by spurning the sand" [*Æneid*].

When I am angry, my anger is very sharp but withal very short, and as private as I can; I lose myself indeed in promptness and violence, but not in trouble; so that I throw out all sorts of injurious words at random, and without choice, and never consider pertinently to dart my language where I think it will deepest wound, for I commonly make use of no other weapon in my anger than my tongue. My servants have a better bargain of me in great occasions than in little; the light ones surprise me; and the mischief on't is, that when you are once upon the precipice, 'tis no matter who gave you the push, for you always go to the bottom; the fall urges, moves, and makes haste of itself. In great occasions this satisfies me, that they are so just every one expects a reasonable indignation, and then I glorify myself in deceiving their expectation; against these, I fortify and prepare myself; they disturb my head, and threaten to transport me very far, should I follow them. I can easily contain myself from entering into one of these passions, and am strong enough, when I expect them, to repel their violence, be the cause never so great; but if a passion once prepossess and seize me, it carries me away, be the cause never so small. I bargain thus with those who may contend with me; when you see me moved first, let me alone, right or wrong; I'll do the same for you. The storm is only begot by a concurrence of angers, which easily spring from one another, and are not born together. Let every one have his own way, and we shall be always at peace.

A profitable advice, but hard to execute. Sometimes also it falls out that I put on a seeming anger, for the better governing of my house, without any real emotion. As age renders my humors more sharp, I study to oppose them, and will, if I can, order it so, that for the future I may be so much the less peevish and hard to please, as I have more excuse and inclination to be so, although I have heretofore been reckoned among those who have the greatest patience.

A word more to conclude this chapter. Aristotle says, that anger sometimes serves for arms to virtue and valor. 'Tis likely it may be so, nevertheless, they who contradict him pleasantly answer, that 'tis a weapon of novel use, for we move all other arms, this moves us; our hands guide it not, 'tis it that guides our hands; it holds us, we hold not it.

OF PROFIT AND HONESTY.

No man is free from speaking foolish things; but the worst on't is, when a man studies to play the fool. "Truly he, with a great effort, will say some mighty trifle," says Terence.

This does not concern me; mine slip from me with as little care as they are of little value, and 'tis the better for them. I would presently part with them for what they are worth, and neither buy nor sell them, but as they weigh. I speak on paper as I do to the first person I meet; and that this is true, observe what follows.

To whom ought not treachery to be hateful when Tiberius refused it in a thing of so great importance to him? He had word sent him from Germany that if he thought fit, they would rid him of Arminius by poison: this was the most potent enemy the Romans had, who had defeated them so ignominiously under Varus, and who alone prevented their aggrandizement in those parts. He returned answer, "that the people of Rome were wont to revenge themselves of their enemies by open ways, and with their swords in their hands, and not clandestinely and by fraud: "wherein he quitted the profitable for the honest. You will tell me that he was a braggadocio; I believe so too: and 'tis no great miracle in men of his profession. But the acknowledgment of virtue is not less valid in the mouth of him who hates it, forasmuch as truth forces it from him, and if he will not inwardly receive it, he at least puts it on for a decoration.

Our outward and inward structure is full of imperfection; but there is nothing useless in nature, not even inutility itself; nothing has insinuated itself into this universe that has not therein some fit and proper place. Our being is cemented with sickly qualities: ambition, jealousy, envy, revenge, superstition, and despair have so natural a possession in us, that its image is discerned in beasts; nay, and cruelty, so unnatural a vice; for even in the midst of compassion we feel within I know not what tart-sweet titillation of ill-natured pleasure in seeing others suffer; and the children feel it: "It is sweet, when the winds disturb the waters of the vast sea, to witness from land the peril of other persons "[Lucretius]; of the seeds of which qualities, whoever should divest men would destroy the fundamental conditions of human life.

Likewise, in all governments there are necessary offices, not only abject, but vicious also. Vices there help to make up the seam in our piecing, as poisons are useful for the conservation of health. If they become excusable because they are of use to us, and that the common necessity covers their true qualities, we are to resign this part to the strongest and boldest citizens, who sacrifice their honor and conscience as others of old sacrificed their lives, for the good of their country: we who are weaker, take upon us parts both that are more easy and less hazardous. The public weal requires that men should betray, and lie, and massacre; let us leave this commission to men who are more obedient and more supple.

In earnest, I have often been troubled to see judges, by fraud and false hopes of favor or pardon, allure a criminal to confess his fact, and therein to make use of cozenage and impudence. It would become justice, and Plato himself, who countenances this manner of proceeding, to furnish me with other means more suitable to my own liking: this is a malicious kind of justice; and I look upon it as no less wounded by itself than by others. I said not long since to some company in discourse, that I should hardly be drawn to betray my prince for a particular man, who should be much ashamed to betray any particular man for my prince; and I do not only hate deceiving myself, but that any one should deceive through me; I will neither afford matter nor occasion to any such thing.

In the little I have had to mediate between our princes[1] in the divisions and subdivisions by which we are at this time torn to pieces, I have been very careful that they should neither be deceived in me, nor deceive others by me. People of that kind of trading are very reserved, and pretend to be the most moderate imaginable and nearest to the opinions of those with whom they have to do; I expose myself in my stiff opinion, and after a method the most my own; a tender negotiator, a novice, who had rather fail in the affair than be wanting to myself. And yet it has been hitherto with so good luck (for fortune has doubtless the best share in it), that few things have passed from hand to hand with less suspicion or more favor and privacy. I have a free and open way that easily insinuates itself and obtains belief with those with whom I am to deal, at the first meeting.

Sincerity and pure truth, in what age soever, pass for current: and besides, the liberty and freedom of a man who treats without any interest of his own, is never hateful or suspected, and he may very well make use of the answer of Hyperides to the Athenians, who complained of his blunt way of speaking: "My masters, do not consider whether or no I am free, but whether I am so without a bribe, or without any advantage to my own affairs." My liberty of speaking has also easily cleared me from all suspicion of dissembling by its vehemency, leaving nothing unsaid, how harsh and bitter soever (so that I could have said no worse behind their backs), and in that it carried along with it a manifest show of simplicity and indifference. I pretend

---

[1] Between the King of Navarre, afterward Henry IV., and the Duc de Guise.

to no other fruit by acting than to act, and add to it no long arguments or propositions; every action plays its own game, win if it can.

As to the rest, I am not swayed by any passion, either of love or hatred, toward the great, nor have my will captivated either by particular injury or obligation. I look upon our kings with an affection simply loyal and respectful, neither prompted nor restrained by any private interest, and I love myself for it. Nor does the general and just cause attract me otherwise than with moderation, and without heat. I am not subject to those penetrating and close compacts and engagements. Anger and hatred are beyond the duty of justice; and are passions only useful to those who do not keep themselves strictly to their duty by simple reason: "*Utatur motu animi, qui uti ratione non potest.*" All legitimate and equitable intentions are temperate and equable of themselves; if otherwise, they degenerate into seditious and unlawful. This is it which makes me walk everywhere with my head erect, my face and my heart open. To confess the truth, and I am not afraid to confess it, I should easily, in case of need, hold up one candle to St. Michael and another to his dragon, like the old woman; I will follow the right side even to the fire, but excluding the fire if I can. Let Montaigne be overwhelmed in the public ruin, if need be; but if there be no need, I should think myself obliged to fortune to save me, and I will make use of all the length of line my duty allows for his preservation.

Was it not Atticus, who being of the just but losing side, preserved himself by his moderation in that universal shipwreck of the world, among so many mutations and diversities? For private man, as he was, it is more easy; and in such kind of work, I think a man may justly not be ambitious to offer and insinuate himself. For a man, indeed, to be wavering and irresolute, to keep his affection unmoved and without inclination in the troubles of his country and public divisions, I neither think it handsome nor honest: "That is not a middle way, but no way, to await events, by which they refer their resolutions to fortune" [Livy]. This may be allowed in our neighboring affairs, and thus Gelo the tyrant of Syracuse suspended his inclination in the war between the Greeks and barbarians, keeping a resident ambassador with presents at Delphos, to watch and see which way fortune would incline, and then take fit occasion to fall in with the victors.

It would be a kind of treason to proceed after this manner in our own domestic affairs, wherein a man must of necessity be of the one side or the other; though for a man who has no office or express command to call him out, to sit still, I hold it more excusable (and yet I do not excuse myself upon these terms) than in foreign expeditions,

to which, however, according to our laws, no man is pressed against his
will. And yet even those who wholly engage themselves in such a war,
may behave themselves with such temper and moderation that the
storm may fly over their heads without doing them any harm.

Had we not reason to hope such an issue in the person of the late
Sieur de Morvilliers, bishop of Orleans? And I know among those
who behave themselves most bravely in the present war, some whose
manners are so gentle, obliging, and just, that they will certainly stand
firm, whatever event Heaven is preparing for us. I am of opinion that
it properly belongs to kings only to quarrel with kings; and I laugh at
those bully-rooks who, out of wantonness of courage, present themselves to so disproportioned disputes; for a man has never the more
particular quarrel with a prince, by marching openly and boldly
against him for his own honor and according to his duty; if he does
not love such a person, he does better, he esteems him. And notably
the cause of the laws and of the ancient government of a kingdom has
this always annexed to it, that even those, who for their own private
interest invade them, excuse, if they do not honor, the defenders.

But we are not, as we nowadays do, to call peevishness and inward
discontent, that spring from private interest and passion, duty: nor a
treacherous and malicious conduct, courage. They call their propension to mischief and violence, zeal: 'tis not the cause, but their
interest, that inflames them; they kindle and begin a war, not because
it is just, but because it is war.

A man may very well behave himself commodiously, and loyally
too, among those of the adverse party; carry yourself if not with the
same equal affection (for that is capable of different measure), at least
with an affection moderate, well-tempered, and such as shall not so
engage you to one party, that it may demand all you are able to do
for that side, content yourself with a moderate proportion of their
favor and good-will; and to swim in troubled waters without fishing
in them.

The other way, of offering a man's self and the utmost service he
is able to do, both to one party and the other, has still less of prudence
in it than conscience. Does not he to whom you betray another, to
whom you were as welcome as to himself, know that you will at
another time do as much for him? He holds you for a villain; and in
the meantime hears what you will say, gathers intelligence from you,
and works his own ends out of your disloyalty; double-dealing men
are useful for bringing in, but we must have a care they carry out as
little as is possible.

I say nothing to one party, that I may not, upon occasion, say to
the other, with a little alteration of accent; and report nothing but

things either indifferent or known, or what is of common consequence. I cannot permit myself, for any consideration, to tell them a lie. What is intrusted to my secrecy, I religiously conceal; but I take as few trusts of that nature upon me as I can. The secrets of princes are a troublesome burthen to such as are not interested in them. I very willingly bargain that they trust me with little, but confidently rely upon what I tell them. I have ever known more than I desired. One open way of speaking introduces another open way of speaking, and draws out discoveries, like wine and love. Phillipides, in my opinion, answered King Lysimachus very discreetly, who, asking him what of his estate he should bestow upon him? "What you will," said he, "provided it be none of your secrets." I see every one is displeased if the bottom of the affair be concealed from him wherein he is employed, or that there be any reservation in the thing: for my part, I am content to know no more of the business than what they would have me employ myself in, nor desire that my knowledge should exceed or restrict what I have to say. If I must serve for an instrument of deceit, let it be at least with a safe conscience; I will not be reputed a servant either so affectionate, or so loyal, as to be fit to betray any one: he who is unfaithful to himself, is excusably so to his master.

But they are princes who do not accept men by halves, and despise limited and conditional services; I cannot help it; I frankly tell them how far I can go; for a slave I should not be, but to reason, and I can hardly submit even to that. And they also are to blame to exact from a freeman the same subjection and obligation to their service that they do from him they have made and bought, or whose fortune particularly and expressly depends upon theirs. The laws have delivered me from a great anxiety; they have chosen a side for me, and given me a master; all other superiority and obligation ought to be relative to that, and cut off from all other. Yet this is not to say, that if my affection should otherwise incline me, my hand should presently obey it; the will and desire are a law to themselves; but actions must receive commission from the public appointment.

All this proceeding of mine is a little dissonant from the ordinary forms; it would produce no great effects, nor be of any long duration; innocence itself could not, in this age of ours, either negotiate without dissimulation, or traffic without lying; and, indeed, public employments are by no means for my palate; what my profession requires, I perform after the most private manner that I can. Being young, I was engaged up to the ears in business, and it succeeded well; but I disengaged myself in good time. I have often since avoided meddling in it, rarely accepted, and never asked it; keeping my back still turned to ambition; but, if not like rowers who so advance

backward, yet so, at the same time, that I am less obliged to my resolution than to my good fortune, that I was not wholly embarked in
it. For there are ways less displeasing to my taste, and more suitable
to my ability, by which, if she had formerly called me to the public
service, and my own advancement toward the world's opinion, I
know I should, in spite of all my own arguments to the contrary, have
pursued them. Such as commonly say, in opposition to what I profess,
that what I call freedom, simplicity, and plainness in my manners, is
art and subtlety, and rather prudence than goodness, industry than
nature, good sense than good luck, do me more honor than disgrace;
but, certainly, they make my subtlety too subtle: and whoever has
followed me close, and pried narrowly into me, I will give him the
victory, if he does not confess that there is no rule in their school that
could match this natural motion, and maintain an appearance of liberty and license, so equal and inflexible, through so many various and
crooked paths, and that all their wit and endeavor could never have
led them through.

The way of truth is one and simple; that of particular profit, and
the commodity of affairs a man is intrusted with, is double, unequal,
and casual. I have often seen these counterfeit and artificial liberties
practised, but for the most part, without success; they relish of Æsop's
ass who, in emulation of the dog, obligingly clapped his two fore feet
upon his master's shoulders; but as many caresses as the dog had for
such an expression of kindness, twice as many blows with a cudgel
had the poor ass for his compliment. Says Cicero, "That best becomes
every man, that he is best at." I will not deprive deceit of its due; that
were but ill to understand the world; I know it has often been of great
use, and that it maintains and supplies most men's employment.
There are vices that are lawful, as there are many actions, either good
or excusable, that are not lawful in themselves.

The justice which in itself is natural and universal, is otherwise and
more nobly ordered, than that other justice, which is special, national,
and constrained to the ends of government. Cicero says further, "We
retain no solid and express effigies of true right and justice; we have
only the shadow and images of it." Insomuch that the sage Dandamis,
hearing the lives of Socrates, Pythagoras, and Diogenes read, judged
them to be great men every way, excepting that they were too much
subjected to the reverence of the laws which, to second and authorize, true virtue must abate very much of its original vigor; many
vicious actions are introduced, not only by their permission, but by
their advice. "Crimes are committed by the consent of the magistrates
and the common laws," says Seneca. I follow the common phrase that
distinguishes between profitable and honest things, so as to call some

natural actions, that are not only profitable but necessary, dishonest, and foul.

But let us proceed in our examples of treachery: Two pretenders to the kingdom of Thrace were fallen into dispute about their title; the emperor hindered them from proceeding to blows: but one of them, under color of bringing things to a friendly issue by an interview, having invited his competitor to an entertainment in his own house, imprisoned and killed him. Justice required that the Romans should have satisfaction for this offence; but there was a difficulty in obtaining it by ordinary ways; what, therefore, they could not do legitimately, without war and without danger, they resolved to do by treachery; and what they could not honestly do, they did profitably. For which end, one Pomponius Flaccus was found to be a fit instrument. This man, by dissembled words and assurances, having drawn the other into his toils, instead of the honor and favor he had promised him, sent him bound hand and foot to Rome. Here one traitor betrayed another, contrary to common custom: for they are full of mistrust, and 'tis hard to overreach them in their own art: witness the sad experience we have lately had.[1]

Let who will be Pomponius Flaccus, and there are enough who would: for my part, both my word and my faith are, like all the rest, parts of this common body: their best effect is the public service; this I take for presupposed. But should one command me to take charge of the courts of law and lawsuits, I should make answer, that I understood it not; or the place of a leader of pioneers, I would say, that I was called to a more honorable employment; so likewise, he that would employ me to lie, betray, and forswear myself, though not to assassinate or to poison, for some notable service, I should say, "If I have robbed or stolen anything from any man, send me rather to the galleys." For it is permissible in a man of honor to say, as the Lacedæmonians did, having been defeated by Antipater, when just upon concluding an agreement: "You may impose as heavy and ruinous taxes upon us as you please, but to command us to do shameful and dishonest things, you will lose your time, for it is to no purpose."

Every one ought to make the same vow to himself, that the kings of Egypt made their judges solemnly swear, that they would not do anything contrary to their consciences, though never so much commanded to it by themselves. In such commissions, there is evident mark of ignominy and condemnation; and he who gives it, at the

---

[1] Montaigne here probably refers to the feigned reconciliation between Catherine de Medici and Henry, Duc de Guise, in 1588.

same time accuses you, and gives it, if you understand it right, for a burden and a punishment. As much as the public affairs are bettered by your exploit, so much are your own the worse, and the better you behave yourself in it, 'tis so much the worse for yourself; and it will be no new thing, nor, peradventure, without some color of justice, if the same person ruin you, who set you on work.

If treachery can be in any case excusable, it must be only so when it is practised to chastise and betray treachery. There are examples enough of treacheries, not only rejected, but chastised and punished by those in favor of whom they were undertaken. Who is ignorant of Fabricius' sentence against the physician of Pyrrhus?

But this we also find recorded, that some persons have commanded a thing, who afterward have severely avenged the execution of it upon him they had employed, rejecting the reputation of so unbridled an authority, and disowning so abandoned and base a servitude and obedience. Jaropelc, duke of Russia, tampered with a gentleman of Hungary to betray Boleslaus, king of Poland, either by killing him, or by giving the Russians opportunity to do him some notable mischief. This worthy went ably to work; he was more assiduous than before in the service of that king, so that he obtained the honor to be of his council, and one of the chiefest in his trust. With these advantages, and taking an opportune occasion of his master's absence, he betrayed Vislicza, a great and rich city, to the Russians, which was entirely sacked and burned, and not only all the inhabitants of both sexes, young and old, put to the sword, but moreover a great number of neighboring gentry, whom he had drawn thither to that end. Jaropelc, his revenge being thus satisfied and his anger appeased, which was not, indeed, without pretence (for Boleslaus had highly offended him, and after the same manner) and sated with the fruit of this treachery, coming to consider the foulness of it, with a sound judgment and clear from passion, looked upon what had been done with so much horror and remorse, that he caused the eyes to be bored out and the tongue and shameful parts to be cut off of him who had performed it.

Antigonus persuaded the Argyraspidian soldiers to betray Eumenes, their general, his adversary, into his hands; but after he had caused him, so delivered, to be slain, he would himself be the commissioner of the divine justice for the punishment of so detestable a crime and committed them into the hands of the governor of the province, with express command, by whatever means, to destroy and bring them all to an evil end, so that of that great number of men, not so much as one ever returned again into Macedonia; the better he had been served, the more wickedly he judged it to be, and meriting greater punishment.

The slave who betrayed the place where his master P. Sulpicius lay concealed, was, according to the promise of Sylla's proscription, manumitted for his pains; but according to the promise of the public justice, which was free from any such engagement, he was thrown headlong from the Tarpeian rock.

Our King Clovis, instead of the arms of gold he had promised them, caused three of Canacre's servants to be hanged after they had betrayed their master to him, though he had debauched them to it; he hanged them with the purse of their reward about their necks: after having satisfied his second and special faith, he satisfied the general and first.

Mohammed II. having resolved to rid himself of his brother, out of jealousy of state, according to the practice of the Ottoman family, he employed one of his officers in the execution; who, pouring a quantity of water too fast into him, choked him. This being done, to expiate the murder, he delivered the murderer into the hands of the mother of him he had so caused to be put to death, for they were only brothers by the father's side; she, in his presence, ripped up the murderer's bosom, and with her own hands rifled his breast for his heart, tore it out, and threw it to the dogs. And even to the worst people it is the sweetest thing imaginable, having once gained their end by a vicious action, to foist, in all security, into it some show of virtue and justice, as by way of compensation and conscientious correction; to which may be added, that they look upon the ministers of such horrid crimes as upon men who reproach them with them, and think by their deaths to erase the memory and testimony of such proceedings.

Or if, perhaps, you are rewarded, not to frustrate the public necessity for that extreme and desperate remedy, he who does it cannot for all that, if he be not such himself, but look upon you as an accursed and execrable fellow, and conclude you a greater traitor than he does, against whom you are so; for he tries the malignity of your disposition by your own hands, where he cannot possibly be deceived, you having no object of preceding hatred to move you to such an act; but he employs you as they do condemned malefactors in executions of justice, an office as necessary as dishonorable. Besides the baseness of such commissions, there is, moreover, a prostitution of conscience. Seeing that the daughter of Sejanus could not be put to death by the law of Rome because she was a virgin, she was, to make it lawful, first ravished by the hangman and then strangled: not only his hand but his soul is slave to the public convenience.

When Amurath I., more grievously to punish his subjects who had taken part in the parricide rebellion of his son, ordained that their nearest kindred should assist in the execution, I find it very handsome in some of them to have rather chosen to be unjustly thought guilty of the parricide of another than to serve justice by a parricide of their own. And where I have seen, at the taking of some little fort by assault in my time, some rascals who to save their own lives, would consent to hang their friends and companions, I have looked upon them to be of worse condition than those who were hanged. 'Tis said that Witold, prince of Lithuania, introduced into that nation the practice that the criminal condemned to death should with his own hand execute the sentence, thinking it strange that a third person, innocent of the fault, should be made guilty of homicide.

A prince, when by some urgent circumstance or some impetuous and unforeseen accident that very much concerns his state, compelled to forfeit his word and break his faith, or otherwise forced from his ordinary duty, ought to attribute this necessity to a lash of the divine rod; vice it is not, for he has given up his own reason to a more universal and more powerful reason; but, certainly, 'tis a misfortune; so that if any one should ask me what remedy? "None," say I, "if he were really racked between these two extremes; *sed videat, ne quœratur latebra perjurio*, he must do it; but if he did it without regret, if it did not grieve him to do it, 'tis a sign his conscience is in a scurvy condition." If there be a person to be found of so tender a conscience as to think no cure whatever worth so important a remedy, I shall like him never the worse; he could not more excusably or more decently perish. We cannot do all we would, so that we must often, as the last anchorage, commit the protection of our vessels to the simple conduct of heaven. To what more just necessity does he reserve himself? What is less possible for him to do than what he cannot do but at the expense of his faith and honor, things that, perhaps, ought to be dearer to him than his own safety, or even the safety of his people. Though he should, with folded arms, only call God to his assistance, has he not reason to hope that the divine goodness will not refuse the favor of an extraordinary arm to just and pure hands? These are dangerous examples, rare and sickly exceptions to our natural rules; we must yield to them, but with great moderation and circumspection; no private utility is of such importance that we should upon that account strain our consciences to such a degree: the public may be, when very manifest and of very great concern.

Timoleon made a timely expiation for his strange exploit by the tears he shed, calling to mind that it was with a fraternal hand that he had slain the tyrant; and it justly pricked his conscience that he had been necessitated to purchase the public utility at so great a price as the violation of his private morality. Even the senate itself, by his means delivered from slavery, dared not positively determine of so high a fact, and divided into two so important and contrary aspects; but the Syracusans, sending at the same time to the Corinthians to solicit their protection, and to require of them a captain fit to reestablish their city in its former dignity and to clear Sicily of several little tyrants by whom it was oppressed, they deputed Timoleon for that service, with this cunning declaration; "that according as he should behave himself well or ill in his employment, their sentence should incline either to favor the deliverer of his country, or to disfavor the murderer of his brother."

This fantastic conclusion carries along with it some excuse, by reason of the danger of the example, and the importance of so strange an action; and they did well to discharge their own judgment of it, and to refer it to others who were not so much concerned. But Timoleon's comportment in this expedition soon made his cause more clear, so worthily and virtuously he demeaned himself upon all occasions; and the good fortune that accompanied him in the difficulties he had to overcome in this noble employment, seemed to be strewed in his way by the gods, favorably conspiring for his justification.

The end of this matter is excusable, if any can be so; but the profit of the augmentation of the public revenue, that served the Roman senate for a pretence to the foul conclusion I am going to relate, is not sufficient to warrant any such injustice.

Certain cities had redeemed themselves and their liberty by money, by the order and consent of the senate, out of the hands of L. Sylla: the business coming again in question, the senate condemned them to be taxable as they were before, and that the money they had disbursed for their redemption should be lost to them. Civil war often produces such villanous examples; that we punish private men for confiding in us when we were public ministers: and the selfsame magistrate makes another man pay the penalty of his change, that has nothing to do with it; the pedagogue whips his scholar for his docility; and the guide beats the blind man whom he leads by the hand; a horrid image of justice.

There are rules in philosophy that are both false and weak. The example that is proposed to us for preferring private utility before faith given, has not weight enough by the circumstance they put to it; robbers have seized you, and after having made you swear to pay them a certain sum of money, dismiss you. 'Tis not well done to say, that an honest man can be quit of his oath without payment, being out of their hands. 'Tis no such thing; what fear has once made me willing to do, I am obliged to do it, when I am no longer in fear; and though that fear only prevailed with my tongue without forcing my will, yet am I bound to keep my word. For my part, when my tongue has sometimes inconsiderately said something that I did not think, I have made a conscience of disowning it: otherwise, by degrees, we shall abolish all the right another derives from our promises and oaths. "*Quasi vero forti viro vis possit adhiberi.*" And 'tis only lawful, upon the account of private interest to excuse breach of promise when we have promised something that is unlawful and wicked in itself; for the right of virtue ought to take place of the right of any obligation of ours.

I have formerly placed Epaminondas in the first rank of excellent men and do not repent it. How high did he stretch the consideration of his own particular duty? he who never killed a man whom he had overcome; who, for the inestimable benefit of restoring the liberty of his country, made conscience of killing a tyrant or his accomplices, without due form of justice: and who concluded him to be a wicked man, how good a citizen soever otherwise, who among his enemies in battle spared not his friend and his guest. This was a soul of a rich composition: he married goodness and humanity, nay, even the tenderest and most delicate in the whole school of philosophy, to the roughest and most violent human actions. Was it nature or art that had intenerated that great courage of his, so full, so obstinate against pain and death and poverty, to such an extreme degree of sweetness and compassion? Dreadful in arms and blood, he overran and subdued a nation invincible by all others but by him alone; and yet in the heat of an encounter, could turn aside from his friend and guest. Certainly he was fit to command in war, who could so rein himself with the curb of good nature, in the height and heat of his fury, a fury inflamed and foaming with blood and slaughter.

'Tis a miracle to be able to mix any image of justice with such violent actions: and it was only possible for such a steadfastness of mind as that of Epaminondas, therein to mix sweetness and the facility of the gentlest manners and purest innocence. And whereas one told the Mamertines, that statutes were of no resistance against armed men; and another told the tribune of the people, that the time of justice and of war were distinct things; and a third said that the noise of arms deafened the voice of laws, this man in all such rattle was not deaf to that of civility and pure courtesy. Had he not borrowed from his enemies the custom of sacrificing to the Muses when he went to war, that they might, by their sweetness and gayety, soften his martial and rigorous fury?

Let us not fear, by the example of so great a master, to believe that there is something unlawful, even against an enemy; and that the common concern ought not to require all things of all men, against private interest. Livy says, "The memory of private right still remains amid public dissensions"; and Ovid, "No power on earth can sanction treachery against a friend." All things are not lawful to an honest man for the service of his prince, the laws, or the general quarrel. "The duty to one's country does not supersede all other duties," says Cicero; "the country itself requires that its citizens should act piously toward their parents." 'Tis an instruction proper for the time wherein we live; we need not harden our courage with these arms of steel; 'tis enough that our shoulders are inured to them; 'tis enough to dip our pens in ink, without dipping them in blood. If it be grandeur of courage, and the effect of a rare and singular virtue, to contemn friendship, private obligations, a man's word and relationship, for the common good and obedience to the magistrate, 'tis certainly sufficient to excuse us, that 'tis a grandeur that could have no place in the grandeur of Epaminondas' courage.

I abominate those mad exhortations of this other discomposed soul.[1] "When swords are drawn, let no idea of love, nor the face even of a father presented to you, move you: mutilate with your sword those venerable features" [Lucan].

Let us deprive wicked, bloody, and treacherous natures of such a pretence of reason; let us set aside this guilty and extravagant justice, and stick to more human imitations. How great things can time and example do! In an encounter of the civil war against Cinna, one of Pompey's soldiers having unawares killed his brother, who was of the contrary party, he immediately for shame and sorrow killed himself; and some years after in another civil war of the same people a soldier demanded a reward of his officer for having killed his brother.

A man but ill proves the honor and beauty of an action by its utility; and very erroneously concludes that every one is obliged to it, and that it becomes every one to do it, if it be of utility. "All things are not equally fit for all men," says Propertius. Let us take that which is most necessary and profitable for human society; it will be marriage; and yet the council of the saints find the contrary much better, excluding from it the most venerable vocation of man; as we design those horses for stallions, of which we have the least esteem.

OF REPENTANCE.

Others form man; I only report him: and represent a particular one, ill fashioned enough, and whom, if I had to model him anew, I should certainly make something else than what he is: but that's past

---

[1] Julius Cæsar.

recalling. Now, though the features of my picture alter and change, 'tis not, however, unlike: the world eternally turns round; all things therein are incessantly moving, the earth, the rocks of Caucasus, and the pyramids of Egypt, both by the public motion and their own. Even constancy itself is no other but a slower and more languishing motion. I cannot fix my object; 'tis always tottering and reeling by a natural giddiness: I take it as it is at the instant I consider it; I do not paint its being, I paint its passage; not a passing from one age to another, or, as the people say, from seven to seven years, but from day to day, from minute to minute. I must accommodate my history to the hour: I may presently change, not only by fortune, but also by intention. 'Tis a counterpart of various and changeable accidents, and of irresolute imaginations, and, as it falls out, sometimes contrary: whether it be that I am then another self, or that I take subjects by other circumstances and considerations: so it is, that I may peradventure contradict myself, but, as Demades said, I never contradict the truth. Could my soul once take footing, I would not essay but resolve: but it is always learning and making trial.

I propose a life ordinary and without lustre: 'tis all one; all moral philosophy may as well be applied to a common and private life, as to one of richer composition: every man carries the entire form of human condition. Authors communicate themselves to the people by some especial and extrinsic mark; I, the first of any, by my universal being; as Michel de Montaigne, not as a grammarian, a poet, or a lawyer. If the world find fault that I speak too much of myself, I find fault that they do not so much as think of themselves. But is it reason, that being so particular in my way of living, I should pretend to recommend myself to the public knowledge? And is it also reason that I should produce to the world, where art and handling have so much credit and authority, crude and simple effects of nature, and of a weak nature to boot? Is it not to build a wall without stone or brick, or some such thing, to write books without learning and without art?

The fancies of music are carried on by art; mine by chance. I have this, at least, according to discipline, that never any man treated of a subject he better understood and knew, than I what I have undertaken, and that in this I am the most understanding man alive: secondly, that never any man penetrated farther into his matter, nor better and more distinctly sifted the parts and sequences of it, nor ever more exactly and fully arrived at the end he proposed to himself. To perfect it, I need bring nothing but fidelity to the work; and that is there, and the most pure and sincere that is anywhere to be found. I speak truth, not so much as I would, but as much as I dare; and I dare a little the more, as I grow older; for, methinks, custom allows to age more liberty of prating, and more indiscretion of talking of a man's self. That cannot fall out here, which I often see elsewhere, that the work and the artificer contradict one another: "Can a man of such sober conversation have written so foolish a book?" Or "Do so learned writings proceed from a man of so weak conversation?" He who talks at a very ordinary rate, and writes rare matter, 'tis to say that his capacity is borrowed and not his own.

A learned man is not learned in all things: but a sufficient man is sufficient throughout, even to ignorance itself; here my book and I go hand in hand together. Elsewhere men may commend or censure the work, without reference to the workman; here they cannot: who touches the one, touches the other. He who shall judge of it without knowing him, will more wrong himself than me; he who does know him, gives me all the satisfaction I desire. I shall be happy beyond my desert, if I can obtain only thus much from the public approbation, as to make men of understanding perceive that I was capable of profiting by knowledge, had I had it; and that I deserved to have been assisted by a better memory.

Be pleased here to excuse what I often repeat, that I very rarely repent, and that my conscience is satisfied with itself, not as the conscience of an angel, or that of a horse, but as the conscience of a man; always adding this clause, not one of ceremony, but a true and real submission, that I speak inquiring and doubting, purely and simply referring myself to the common and accepted beliefs for the resolution. I do not teach, I only relate.

There is no vice that is absolutely a vice which does not offend, and that a sound judgment does not accuse; for there is in it so manifest a deformity and inconvenience, that, peradventure, they are in the right who say that it is chiefly begotten by stupidity and ignorance: so hard is it to imagine that a man can know without abhorring it. Malice sucks up the greatest part of its own venom, and poisons itself. Vice leaves repentance in the soul, like an ulcer in the flesh, which is always scratching and lacerating itself: for reason effaces all other grief and sorrows, but it begets that of repentance, which is so much the more grievous, by reason it springs within, as the cold and heat of fevers are more sharp than those that only strike upon the outward skin. I hold for vices (but every one according to its proportion), not only those which reason and nature condemn, but those also which the opinion of men, though false and erroneous, have made such, if authorized by law and custom.

There is likewise no virtue which does not rejoice a well-descended nature; there is a kind of, I know not what, congratulation in well doing that gives us an inward satisfaction, and a generous boldness that accompanies a good conscience: a soul daringly vicious may, peradventure, arm itself with security, but it cannot supply itself with this complacency and satisfaction. 'Tis no little satisfaction to feel a man's self preserved from the contagion of so depraved an age, and to say to himself: "Whoever could penetrate into my soul would not there find me guilty either of the affliction or ruin of any one, or of revenge or envy, or any offence against the public laws, or of innovation or disturbance, or failure of my word; and though the license of the time permits and teaches every one so to do, yet have I not plundered any Frenchman's goods, or taken his money, and have lived upon what is my own, in war as well as in peace; neither have I set any man to work without paying him his hire." These testimonies of a good conscience please, and this natural rejoicing is very beneficial to us, and the only reward that we can never fail of.

To ground the recompense of virtuous actions upon the approbation of others is too uncertain and unsafe a foundation, especially in so corrupt and ignorant an age as this, wherein the good opinion of the vulgar is injurious: upon whom do you rely to show you what is recommendable? God defend me from being an honest man, according to the descriptions of honor I daily see every one make of himself. "*Quæ fuerant vitia, mores sunt.*" Some of my friends have at times schooled and scolded me with great sincerity and plainness, either of their own voluntary motion, or by me entreated to it as to an office, which to a well-composed soul surpasses not only in utility, but in kindness all other offices of friendship: I have always received them with the most open arms, both of courtesy and acknowledgment; but, to say the truth, I have often found so much false measure, both in their reproaches and praises, that I had not done much amiss, rather to have done ill, than to have done well according to their notions.

We, who live private lives, not exposed to any other view than our own, ought chiefly to have settled a pattern within ourselves by which to try our actions; and according to that, sometimes to encourage and sometimes to correct ourselves. I have my laws and my judicature to judge of myself, and apply myself more to these than to any other rules: I do, indeed, restrain my actions according to others; but extend them not by any other rule than my own. You yourself only know if you are cowardly and cruel, loyal and devout: others see you not, and only guess at you by uncertain conjectures, and do not so much see your nature as your art; rely not therefore upon their opinions, but stick to your own. "Thou must employ thy own judgment upon thyself; great is the weight of thy own conscience in the discovery of thy own virtues and vices; that being taken away, all things are lost," says Cicero.

But the saying that repentance immediately follows the sin seems not to have respect to sin in its high estate, which is lodged in us as in its own proper habitation. One may disown and retract the vices that surprise us, and to which we are hurried by passions; but those which by a long habit are rooted in a strong and vigorous will are not subject to contradiction. Repentance is no other but a recanting of the will and an opposition to our fancies, which lead us which way they please. It makes this person disown his former virtue and continency, and say with Horace, "Why was I not of the same mind when I was a boy that I am now? or why do not the ruddy cheeks of my youth return to help me now?"

'Tis an exact life that maintains itself in due order in private. Every one may juggle his part, and represent an honest man upon the stage: but within, and in his own bosom, where all may do as they list, where all is concealed, to be regular—there's the point. The next degree is to be so in his house, and in his ordinary actions, for which we are accountable to none, and where there is no study nor artifice. And therefore Bias, setting forth the excellent state of a private family, says: "of which the master is the same within, by his own virtue and temper, that he is abroad, for fear of the laws and report of men." And it was a worthy saying of Julius Drusus, to the masons who offered him, for three thousand crowns, to put his house in such a posture that his neighbors should no longer have the same inspection into it as before; "I will give you," said he, "six thousand to make it so that everybody may see into every room." 'Tis honorably recorded of Agesilaus, that he used in his journeys always to take up his lodgings in temples, to the end that the people and the gods themselves might pry into his most private actions.

Such a one has been a miracle to the world, in whom neither his wife nor servant has ever seen anything so much as remarkable; few men have been admired by their own domestics; no one was ever a prophet, not merely in his own house, but in his own country, says the experience of histories: 'tis the same in things of naught, and in this low example the image of a greater is to be seen. In my country of Gascony, they look upon it as a drollery to see me in print; the further off I am read from my own home, the better I am esteemed. I am fain to purchase printers in Guienne; elsewhere they purchase me. Upon this it is that they lay their foundation who conceal themselves present and living, to obtain a name when they are absent and dead.

I had rather have a great deal less in hand, and do not expose myself to the world upon any other account than my present share; when I leave it I quit the rest. See this functionary whom the people escort in state, with wonder and applause, to his very door; he puts off the pageant with his robe, and falls so much the lower by how much he was higher exalted: in himself within, all is tumult and degraded. And though all should be regular there, it will require a vivid and well-chosen judgment to perceive it in these low and private actions; to which may be added, that order is a dull, sombre virtue. To enter a breach, conduct an embassy, govern a people, are actions of renown: to reprehend, laugh, sell, pay, love, hate, and gently and justly converse with a man's own family, and with himself; not to relax, not to give a man's self the lie is more rare and hard, and less remarkable. By which means, retired lives, whatever is said to the contrary, undergo duties of as great or greater difficulty than the others do; and private men, says Aristotle, serve virtue more painfully and highly, than those in authority do: we prepare ourselves for eminent occasions, more out of glory than conscience.

The shortest way to arrive at glory, would be to do that for conscience which we do for glory: and the virtue of Alexander appears to me of much less vigor in his great theatre, than that of Socrates in his mean and obscure employment. I can easily conceive Socrates in the place of Alexander, but Alexander in that of Socrates, I cannot. Who shall ask the one what he can do, he will answer, "Subdue the world:" and who shall put the same question to the other, he will say, "Carry on human life conformably with its natural condition;" a much more general, weighty, and legitimate science than the other.

The virtue of the soul does not consist in flying high, but in walking orderly; its grandeur does not exercise itself in grandeur, but in mediocrity. As they who judge and try us within make no great account of the lustre of our public actions, and see they are only streaks and rays of clear water springing from a slimy and muddy bottom: so, likewise, they who judge of us by this gallant outward appearance in like manner conclude of our internal constitution; and cannot couple common faculties, and like their own, with the other faculties that astonish them, and are so far out of their sight. Therefore it is, that we give such savage forms to demons: and who does not give Tamerlane great eyebrows, wide nostrils, a dreadful visage, and a prodigious stature, according to the imagination he has conceived by the report of his name? Had any one formerly brought me to Erasmus, I should hardly have believed but that all was adage and apothegm he spoke to his man or his hostess. As vicious souls are often incited by some foreign impulse to do well, so are virtuous souls to do ill; they are therefore to be judged by their settled state, when they arc at home, whenever that may be; and, at all events, when they are nearer repose, and in their native station.

Natural inclinations are much assisted and fortified by education: but they seldom alter and overcome their institution: a thousand natures of my time have escaped toward virtue or vice, through a quite contrary discipline. "So savage beasts, when shut up in cages, and grown unaccustomed to the woods, become tame, and lay aside their fierce looks, and submit to the rule of man; if again they taste blood, their rage and fury return, their jaws are erected by thirst of blood, and they scarcely forbear to assail their trembling masters," says Lucan.

These original qualities are not to be rooted out; they may be covered and concealed. The Latin tongue is as it were natural to me; I understand it better than French; but I have not been used to speak it, nor hardly to write it these forty years. Yet, upon extreme and sudden emotions which I have fallen into twice or thrice in my life, and once, seeing my father in perfect health fall upon me in a swoon, I have always uttered my first outcries and ejaculations in Latin; nature starting up, and forcibly expressing itself, in spite of so long a discontinuation; and this example is said of many others.

They who in my time have attempted to correct the manners of the world by new opinions, reform seeming vices, but the essential vices they leave as they were, if indeed they do not augment them; and augmentation is, therein, to be feared; we defer all other well doing upon the account of these external reformations of less cost and greater show, and thereby expiate cheaply, for the other natural consubstantial and intestine vices. Look a little into our experience: there is no man, if he listen to himself, who does not in himself discover a particular and governing form of his own, that jostles his education, and wrestles with the tempest of passions that are contrary to it. For my part, I seldom find myself agitated with surprises; I always find myself in my place, as heavy and unwieldy bodies do; if I am not at home, I am always near at hand; my dissipations do not transport me very far, there is nothing strange nor extreme in the case; and yet I have sound and vigorous turns.

The true condemnation, and which touches the common practice of men, is, that their very retirement itself is full of filth and corruption; the idea of their reformation composed; their repentance sick and faulty, very nearly as much as their sin. Some, either from having been linked to vice by a natural propension, or long practice, cannot see its deformity. Others (of which constitution I am) do indeed feel the weight of vice, but they counterbalance it with pleasure, or some other occasion; and suffer, and lend themselves to it, for a certain price, but viciously and basely. Yet there might, haply, be imagined so vast a disproportion of measure, where with justice the pleasure might excuse the sin, as we say of utility; not only if accidental, and out of sin, as in thefts, but the very exercise of sin, as in the enjoyment of women, where the temptation is violent, and 'tis said, sometimes not to be overcome.

Being the other day at Armaignac, on the estate of a kinsman of mine, I there saw a country fellow who was by every one nicknamed the thief. He thus related the story of his life; that being born a beggar, and finding that he should not be able, so as to be clear of indigence, to get his living by the sweat of his brow, he resolved to turn thief, and by means of his strength of body, had exercised this trade all the time of his youth in great security; for he ever made his harvest and vintage in other men's grounds, but a great way off, and in so great quantities, that it was not to be imagined one man could have carried away so much in one night upon his shoulders; and, moreover, was careful equally to divide and distribute the mischief he did, that the loss was of less importance to every particular man. He is now grown old, and rich for a man of his condition, thanks to his trade, which he openly confesses to every one. And to make his peace with God, he says that he is daily ready by good offices to make satisfaction to the successors of those he has robbed, and if he do not finish (for to do it all at once he is not able) he will then leave it in charge to his heirs to perform the rest, proportionably to the wrong he himself only knows he has done to each. By this description, true or false, this man looks upon theft as a dishonest action, and hates it, but less than poverty, and simply repents; but to the extent he has thus recompensed, he repents not. This is not that habit which incorporates us into vice, and conforms even our understanding itself to it; nor is it that impetuous whirlwind that by gusts troubles and blinds our souls and for the time precipitates us, judgment and all, into the power of vice.

I customarily do what I do thoroughly and make but one step on't; I have rarely any movement that hides itself and steals away from my reason, and that does not proceed in the matter by the consent of all my faculties, without division or intestine sedition; my judgment is to have all the blame or all the praise; and the blame it once has, it has always; for almost from my infancy it has ever been one; the same inclination, the same turn, the same force; and as to universal opinions, I fixed myself from my childhood in the place where I resolved to stick. There are some sins that are impetuous, prompt, and sudden; let us set them aside; but in these other sins so often repeated, deliberated, and contrived, whether sins of complexion or sins of profession and vocation, I cannot conceive that they should have so long been settled in the same resolution, unless the reason and conscience of him who has them be constant to have them; and the repentance he boasts to be inspired with on a sudden is very hard for me to imagine or form. I follow not the opinion of the Pythagorean sect, "that men take up a new soul when they repair to the images of the gods to receive their oracles," unless he mean that it must needs be extrinsic, new, and lent for the time; our own showing so little sign of purification and cleanness, fit for such an office.

They act quite contrary to the stoical precepts, who do indeed command us to correct the imperfections and vices we know ourselves guilty of, but forbid us therefore to disturb the repose of our souls; these make us believe that they have great grief and remorse within; but of amendment, correction, or interruption, they make nothing appear. It cannot be a cure if the malady be not wholly discharged; if repentance were laid upon the scale of the balance, it would weigh down sin. I find no quality so easy to counterfeit as devotion, if men do not conform their manners and life to the profession; its essence is abstruse and occult; the appearances easy and ostentatious.

For my own part, I may desire in general to be other than I am; I may condemn and dislike my whole form, and beg of Almighty God for an entire reformation, and that He will please to pardon my natural infirmity: but I ought not to call this repentance, methinks, no more, than the being dissatisfied that I am not an angel or Cato. My actions are regular, and conformable with what I am, and to my condition; I can do no better; and repentance does not properly touch things that are not in our power; sorrow does. I imagine an infinite number of natures more elevated and regular than mine; and yet I do not for all that improve my faculties, no more than my arm or will grows more strong and vigorous for conceiving those of another to be so. If to conceive and wish a nobler way of acting than that we have should produce a repentance of our own, we must then repent us of our most innocent actions, forasmuch as we may well suppose that in a more excellent nature they would have been carried on with greater dignity and perfection; and we would that ours were so.

When I reflect upon the deportments of my youth, with that of my old age, I find that I have commonly behaved myself with equal order in both, according to what I understand: this is all that my resistance can do. I do not flatter myself; in the same circumstances I should do the same things. It is not a patch, but rather an universal tincture, with which I am stained. I know no repentance, superficial, halfway and ceremonious; it must sting me all over before I can call it so, and must prick my bowels as deeply and universally as God sees into me.

As to business, many excellent opportunities have escaped me for want of good management; and yet my deliberations were sound enough, according to the occurrences presented to me: 'tis their way to choose always the easiest and safest course. I find that, in my former resolves, I have proceeded with discretion, according to my own rule, and according to the state of the subject proposed, and should do the same a thousand years hence in like occasions; I do not consider what it is now, but what it was then, when I deliberated on it: the force of all counsel consists in the time; occasions and things eternally shift and change. I have in my life committed some important errors, not for want of good understanding, but for want of good luck. There are secret, and not to be foreseen, parts in matters we have in hand, especially in the nature of men; mute conditions, that make no show, unknown sometimes even to the possessors themselves, that spring and start up by incidental occasions; if my prudence could not penetrate into nor foresee them, I blame it not: 'tis commissioned no farther than its own limits; if the event be too hard for me, and take the side I have refused, there is no remedy; I do not blame myself, I accuse my fortune, and not my work; this cannot be called repentance.

Phocion, having given the Athenians an advice that was not followed, and the affair nevertheless succeeding contrary to his opinion, some one said to him; "Well, Phocion, art thou content that matters go so well?" "I am very well content," replied he, "that this has happened so well, but I do not repent that I counselled the other." When any of my friends address themselves to me for advice, I give it candidly and clearly, without sticking, as almost all other men do, at the hazard of the thing's falling out contrary to my opinion, and that I may be reproached for my counsel; I am very indifferent as to that, for the fault will be theirs for having consulted me, and I could not refuse them that office.

I, for my own part, can rarely blame any one but myself for my oversights and misfortunes, for indeed I seldom solicit the advice of another, if not by honor of ceremony, or excepting where I stand in need of information, special science, or as to matter of fact. But in things wherein I stand in need of nothing but judgment, other men's reasons may serve to fortify my own, but have little power to dissuade me; I hear them all with civility and patience: but to my recollection, I never made use of any but my own. With me, they are but flies and atoms, that confound and distract my will; I lay no great stress upon my opinions; but I lay as little upon those of others, and fortune rewards me accordingly: if I receive but little advice, I also give but little. I am seldom consulted, and still more seldom believed, and know no concern, either public or private, that has been mended or bettered by my advice. Even they whom fortune had in some sort tied to my direction, have more willingly suffered themselves to be governed by any other counsels than mine. And as a man who am as jealous of my repose as of my authority, I am better pleased that it should be so; in leaving me there, they humor what I profess, which is to settle and wholly contain myself within myself. I take a pleasure in being uninterested in other men's affairs, and disengaged from being their warranty, and responsible for what they do.

In all affairs that are past, be it how it will, I have very little regret; for this imagination puts me out of my pain, that they were so to fall out; they are in the great revolution of the world, and in the chain of stoical causes: your fancy cannot, by wish and imagination, move one tittle, but that the great current of things will not reverse both the past and the future.

As to the rest, I abominate that incidental repentance which old age brings along with it. He, who said of old,[1] that he was obliged to his age for having weaned him from pleasure, was of another opinion than I am; I can never think myself beholden to impotency, for any good it can do to me; "Nor can Providence ever be seen so averse to her own work, that debility should be ranked among the best things" [Quintilian]. Our appetites are rare in old age; a profound satiety seizes us after the act; in this I see nothing of conscience; chagrin and weakness imprint in us a drowsy and rheumatic virtue. We must not suffer ourselves to be so wholly carried away by natural alterations, as to suffer our judgments to be imposed upon by them. Youth and pleasure have not formerly so far prevailed with me, that I did not well enough discern the face of vice in pleasure; neither does the distaste that years have brought me so far prevail with me now, that I cannot discern pleasure in vice. Now that I am no more in my flourishing age, I judge as well of these things as if I were. I, who narrowly and strictly examine it, find my reason the very same it was in my most licentious age, except, perhaps, that 'tis weaker and more decayed by being grown older; and I find that the pleasure it refuses me upon the account of my bodily health, it would no more refuse now, in consideration of the health of my soul, than at any time heretofore. I do not repute it the more valiant for not being able to combat; my temptations are so broken and mortified, that they are not worth its opposition; holding but out my hands, I repel them. Should one present the old concupiscence before it, I fear it would have less power to resist it than heretofore; I do not discern that in itself it judges anything otherwise now, than it formerly did, nor that it has acquired any new light: wherefore, if there be convalescence, 'tis an enchanted one.

---

[1] Sophocles. Cicero, *De Senectute*, c. 14.

Miserable kind of remedy, to owe one's health to one's disease! 'Tis not that our misfortune should perform this office, but the good fortune of our judgment. I am not to be made to do anything by persecutions and afflictions, but to curse them: that is for people who cannot be roused but by a whip. My reason is much more free in prosperity, and much more distracted, and put to't to digest pains than pleasures: I see best in a clear sky; health admonishes me more cheerfully, and to better purpose, than sickness. I did all that in me lay to reform and regulate myself from pleasures, at a time when I had health and vigor to enjoy them; I should be ashamed and envious, that the misery and misfortune of my old age should have credit over my good, healthful, sprightly, and vigorous years; and that men should estimate me, not by what I have been, but by what I have ceased to be.

In my opinion, 'tis the happy living, and not (as Antisthenes said) the happy dying, in which human felicity consists. I have not made it my business to make a monstrous addition of a philosopher's tail to the head and body of a libertine; nor would I have this wretched remainder give the lie to the pleasant, sound, and long part of my life: I would present myself uniformly throughout. Were I to live my life over again, I should live it just as I have lived it; I neither complain of the past, nor do I fear the future; and if I am not much deceived, I am the same within that I am without. 'Tis one main obligation I have to my fortune, that the succession of my bodily estate has been carried on according to the natural seasons; I have seen the grass, the blossom, and the fruit; and now see the withering; happily, however, because naturally. I bear the infirmities I have the better, because they came not till I had reason to expect them, and because also they make me with greater pleasure remember that long felicity of my past life. My wisdom may have been just the same in both ages; but it was more active, and of better grace while young and sprightly, than now it is when broken, peevish, and uneasy. I repudiate, then, these casual and painful reformations. God must touch our hearts; our consciences must amend of themselves, by the aid of our reason, and not by the decay of our appetites; pleasure is, in itself, neither pale nor discolored, to be discerned by dim and decayed eyes.

We ought to love temperance for itself, and because God has commanded that and chastity; but that which we are reduced to by catarrhs, and for which I am indebted to the stone, is neither chastity nor temperance; a man cannot boast that he despises and resists pleasure, if he cannot see it, if he knows not what it is, and cannot discern its graces, its force, and most alluring beauties; I know both the one and the other, and may therefore the better say it. But, methinks, our souls, in old age, are subject to more troublesome maladies and imperfections than in youth; I said the same when young and when I was reproached with the want of a beard; and I say so now that my gray hairs give me some authority. We call the difficulty of our humors and the disrelish of present things wisdom; but, in truth, we do not so much forsake vices as we change them, and, in my opinion, for worse. Besides a foolish and feeble pride, an impertinent prating, forward and insociable humors, superstition, and a ridiculous desire of riches when we have lost the use of them, I find there more envy, injustice and malice.

Age imprints more wrinkles in the mind than it does on the face; and souls are never, or very rarely seen, that in growing old do not smell sour and musty. Man moves all together, both toward his perfection and decay. In observing the wisdom of Socrates, and many circumstances of his condemnation, I should dare to believe, that he in some sort himself purposely, by collusion, contributed to it, seeing that, at the age of seventy years, he might fear to suffer the lofty motions of his mind to be cramped, and his wonted lustre obscured.

What strange metamorphoses do I see age every day make in many of my acquaintance! 'Tis a potent malady, and that naturally and imperceptibly steals into us; a vast provision of study and great precaution are required to evade the imperfections it loads us with, or at least, to weaken their progress. I find that, notwithstanding all my entrenchments, it gets foot by foot upon me; I make the best resistance I can, but I do not know to what at last it will reduce me. But fall out what will, I am content the world may know, when I am fallen, from what I fell.

OF THE INCONVENIENCE OF GREATNESS.

Since we cannot attain unto it, let us revenge ourselves by railing at it; and yet it is not absolutely railing against anything, to proclaim its defects, because they are in all things to be found, how beautiful or how much to be coveted soever. Greatness has, in general, this manifest advantage, that it can lower itself when it pleases, and has, very near, the choice of both the one and the other condition; for a man does not fall from all heights; there are several from which one may descend without falling down.

It does, indeed, appear to me that we value it at too high a rate, and also overvalue the resolution of those whom we have either seen, or heard, have contemned it, or displaced themselves of their own accord: its essence is not so evidently commodious that a man may not, without a miracle, refuse it. I find it a very hard thing to undergo misfortunes, but to be content with a moderate measure of fortune and to avoid greatness I think a very easy matter. 'Tis, methinks, a virtue to which I, who am no conjurer, could without any great endeavor arrive. What, then, is to be expected from them that would yet put into consideration the glory attending this refusal, wherein there may lurk worse ambition than even in the desire itself, and fruition of greatness? Forasmuch as ambition never comports itself better, according to itself, than when it proceeds by obscure and unfrequented ways.

I incite my courage to patience, but I rein it as much as I can toward desire. I have as much to wish for as another, and allow my wishes as much liberty and indiscretion; but, yet it never befell me to wish for either empire or royalty, or the eminency of those high and commanding fortunes: I do not aim that way; I love myself too well. When I think to grow greater 'tis but very moderately, and by a compelled and timorous advancement, such as is proper for me in resolution, in prudence, in health, in beauty, and even in riches too; but this supreme reputation, this mighty authority, oppress my imagination; and, quite contrary to that other,[1] I should, peradventure, rather choose to be the second or third in Perigord, than the first at Paris: at least, without lying, rather the third at Paris than the first. I would neither dispute, a miserable unknown, with a nobleman's porter, nor make crowds open in adoration as I pass. I am trained up to a moderate condition, as well by my choice as fortune; and have made it appear, in the whole conduct of my life and enterprises, that I have rather avoided than otherwise the climbing above the degree of fortune wherein God has placed me by my birth: all natural constitution is equally just and easy. My soul is so sneaking that I measure not good fortune by the height, but by the facility.

But if my heart be not great enough, 'tis open enough to make amends, at any one's request, freely to lay open its weakness. Should any one put me upon comparing the life of L. Thorius Balbus, a brave man, handsome, learned, healthful, understanding, and abounding in all sorts of conveniences and pleasures, leading a quiet life, and all his own, his mind well prepared against death, superstition, pain, and other incumbrances of human necessity, dying at last, in battle, with his sword in his hand, for the defence of his country, on the one part; and on the other part, the life of M. Regulus, so great and high as is known to every one, and his end admirable; the one without name and without dignity, the other exemplary, and glorious to wonder,—I should doubtless say as Cicero did, could I speak as well as he. But if

---

[1] Julius Cæsar.

I was to compare them with my own, I should then also say that the first is as much according to my capacity, and from desire, which I conform to my capacity, as the second is far beyond it; that I could not approach the last but with veneration, the other I could readily attain by use.

But let us return to our temporal greatness, from which we are digressed. I disrelish all dominion, whether active or passive. Otanes, one of the seven who had right to pretend to the kingdom of Persia, did, as I should willingly have done, which was, that he gave up to his concurrents his right of being promoted to it, either by election or by lot, provided that he and his might live in the empire out of all authority and subjection, those of the ancient laws excepted, and might enjoy all liberty that was not prejudicial to these, being as impatient of commanding as of being commanded.

The most painful and difficult employment in the world, in my opinion, is worthily to discharge the office of a king. I excuse more of their mistakes than men commonly do, in consideration of the intolerable weight of their function, which astounds me. 'Tis hard to keep measure in so immeasurable a power; yet so it is, that it is, even to those who are not of the best nature, a singular incitement to virtue, to be seated in a place where you cannot do the least good that shall not be put upon record; and where the least benefit redounds to so many men, and where your talent of administration, like that of preachers, principally addresses itself to the people, no very exact judge, easy to deceive, and easily content. There are few things wherein we can give a sincere judgment, by reason that there are few wherein we have not, in some sort, a private interest. Superiority and inferiority, dominion and subjection, are bound to a natural envy and contest, and must of necessity, perpetually intrench upon one another. I believe neither the one nor the other touching the rights of the other party; let reason, therefore, which is inflexible and without passion, determine when we can avail ourselves of it. 'Tis not above a month ago that I read over two Scotch authors contending upon this subject, of whom he who stands for the people makes kings to be in a worse condition than a carter; and he who writes for monarchy places them some degrees above God Almighty in power and sovereignty.

Now, the inconveniency of greatness that I have made choice of to consider in this place, upon some occasion that has lately put it into my head, is this: there is not, peradventure, anything more pleasant in the commerce of men than the trials that we make against one another, out of emulation of honor and worth, whether in the exercises of the body or in those of the mind, wherein sovereign greatness can

have no true part. And, in earnest, I have often thought that by force
of respect itself men use princes disdainfully and injuriously in that
particular: for the thing I was infinitely offended at in my childhood,
that they who exercised with me forbore to do their best because they
found me unworthy of their utmost endeavor, is what we see happen
to them daily, every one finding himself unworthy to contend with
them.

If we discover that they have the least desire to get the better of us,
there is no one who will not make it his business to give it them, and
who will not rather betray his own glory than offend theirs; and will,
therein, employ so much force only as is necessary to save their
honor. What share have they, then, in the engagement, where every
one is on their side? Methinks I see those Paladins of ancient times
presenting themselves to jousts and battle with enchanted arms and
bodies. Brisson, running against Alexander, purposely missed his
blow, and made a fault in his career; Alexander chid him for it, but
he ought to have had him whipped. Upon this consideration
Carneades said, that "the sons of princes learned nothing right but to
ride; by reason that, in all their other exercises, every one bends and
yields to them; but a horse, that is neither a flatterer nor a courtier,
throws the son of a king with no more ceremony than he would
throw that of a porter."

Homer was fain to consent that Venus, so sweet and delicate a goddess as she was, should be wounded at the battle of Troy, thereby to
ascribe courage and boldness to her; qualities that cannot possibly be
in those who are exempt from danger. The gods are made to be
angry, to fear, to run away, to be jealous, to grieve, to be transported
with passions, to honor them with the virtues that, among us, are
built upon these imperfections. Who does not participate in the hazard and difficulty can claim no interest in the honor and pleasure that
are the consequents of hazardous actions. 'Tis pity a man should be
so potent that all things must give way to him; fortune therein sets
you too remote from society, and places you in too great a solitude.
This easiness and mean facility of making all things bow under you is
an enemy to all sorts of pleasure: 'tis to slide, not to go: 'tis to sleep,
and not to live. Conceive man accompanied with omnipotence: you
overwhelm him; he must beg disturbance and opposition as an alms:
his being and his good are in indigence.

Their good qualities are dead and lost; for they can only be perceived by comparison, and we put them out of this: they have little
knowledge of true praise, having their ears deafened with so continual
and uniform an approbation. Have they to do with the stupidest of
all their subjects? they have no means to take any advantage of him,

if he but say: "'Tis because he is my king," he thinks he has said enough to express, that he, therefore, suffered himself to be overcome. This quality stifles and consumes the other true and essential qualities: they are sunk in the royalty; and leave them nothing to recommend themselves with but actions that directly concern and serve the function of their place; 'tis so much to be a king, that this alone remains to them. The outer glare that environs him conceals and shrouds him; our sight is there repelled and dissipated, being filled and stopped by this prevailing light. The senate awarded the prize of eloquence to Tiberius; he refused it, esteeming that though it had been just, he could derive no advantage from a judgment so partial, and so little free to judge.

As we give them all advantages of honor, so do we soothe and authorize all their vices and defects, not only by approbation, but by imitation also. Every one of Alexander's followers carried his head on one side, as he did; and the flatterers of Dionysius ran against one another in his presence, and stumbled at and overturned whatever was under foot, to show they were as purblind as he. Hernia itself has also served to recommend a man to favor; I have seen deafness affected; and because the master hated his wife, Plutarch has seen his courtiers repudiate theirs, whom they loved: and, which is yet more, uncleanliness and all manner of dissolution have so been in fashion; as also disloyalty, blasphemy, cruelty, heresy, superstition, irreligion, effeminacy, and worse, if worse there be: and by an example yet more dangerous than that of Mithridates' flatterers who, as their master pretended to the honor of a good physician, came to him to have incisions and cauteries made in their limbs; for these others suffered the soul, a more delicate and noble part, to be cauterized.

But to end where I began; the Emperor Adrian, disputing with the philosopher Favorinus about the interpretation of some word, Favorinus soon yielded him the victory; for which his friends rebuking him: "You talk simply," said he, "would you not have him wiser than I, who commands thirty legions?" Augustus wrote verses against Asinius Pollio, and "I," said Pollio, "say nothing, for it is not prudence to write in contest with him who has power to prescribe;" and he had reason; for Dionysius, because he could not equal Philoxenus in poesy and Plato in discourse, condemned the one to the quarries, and sent the other to be sold for a slave into the island of Ægina.

OF MANAGING THE WILL.

Few things, in comparison of what commonly affect other men, move, or to say better, possess me: for 'tis but reason they should

concern a man, provided they do not possess him. I am very solicitous, both by study and argument, to enlarge this privilege of insen-
sibility, which is in me naturally raised to a pretty degree, so that
consequently I espouse and am very much moved with very few
things. I have a clear sight enough, but I fix it upon very few objects;
I have a sense delicate and tender enough; but an apprehension and
application hard and negligent. I am very unwilling to engage myself;
as much as in me lies, I employ myself wholly on myself, and even in
that subject should rather choose to curb and restrain my affection
from plunging itself over head and ears into it, it being a subject that
I possess at the mercy of others, and over which fortune has more
right than I; so that even as to health, which I so much value, 'tis all
the more necessary for me not so passionately to covet and heed it,
than to find diseases so insupportable.

A man ought to moderate himself between the hatred of pain and
the love of pleasure; and Plato lets down a middle path of life between
the two. But against such affections as wholly carry me away from
myself, and fix me elsewhere, against those, I say, I oppose myself
with my utmost power. 'Tis my opinion that a man should lend himself to others, and only give himself to himself. Were my will easy to
lend itself out, and to be swayed, I should not stick there; I am too
tender, both by nature and use: "*Fugax rerum, securaque in otia natus.*"
Hot and obstinate disputes wherein my adversary would at last have
the better, the issue that would render my heat and obstinacy dis-
graceful, would peradventure vex me to the last degree. Should I set
myself to it at the rate that others do, my soul would never have the
force to bear the emotion and alarms of those who grasp at so much;
it would immediately be disordered by this inward agitation. If,
sometimes, I have been put upon the management of other men's
affairs, I have promised to take them in hand, but not into my lungs
and liver; to take them upon me, not to incorporate them: to take
pains, yes; to be impassioned about it, by no means; I have a care of
them, but I will not sit upon them. I have enough to do to order and
govern the domestic throng of those that I have in my own veins and
bowels, without introducing a crowd of other men's affairs; and am
sufficiently concerned about my own proper and natural business,
without meddling with the concerns of others.

Such as know how much they owe to themselves, and how many
offices they are bound to of their own, find that nature has cut them
out work enough of their own to keep them from being idle. "Thou
hast business enough at home, look to that."

Men let themselves out to hire; their faculties are not for themselves, but for those to whom they have enslaved themselves; 'tis their

tenants occupy them, not themselves. This common humor pleases not me. We must be thrifty of the liberty of our souls, and never let it out but upon just occasions, which are very few, if we judge aright. Do but observe such as have accustomed themselves to be at every one's call; they do it indifferently upon all, as well little as great occasions; in that which nothing concerns them, as much as in what imports them most. They thrust themselves in indifferently wherever there is work to do and obligation; and are without life when not in tumultuous bustle: "*In negotiis sunt, negotii causa.*" It is not so much that they will go, as it is that they cannot stand still; like a rolling stone that cannot stop till it can go no farther.

Occupation, with a certain sort of men, is a mark of understanding and dignity; their souls seek repose in agitation, as children do by being rocked in a cradle; they may pronounce themselves as serviceable to their friends, as they are troublesome to themselves. No one distributes his money to others, but every one distributes his time and his life; there is nothing of which we are so prodigal as of these two things, of which to be thrifty would be both commendable and useful. I am of a quite contrary humor; I look to myself, and commonly covet with no great ardor what I do desire; and desire little; and I employ and busy myself at the same rate, rarely and temperately. Whatever they take in hand, they do it with their utmost will and vehemence. There are so many dangerous steps, that, for the more safety, we must a little lightly and superficially glide over the world, and not rush through it. Pleasure itself is painful in profundity: "You tread on fire, hidden under deceitful ashes" [Horace].

The parliament of Bordeaux chose me mayor of their city, at a time when I was at a distance from France, and still more remote from any such thought. I entreated to be excused, but I was told by my friends that I had committed an error in so doing, and the greater because the king had, moreover, interposed his command in that affair. 'Tis an office that ought to be looked upon so much more honorable, as it has no other salary nor advantage than the bare honor of its execution. It continues two years, but may be extended by a second election, which very rarely happens; it was to me, and had never been so but twice before; some years ago to Monsieur de Lanssac, and lately to Monsieur de Biron, marshal of France, in whose place I succeeded; and I left mine to Monsieur de Matignon, marshal of France also; proud of so noble a fraternity — "*Uterque bonus pacis bellique minister.*" Fortune would have a hand in my promotion, by this particular circumstance which she put in of her own, not altogether vain; for Alexander disdained the ambassadors of Corinth, who came to offer him a burgess-ship of their city; but when they proceeded to lay before him that Bacchus and Hercules were also in the register, he graciously accepted the offer.

At my arrival, I faithfully and conscientiously represented myself to them for such as I find myself to be — a man without memory, without vigilance, without experience, and without vigor; but withal, without hatred, without ambition, without avarice, and without violence; that they might be informed of my qualities, and know what they were to expect from my service. And the knowledge they had had of my father, and the honor they had for his memory, having been the only motive to confer this favor upon me, I plainly told them that I should be very sorry anything should make so great an impression upon me, as their affairs and the concerns of their city had made upon him, while he held the government to which they had preferred me. I remembered, when a boy, to have seen him in his old age cruelly tormented with these public affairs, neglecting the soft repose of his own house, to which the declension of his age had reduced him for several years before, the management of his own affairs, and his health; and certainly despising his own life, which was in great danger of being lost, by being engaged in long and painful journeys on their behalf. Such was he; and this humor of his proceeded from a marvellous good nature; never was there a more charitable and popular soul. Yet this proceeding which I commend in others, I do not love to follow myself, and am not without excuse.

He had learned that a man must forget himself for his neighbor, and that the particular was of no manner of consideration in comparison with the general. Most of the rules and precepts of the world run this way; to drive us out of ourselves into the street for the benefit of public society: they thought to do a great feat to divert and remove us from ourselves, assuming we were but too much fixed there, and by a too natural inclination; and have said all they could to that purpose: for 'tis no new thing for the sages to preach things as they serve, not as they are. Truth has its obstructions, inconveniences, and incompatibilities with us; we must often deceive, that we may not deceive ourselves; and shut our eyes and our understandings, to redress and amend them: "For the ignorant judge, and therefore are oft to be deceived lest they should err." When they order us to love three, four, or fifty degrees of things above ourselves, they do like archers, who, to hit the white, take their aim a great deal higher than the butt; to make a crooked stick straight, we bend it the contrary way.

I believe that in the Temple of Pallas, as we see in all other religions, there were apparent mysteries to be exposed to the people; and others, more secret and high, that were only to be shown to such as were professed; 'tis likely that in these the true point of friendship that every one owes to himself is to be found; not a false friendship, that makes us embrace glory, knowledge, riches, and the like, with a principal and immoderate affection, as members of our being; nor an indiscreet and effeminate friendship, wherein it happens, as with ivy, that it decays and ruins the walls it embraces; but a sound and regular friendship, equally useful and pleasant. He who knows the duties of this friendship and practises them, is truly of the cabinet council of the Muses, and has attained to the height of human wisdom and of our happiness; such an one, exactly knowing what he owes to himself, will on his part find that he ought to apply to himself the use of the world and of other men; and to do this, to contribute to public society the duties and offices appertaining to him. He who does not in some sort live for others, does not live much for himself: "He who is his own friend is a friend to everybody else." The principal charge we have, is, to every one his own conduct; and 'tis for this only that we are here. As he who should forget to live a virtuous and holy life, and should think he acquitted himself of his duty in instructing and training others up to it, would be a fool; even so he who abandons his own particular healthful and pleasant living, to serve others therewith, takes, in my opinion, a wrong and unnatural course.

I would not that men should refuse, in the employments they take upon them, their attention, pains, eloquence, sweat, and blood if need be: "Not afraid to die for beloved friends, and for his country:" — but 'tis only borrowed, and accidentally; his mind being always in repose and in health; not without action, but without vexation, without passion. To be simply acting costs him so little, that he acts even sleeping; but it must be set on going with discretion; for the body receives the offices imposed upon it, just according to what they are; the mind often extends and makes them heavier at its own expense, giving them what measure it pleases. Men perform like things with several sorts of endeavor, and different contention of will; the one does well enough without the other: for how many people hazard themselves every day in war without any concern which way it goes; and thrust themselves into the dangers of battles, the loss of which will not break their next night's sleep? and such a man may be at home, out of the danger which he dared not have looked upon, who is more passionately concerned for the issue of this war, and whose soul is more anxious about events, than the soldier who therein stakes his blood and his life. I could have engaged myself in public employments without quitting my own matters a nail's breadth, and have given myself to others, without abandoning myself.

This sharpness and violence of desires more hinder than they advance the execution of what they undertake; fill us with impatience against slow or contrary events, and with heat and suspicion against those with whom we have to do. We never carry on that thing well by which we are prepossessed and led: "Passionate heat carries on things ill." He who therein employs only his judgment and address proceeds more cheerfully: he counterfeits, he gives way, he defers quite at his ease, according to the necessities of occasions; he fails in his attempt without trouble and affliction, ready and entire for a new enterprise; he always marches with the bridle in his hand. In him who is drunk with this violent and tyrannic intention, we discover, of necessity, much imprudence and injustice; the impetuosity of his desire carries him away; these are rash motions, and, if fortune do not very much assist, of very little fruit.

Philosophy directs that, in the revenge of injuries received, we should strip ourselves of choler; not that the chastisement should be less, but, on the contrary, that the revenge may be the better and more heavily laid on, which, it conceives, will be by this impetuosity hindered. For anger not only disturbs, but, of itself, also wearies the arms of those who chastise; this fire benumbs and wastes their force; as in precipitation, "*festinatio tarda est*" — "haste trips up its own heels," fetters, and stops itself; "*Ipsa se velocitas implicat.*" For example, according to what I commonly see, avarice has no greater impediment than itself; the more bent and vigorous it is, the less it rakes together, and commonly sooner grows rich when disguised in a visor of liberality.

A very honest gentleman, and a particular friend of mine, had liked to have cracked his brains by a too passionate attention and affection to the affairs of a certain prince, his master; which master has thus set himself out to me; "that he foresees the weight of accidents as well as another, but that in those for which there is no remedy, he presently resolves upon suffering; in others, having taken all the necessary precautions which by the vivacity of his understanding he can presently do, he quietly awaits what may follow." And, in truth, I have accordingly seen him maintain a great indifferency and liberty of actions and serenity of countenance, in very great and difficult affairs: I find him much greater, and of greater capacity in adverse than in prosperous fortune: his defeats are to him more glorious than his victories, and his mourning than his triumph.

Do but consider, that even in vain and frivolous actions, as at chess, tennis, and the like, this eager and ardent engaging with an impetuous desire, immediately throws the mind and members into indiscretion and disorder: a man astounds and hinders himself; he who carries himself more moderately both toward gain and loss, has always his wits about him; the less peevish and passionate he is at play, he plays much more advantageously and surely.

As to the rest, we hinder the mind's seizure and hold, in giving it so many things to seize upon: some things we should only offer to it; tie it to others, and with others incorporate it. It can feel and discern all things, but ought to feed upon nothing but itself; and should be instructed in what properly concerns itself, and that is properly of its own having and substance. The laws of nature teach us what justly we need. After the sages have told us that no one is indigent according to nature, and that every one is so according to opinion, they very subtly distinguish between the desires that proceed from her, and those that proceed from the disorder of our own fancy: those of which we can see the end are hers; those that fly before us, and of which we can see no end, are our own: the poverty of goods is easily cured; the poverty of the soul is irreparable: "For if what is for man enough, could be enough, it were enough; but since it is not so, how can I believe that any wealth can give my mind content" [Lucilius].

Socrates, seeing a great quantity of riches, jewels, and furniture carried in pomp through the city: "How many things are there," said he, "that I do not want." Metrodorus lived on twelve ounces a day; Epicurus upon less: Metrocles slept in winter abroad among sheep; in summer in the cloisters of churches; "*Sufficit ad id natura, quod poscit.*" Cleanthes lived by the labor of his own hands, and boasted that Cleanthes, if he would, could yet maintain another Cleanthes.

If that which nature exactly and originally requires of us for the conservation of our being be too little (as in truth what it is, and how good cheap life may be maintained, cannot be better expressed than by this consideration that it is so little that by its littleness it escapes the gripe and shock of fortune), let us allow ourselves a little more; let us call every one of our habits and conditions, nature; let us rate and treat ourselves by this measure; let us stretch our appurtenances and accounts so far; for so far, I fancy, we have some excuse. Custom is a second nature, and no less powerful. What is wanting to my custom, I reckon is wanting to me; and I should be almost as well content that they took away my life, as cut me short in the way wherein I have so long lived. I am no longer in condition for any great change, nor to put myself into a new and unwonted course, not even to augmentation. 'Tis past the time for me to become other than what I am; and as I should complain of any great good hap that should now befall me, that it came not in time to be enjoyed: "*Quo mihi fortunas, si non conceditur uti?*" so should I complain of any inward acquisition. It were almost better never, than so late, to become an honest man, and well fit to live, when one has no longer to live. I, who am about to make my exit out of the world, would easily resign to any newcomer, who should desire it, all the prudence I am now acquiring in the world's commerce; after meat, mustard. I have no need of goods, of which I can make no use; of what use is knowledge to him who has lost his head?

'Tis an injury and unkindness in fortune to tender us presents that will only inspire us with a just despite that we had them not in their due season. Guide me no more; I can no longer go. Of so many parts as make up a sufficiency, patience is the most sufficient. Give the capacity of an excellent treble to a chorister who has rotten lungs, and eloquence to a hermit, exiled into the deserts of Arabia. There needs no art to help a fall; the end finds itself of itself at the conclusion of every affair. My world is at an end, my form expired; I am totally of the past, and am bound to authorize it, and to conform my outgoing to it.

I will here declare, by way of example, that the pope's late ten days' diminution[1] has taken me so aback that I cannot well reconcile myself to it; I belong to the years wherein we kept another kind of account. So ancient and so long a custom challenges my adherence to it, so that I am constrained to be somewhat heretical on that point: incapable of any, though corrective, innovation. My imagination, in spite of my teeth, always pushes me ten days forward or backward, and is ever murmuring in my ears: "This rule concerns those who are to begin to be." If health itself, sweet as it is, returns to me by fits, 'tis rather to give me cause of regret than possession of it; I have no place left to keep it in. Time leaves me; without which nothing can be possessed. Oh, what little account should I make of those great elective dignities that I see in such esteem in the world, that are never conferred but upon men who are taking leave of it; wherein they do not so much regard how well the man will discharge his trust, as how short his administration will be: from the very entry they look at the exit. In short, I am about finishing this man, and not rebuilding another. By long use, this form is in me turned into substance, and fortune into nature.

I say, therefore, that every one of us feeble creatures is excusable in thinking that to be his own which is comprised under this measure; but withal, beyond these limits, 'tis nothing but confusion; 'tis the largest extent we can grant to our own claims. The more we amplify our need and our possession, so much the more do we expose ourselves to the blows and adversities of fortune. The career of our desires ought to be circumscribed and restrained to a short limit of near and contiguous commodities; and their course ought, moreover, to

---

[1] Gregory XIII., in 1582, reformed the Calendar, passing from the 9th to the 20th of December.

be performed not in a right line that ends elsewhere, but in a circle, of which the two points, by a short wheel, meet and terminate in ourselves. Actions that are carried on without this reflection — a near and essential reflection, I mean — such as those of ambitious and avaricious men, and so many more as run point-blank, and whose career always carries them before themselves, such actions, I say, are erroneous and sickly.

Most of our business is farce: "*Mundus universus exercet histrionam.*" We must play our part properly, but withal as the part of a borrowed personage; we must not make real essence of a mask and outward appearance; nor of a strange person, our own; we cannot distinguish the skin from the shirt: 'tis enough to meal the face, without mealing the breast. I see some who transform and transubstantiate themselves into as many new shapes and new beings as they undertake new employments; and who strut and fume even to the heart and liver, and carry their state along with them even to the close-stool: I cannot make them distinguish the salutations made to themselves from those made to their commission, their train, or their mule. "They forget their very nature in playing their parts." They swell and puff up their souls, and their natural way of speaking, according to the height of their magisterial place. The mayor of Bordeaux and Montaigne have ever been two by very manifest separation. Because one is an advocate or a financier, he must not ignore the knavery there is in such callings; an honest man is not accountable for the vice or absurdity of his employment, and ought not on that account refuse to take the calling upon him: 'tis the usage of his country, and then there is money to be got by it; a man must live by the world, and make his best of it, such as it is. But the judgment of an emperor ought to be above his empire, and see and consider it as a foreign accident; and he ought to know how to enjoy himself apart from it, and to communicate himself as James and Peter, to himself, at all events.

I cannot engage myself so deep and so entire; when my will gives me to anything, 'tis not with so violent an obligation that my judgment is infected with it. In the present broils of this kingdom, my own interest has not made me blind to the laudable qualities of our adversaries, nor to those that are reproachable in those of men of our party. Others adore all of their own side; for my part, I do not so much as excuse most things in those of mine: a good work has never the worse grace with me for being made against me. The knot of the controversy excepted, I have always kept myself in equanimity and pure indifference: "And have no express hatred beyond the necessity of war;" for which I am pleased with myself; and the more, because I see others commonly fail in the contrary direction. Such as extend their anger and hatred beyond the dispute in question, as most men do, show that they spring from some other occasion and private cause; like one, who, being cured of an ulcer, has yet a fever remaining, by which it appears that the ulcer had another more concealed beginning. The reason is that they are not concerned in the common cause; because it is wounding to the state and general interest; but are only nettled by reason of their particular concern.

This is why they are so especially animated, and to a degree so far beyond justice and public reason: "Every one was not so much angry against things in general, as against those that particularly concerned himself" [Livy]. I would have the advantage on our side, but if it be not, I shall not run mad. I am heartily for the right party; but I do not want to be taken notice of as an especial enemy to others, and beyond the general quarrel. I am a mortal enemy to this vicious form of censure: "He is of the League, because he admires the duke of Guise; he is astonished at the king of Navarre's energy, and therefore he is a Huguenot; he finds such and such faults in the king's conduct, he is therefore seditious in his heart;" and I would not grant to the magistrate himself that he did well in condemning a book, because it had placed a heretic among the best poets of the time. Shall we not dare to say of a thief, that he has a handsome leg? If a woman be a strumpet, must it needs follow that she has a stinking breath? Did they in the wisest ages revoke the proud title of Capitolinus they had before conferred on Marcus Manlius, as conservator of religion and the public liberty, and stifle the memory of his liberality, his feats of arms, and military recompenses granted to his valor, because he afterward aspired to the sovereignty, to the prejudice of the laws of his country? If we take a hatred against an advocate, he will not be allowed, the next day, to be eloquent.

I have elsewhere spoken of the zeal that pushed on worthy men to the like faults. For my part, I can say, "Such a one does this thing ill, and another thing virtuously and well." So in the prognostics, or sinister events of affairs, they would have every one in his party blind or a blockhead, and that our persuasion and judgment should subserve not truth, but to the project of our desires. I should rather incline toward the other extreme; so much I fear being suborned by my desire; to which may be added that I am a little tenderly distrustful of things that I wish.

I have, in my time, seen wonders in the indiscreet and prodigious facility of people in suffering their hopes and belief to be led and governed, which way has best pleased and served their leaders, despite a hundred mistakes one upon another, despite mere dreams and phantasms. I no more wonder at those who have been blinded and seduced by the fooleries of Appollonius and Mahomet. Their sense and understanding are absolutely taken away by their passion; their discretion has no more any other choice than that which smiles upon them, and encourages their cause. I had principally observed this in the beginning of our intestine distempers; that other, which has sprung up since, in imitating, has surpassed it; by which I am satisfied that it is a quality inseparable from popular errors; after the first that rolls, opinions drive on one another like waves with the wind: a man is not a member of the body, if it be in his power to forsake it, and if he do not roll the common way. But, doubtless, they wrong the just side, when they go about to assist it with fraud; I have ever been against that practice: 'tis only fit to work upon weak heads; for the sound, there are surer and more honest ways to keep up their courage and to excuse adverse accidents.

Heaven never saw a greater animosity than that between Cæsar and Pompey, nor ever shall; and yet I observe, methinks, in those brave souls, a great moderation toward one another; it was a jealousy of honor and command which did not transport them to a furious and indiscreet hatred, and was without malignity and detraction; in their hottest exploits upon one another, I discover some remains of respect and good will; and am therefore of opinion that, had it been possible, each of them would rather have done his business without the ruin of the other than with it. Take notice how much otherwise matters went with Marius and Sylla.

We must not precipitate ourselves so headlong after our affections and interests. As, when I was young, I opposed myself to the progress of love which I perceived to advance too fast upon me, and had a care lest it should at last become so pleasing as to force, captivate, and wholly reduce me to its mercy; so I do the same upon all other occasions where my will is running on with too warm an appetite. I lean opposite to the side it inclines to, as I find it going to plunge and make itself drunk with its own wine; I evade nourishing its pleasure so far, that I cannot recover it without infinite loss. Souls that, through their own stupidity, only discern things by halves, have this happiness that they smart less with hurtful things; 'tis a spiritual leprosy that has some show of health, and such a health as philosophy does not altogether contemn; but yet we have no reason to call it wisdom, as we often do. And after this manner some one anciently mocked Diogenes, who, in the depth of winter and stark naked, went hugging an image of snow for a trial of his endurance; the other seeing him in this position, "Art thou now very cold?" said he. "Not at all," replied Diogenes. "Why then," said the other, "what difficult and exemplary thing dost thou think thou doest in embracing that snow?" To take a true measure of constancy, one must necessarily know what the suffering is.

But souls that are to meet with adverse events and the injuries of fortune, in their depth and sharpness, that are to weigh and taste them according to their natural weight and bitterness, let such show their skill in avoiding the causes and diverting the blow. What did King Cotys do? He paid liberally for the rich and beautiful vessel that had been presented to him, but, seeing it was exceedingly brittle, he immediately broke it, betimes to prevent so easy a matter of displeasure against his servants. In like manner, I have willingly avoided all confusion in my affairs, and never coveted to have my estate contiguous to those of my relations, and such with whom I coveted a strict friendship; for thence matter of unkindness and falling out often proceeds. I formerly loved the hazardous games of cards and dice; but have long since left them off, only for this reason that, with whatever good air I carried my losses, I could not help feeling vexed within. A man of honor, who ought to be touchingly sensible of the lie or of an insult, and who is not to take a scurvy excuse for satisfaction, should avoid occasions of dispute. I shun melancholy, crabbed men, as I would the plague; and in matters I cannot talk of without emotion and concern, I never meddle, if not compelled by my duty: "*Melius non incipient, quam desinent.*" The surest way, therefore, is to prepare one's self beforehand for occasions.

I know very well that some wise men have taken another way, and have not feared to grapple and engage to the utmost upon several subjects; these are confident of their own strength, under which they protect themselves in all ill successes, making their patience wrestle and contend with disaster: "As a rock standing among the vast billows, exposed to the furious winds and the raging flood, remains unmoved, and defies all the force of seas and skies" [Virgil].

Let us not attempt these examples; we shall never come up to them. They set themselves resolutely, and without agitation, to behold the ruin of their country, which possessed and commanded all their will; this is too much and too hard a task for our commoner souls. Cato gave up the noblest life that ever was, upon this account; we meaner spirits must fly from the storm as far as we can; we must provide for sentiment, and not for patience, and evade the blows we cannot meet. Zeno, seeing Chremonides, a young man whom he loved, draw near to sit down by him, suddenly started up; and Cleanthes demanding of him the reason why he did so, "I hear," said he, "that physicians especially order repose, and forbid emotion in all tumors." Socrates does not say, "Do not surrender to the charms of beauty; stand your ground, and do your utmost to oppose it." "Fly it," says he; "shun the fight and encounter of it, as of a powerful poison that darts and wounds at a distance." And his good disciple, feigning or reciting, but, in my opinion, rather reciting than feigning the rare perfections of the great Cyrus, makes him distrustful of his own strength to resist the charms of the divine beauty of that illustrious Panthea, his captive, and committing the visiting and keeping her to another, who could not have so much liberty as himself. And the Holy Ghost in like manner: "*Ne nos inducas in tentationem.*" We do not pray that our reason may not be combated and overcome by concupiscence, but that it should not be so much as tried by it; that we should not be brought into a state wherein we are so much as to suffer the approaches, solicitations, and temptations of sin; and we beg of Almighty God to keep our consciences quiet, fully and perfectly delivered from all commerce of evil.

Such as say that they have reason for their revenging passion, or any other sort of troublesome agitation of mind, often say true, as things now are, but not as they were: they speak to us when the causes of their error are by themselves nourished and advanced; but look backward — recall these causes to their beginning — and there you will put them to a nonplus. Will they have their faults less, for being of longer continuance; and that of an unjust beginning, the sequel can be just? Whoever shall desire the good of his country, as I do, without fretting or pining himself, will be troubled, but will not swoon to see it threatening either its own ruin, or a no less ruinous continuance; poor vessel, that the waves, the winds, and the pilot toss and steer to so contrary designs!

He who does not gape after the favor of princes, as after a thing he cannot live without, does not much concern himself at the coldness of their reception and countenance, nor at the inconstancy of their wills. He who does not brood over his children or his honors, with a slavish propension, ceases not to live commodiously enough after their loss. He who does good principally for his own satisfaction, will not be much troubled to see men judge of his actions contrary to his merit. A quarter of an ounce of patience will provide sufficiently against such inconveniences. I find ease in this receipt, redeeming myself in the beginning as cheap as I can; and find that by this means I have escaped much trouble and many difficulties. With very little ado I stop the first sally of my emotions, and leave the subject that begins to be troublesome, before it transports me. He who stops not the start, will never be able to stop the career; he, who cannot keep them out, will never get them out when they are once got in; and he who cannot crush them at the beginning, will never do it after; nor ever keep himself from falling, if he cannot recover himself when he first begins to totter: "For they throw themselves headlong when once they loose their reason, and frailty so far indulges itself, that it is unawares carried out into the deep, and can find no port wherein to come to an anchor" [Cicero]. I am betimes sensible of the little breezes that begin to sing and whistle in the shrouds, the fore-runners of the storm: "As when the rising winds, checked by woods, send out dull murmurs, portending a storm to the mariner" [*Æneid*].

How often have I done myself a manifest injustice, to avoid the hazard of having yet a worse done me by the judges, after an age of vexations, dirty and vile practices, more enemies to my nature than fire or the rack? "A man should be an enemy to all lawsuits as much as he may, and I know not whether not something more; for 'tis not only liberal, but sometimes also advantageous, too, a little to recede from one's right" [Cicero]. Were we wise, we ought to rejoice and boast, as I one day heard a young gentleman of a good family very innocently do, that his mother had lost her cause, as if it had been a cough, a fever, or something very troublesome to keep. Even the favors that fortune might have given me through relationship or acquaintance with those who have sovereign authority in those affairs, I have very conscientiously and very carefully avoided employing them to the prejudice of others, and of advancing my pretensions above their true right. In fine, I have so much prevailed by my endeavors (and happily I may say it), that I am to this day a virgin from all suits in law; though I have had very fair offers made me, and with very just title would I have hearkened to them; and a virgin from quarrels too. I have almost passed over a long life without any offence of moment, either active or passive, or without ever hearing a worse word than my own name: a rare favor of heaven.

Our greatest agitations have ridiculous springs and causes: what ruin did our last duke of Burgundy run into about a cartload of sheepskins? And was not the graving of a seal the first and principal cause of the greatest commotion that this machine of the world ever underwent?[1] for Pompey and Cæsar were but the offsets and continuation of the two others: and I have in my time seen the wisest heads in this kingdom assembled with great ceremony, and at the public expense, about treaties and agreements, of which the true decision, in the meantime, absolutely depended upon the ladies' cabinet council, and the inclination of some foolish woman.

The poets very well understood this, when they put all Greece and Asia to fire and sword about an apple. Inquire why that man hazards his life and honor upon the fortune of his rapier and dagger; let him

---

[1] The civil war between Marius and Sylla.

acquaint you with the occasion of the quarrel; he cannot do it without blushing; 'tis so idle and frivolous.

A little thing will engage you in it; but being once embarked, all the cords draw; great provisions are then required, more hard and more important. How much easier is it not to enter in, than it is to get out? Now we should proceed contrary to the reed, which at its first springing produces a long and straight shoot, but afterward, as if tired and out of breath, it runs into thick and frequent joints and knots, as so many pauses which demonstrate that it has no more its first vigor and firmness; 'twere better to begin gently and coldly, and to keep one's breath and vigorous efforts for the height and stress of the business. We guide affairs in their beginnings, and have them in our own power; but afterward, when they are once at work, 'tis they that guide and govern us, and we are to follow them.

Yet do I not mean to say that this counsel has discharged me of all difficulty, and that I have not often had enough to do to curb and restrain my passions; they are not always to be governed according to the measure of occasions, and often have their entries very sharp and violent. But still good fruit and profit may thence be reaped; except for those who in well-doing are not satisfied with any benefit, if reputation be wanting; for, in truth, such an effect is not valued but by every one to himself; you are better contented, but not more esteemed, seeing you reformed yourself before you got into the whirl of the dance, or that the provocative matter was in sight. Yet not in this only, but in all other duties of life also, the way of those who aim at honor is very different from that they proceed by, who propose to themselves order and reason. I find some, who rashly and furiously rush into the lists, and cool in the course. As Plutarch says, that those who, through false shame, are soft and facile to grant whatever is desired of them, are afterward as facile to break their word and to recant; so he who enters lightly into a quarrel is apt to go as lightly out of it.

The same difficulty that keeps me from entering into it, would, when once hot and engaged in quarrel, incite me to maintain it with great obstinacy and resolution. 'Tis the tyranny of custom; when a man is once engaged, he must go through with it, or die. "Undertake coldly," said Bias, "but pursue with ardor." For want of prudence, men fall into want of courage, which is still more intolerable.

Most accommodations of the quarrels of these days of ours are shameful and false; we only seek to save appearances, and in the meantime betray and disavow our true intentions; we salve over the fact. We know very well how we said the thing, and in what sense we spoke it, and the company know it, and our friends whom we have wished to make sensible of our advantage understand it well enough too: 'tis at the expense of our frankness and of the honor of our courage, that we disown our thoughts, and seek refuge in falsities, to make matters up. We give ourselves the lie, to excuse the lie we have given to another. You are not to consider if your word or action may admit of another interpretation; 'tis your own true and sincere interpretation, your real meaning in what you said or did, that you are thenceforward to maintain, whatever it cost you. Men speak to your virtue and conscience, which are not things to be put under a mask; let us leave these pitiful ways and expedients to the jugglers of the law. The excuses and reparations that I see every day made and given to repair indiscretion, seem to me more scandalous than the indiscretion itself.

It were better to affront your adversary a second time, than to offend yourself by giving him so unmanly a satisfaction. You have braved him in your heat and anger, and you would flatter and appease him in your cooler and better sense; and by that means lay yourself lower and at his feet, whom before you pretended to overtop. I do not find anything a gentleman can say so vicious in him, as unsaying what he has said is infamous, when to unsay it is authoritatively extracted from him; forasmuch as obstinacy is more excusable in a man of honor than pusillanimity. Passions are as easy for me to evade, as they are hard for me to moderate: "*Exscinduntur facilius animo, quam temperantur.*"

He who cannot attain the noble Stoical impassibility, let him secure himself in the bosom of this popular stolidity of mine; what they performed by virtue, I inure myself to do by temperament. The middle region harbors storms and tempests; the two extremes, of philosophers and peasants, concur in tranquillity and happiness. Says Virgil: "Happy is he who has discovered the causes of things, and tramples under foot all fear, all concern, as to inexorable fate, or as to the roaring of greedy Acheron: he is blest who knows the country gods, Pan, old Sylvanus, and the sister nymphs."

The births of all things are weak and tender; and therefore we should have our eyes intent on beginnings; for as when, in its infancy, the danger is not perceived, so when it is grown up, the remedy is as little to be found. I had every day encountered a million of crosses, harder to digest in the progress of ambition, than it has been hard for me to curb the natural propension that inclined me to it: "I ever justly feared to raise my head too high" [Horace].

All public actions are subject to various and uncertain interpretations; for too many heads judge of them. Some say of this civic employment of mine (and I am willing to say a word or two about it, not that it is worth so much, but to give an account of my manners in such things), that I have behaved myself in it as a man not sufficiently easy to be moved, and with a languishing affection; and they have some color for what they say. I endeavored to keep my mind and my thoughts in repose, "*Cum semper natura, tum etiam œtate jam quietus;*" and if they sometimes lash out upon some rude and sensible impression, 'tis in truth without my advice. Yet from this natural heaviness of mine, men ought not to conclude a total inability in me (for want of care and want of sense are two very different things), and much less any unkindness or ingratitude toward that corporation, who employed the utmost means they had in their power to oblige me, both before they knew me and after; and they did much more for me in choosing me anew, than in conferring that honor upon me at first. I wish them all imaginable good; and assuredly had occasion been, there is nothing I would have spared for their service; I did for them, as I would have done for myself. 'Tis a good, warlike, and generous people, but capable of obedience and discipline, and of whom the best use may be made, if well guided.

They say also that my administration passed over without leaving any mark or trace. Good! They moreover accuse my cessation in a time when everybody almost was convicted of doing too much. I am impatient to be doing where my will spurs me on; but this itself is an enemy to perseverance. Let him who will make use of me according to my own way, employ me in affairs where vigor and liberty are required, where a direct, short, and, moreover, a hazardous conduct are necessary; I may do something; but if it must be long, subtle, laborious, artificial, and intricate, he had better call in somebody else. All important offices are not necessarily difficult: I came prepared to do somewhat rougher work, had there been great occasion; for it is in my power to do something more than I do, or than I love to do. I did not, to my knowledge, omit anything that my duty really required. I easily forgot those offices that ambition mixes with duty and palliates with its title; these are they that, for the most part, fill the eyes and ears, and give men the most satisfaction; not the thing but the appearance contents them; if they hear no noise, they think men sleep.

My humor is no friend to tumult; I could appease a commotion without commotion and chastise a disorder without being myself disorderly; if I stand in need of anger and inflammation, I borrow it, and put it on. My manners are languid, rather faint than sharp. I do not condemn a magistrate who sleeps, provided the people under his charge sleep as well as he: the laws in that case sleep too. For my part, I commend a gliding, staid, and silent life: "*Neque submissam et abjectam, neque se efferentem;*" my fortune will have it so. I am descended from a family that has lived without lustre or tumult, and, time out of mind, particularly ambitious of a character for probity.

Our people nowadays are so bred up to bustle and ostentation, that good nature, moderation, equability, constancy, and such like quiet and obscure qualities, are no more thought on or regarded. Rough bodies make themselves felt; the smooth are imperceptibly handled: sickness is felt, health little or not at all; no more than the oils that foment us, in comparison of the pains for which we are fomented. 'Tis acting for one's particular reputation and profit, not for the public good, to refer that to be done in the public squares which one may do in the council chamber; and to noonday what might have been done the night before; and to be jealous to do that himself which his colleague can do as well as he; so were some surgeons of Greece wont to perform their operations upon scaffolds in the sight of the people, to draw more practice and profit. They think that good rules cannot be understood, but by the sound of trumpet.

Ambition is not a vice of little people, nor of such modest means as ours. One said to Alexander: "Your father will leave you a great dominion, easy and pacific;" this youth was emulous of his father's victories, and of the justice of his government; he would not have enjoyed the empire of the world in ease and peace. Alcibiades, in Plato, had rather die young, beautiful, rich, noble, and learned, and all this in full excellence, than to stop short of such condition; this disease is, peradventure, excusable in so strong and so full a soul.

When wretched and dwarfish souls gull and deceive themselves, and think to spread their fame for having given right judgment in an affair, or maintained the discipline of the guard of a gate of their city, the more they think to exalt their heads the more they show their tails. This little well-doing has neither body nor life; it vanishes in the first mouth, and goes no farther than from one street to another. Talk of it by all means to your son or your servant, like that old fellow who, having no other auditor of his praises, nor approver of his valor, boasted to his chambermaid, crying, "Oh, Perrette, what a brave, clever man hast thou for thy master!" At the worst, talk of it to yourself, like a councillor of my acquaintance, who, having disgorged a whole cartful of law jargon with great heat and as great folly, coming out of the council chamber, was heard very complacently to mutter between his teeth; "*Non nobis, domine, non nobis, sed nomini tuo da gloriam.*" He who gets it of nobody else, let him pay himself out of his own purse.

Fame is not prostituted at so cheap a rate; rare and exemplary actions, to which it is due, would not endure the company of this prodigious crowd of petty daily performances. Marble may exalt your titles, as much as you please, for having repaired a rod of wall or cleansed a public sewer; but not men of sense. Renown does not follow all good deeds, if novelty and difficulty be not conjoined; nay, so much as mere esteem, according to the Stoics, is not due to every action that proceeds from virtue; nor will they allow him bare thanks, who, out of temperance, abstains from an old blear-eyed hag. Those who have known the admirable qualities of Scipio Africanus, deny him the glory that Panætius attributes to him, of being abstinent from gifts, as a glory not so much his as that of the age he lived in. We have pleasures suitable to our lot; let us not usurp those of grandeur; our own are more natural, and by so much more solid and sure, as they are lower. If not for that of conscience, yet at least for ambition's sake, let us reject ambition; let us disdain that thirst of honor and renown, so low and mendicant, that it makes us beg it of all sorts of people by abject means, and at what cheap rate soever: 'tis dishonor to be so honored.

Let us learn to be no more greedy, than we are capable, of glory. To be puffed up with every action that is innocent or of use, is only for those with whom such things are extraordinary and rare; they will value it as it costs them. The more a good effect makes a noise, the more do I abate of its goodness as I suspect that it was more performed for the noise, than upon account of the goodness; exposed upon the stall, 'tis half sold. Those actions have much more grace and lustre, that slip from the hand of him that does them, negligently and without noise, and that some honest man thereafter finds out and raises from the shade, to produce it to the light upon its own account. "All things truly seem more laudable to me that are performed without ostentation, and without the testimony of the people," says the most ostentatious man[1] that ever lived.

I had but to conserve and to continue, which are silent and insensible effects; innovation is of great lustre; but 'tis interdicted in this age, when we are pressed upon and have nothing to defend ourselves from but novelties. To forbear doing is often as generous as to do; but 'tis less in the light, and the little good that I have in me is of this kind. In fine, occasions in this employment of mine have been confederate with my humor, and I heartily thank them for it. Is there any who desires to be sick, that he may see his physician at work? and would not that physician deserve to be whipped, who should wish the plague among us, that he might put his art in practice? I have never been of that wicked humor, and common enough, to desire that

---

[1] Cicero.

troubles and disorders in this city should elevate and honor my government; I have ever heartily contributed all I could to their tranquillity and ease. He who will not thank me for the order, the sweet and silent calm that has accompanied my administration, cannot, however, deprive me of the share that belongs to me, by title of my good fortune.

And I am of such a composition that I would as willingly be lucky as wise, and had rather owe my successes purely to the favor of Almighty God than to any operation of my own. I had sufficiently published to the world my unfitness for such public offices; but I have something in me yet worse than incapacity itself; which is, that I am not much displeased at it, and that I do not much go about to cure it, considering the course of life that I have proposed to myself. Neither have I satisfied myself in this employment; but I have very near arrived at what I expected from my own performance, and have much surpassed what I promised them with whom I had to do; for I am apt to promise something less than what I am able to do and than what I hope to make good.

I assure myself that I have left no offence or hatred behind me; to leave regret or desire for me among them, I at least know very well that I never much aimed at it. But, says Virgil: "Should I place confidence in this monster? Should I be ignorant of the dangers of that seeming placid sea, those now quiet waves?"